MAINE QUILTS

250 Years of Comfort and Community

Laureen A. LaBar

With Essays by Lynne Z. Bassett and Pamela Weeks

Augusta, Maine

Camden, Maine

Maine State Museum
230 State Street
83 State House Station
Augusta, ME 04333-0083
www.mainestatemuseum.org

Down East Books

An imprint of The Rowman & Littlefield Publishing Group, Inc.
4501 Forbes Blvd., Ste. 200
Lanham, MD 20706
www.rowman.com

Co-published with the Maine State Museum, Augusta, Maine

Distributed by NATIONAL BOOK NETWORK

Copyright © 2021 Maine State Museum

All rights reserved. No part of this book may be reproduced in any form or by any electronic or mechanical means, including information storage and retrieval systems, without written permission from the publisher, except by a reviewer who may quote passages in a review.

British Library Cataloguing in Publication Information available

Library of Congress Cataloging-in-Publication Data available

Names: LaBar, Laureen A., author. | Bassett, Lynne Z., 1961- writer of introduction. | Weeks, Pamela. | Maine State Museum, organizer, host institution.
Title: Maine quilts : 250 years of comfort and community / Laureen A. LaBar ; with essays by Lynne Z. Bassett and Pamela Weeks.
Description: Lanham, MD : Down East Books, [2020] | Issued in connection with the exhibition Comfort and community : 250 years of Maine quilts, at the Maine State Museum. | Includes bibliographical references and index. | Summary: "The history of quilting in Maine is a story of community and Maine State Museum curator Laureen A. LaBar coaxes stories out of objects and uses those stories to enlighten, entertain, and to bring new voices to Maine history"— Provided by publisher.
Identifiers: LCCN 2019059440 (print) | LCCN 2019059441 (ebook) | ISBN 9781608937301 (cloth) | ISBN 9781608937318 (epub)
Subjects: LCSH: Quilts—Maine—Exhibitions.
Classification: LCC NK9112 .L27 2020 (print) | LCC NK9112 (ebook) | DDC 746.4609741—dc23
LC record available at https://lccn.loc.gov/2019059440
LC ebook record available at https://lccn.loc.gov/2019059441

∞™ The paper used in this publication meets the minimum requirements of American National Standard for Information Sciences—Permanence of Paper for Printed Library Materials, ANSI/NISO Z39.48-1992.

For Joan LaBar
Who loved to quilt

CONTENTS

PREFACE		vii
INTRODUCTION		ix
1	TRADITION AND COLONIAL TIES	1
2	A TIME OF REVOLUTION	32
3	ANTEBELLUM ALBUM QUILTS	57
4	COMMUNITY AND UNION IN THE CIVIL WAR	91
5	COTTONS GALORE	105
6	THAT'S JUST CRAZY	132
7	THE TWENTIETH CENTURY: COMMUNITY AND CHANGE	151
8	MAINE QUILTS TODAY	174
NOTES		216
BIBLIOGRAPHY		226
INDEX		232
ACKNOWLEDGMENTS		239

PREFACE

Folk art in Maine, as defined for a century past, has included a number of iconic categories of craft or artistic creation. Decoys, baskets, rugs, and paintings of a certain kind are among them. But of all the possible varieties of hand-made artistry that might be included under this heading, quilts are perhaps the most widely recognized and most widely enjoyed by the public. Perhaps that is because quilts are an almost ideal combination of creative craftsmanship and utility: they can be decorative in endless ways, but are universally attached to an essentially utilitarian form that at least theoretically allows them to be used as coverlets or bed clothes. Perhaps it is because quiltmaking can be a group or social activity as well as a solitary, individualistic one. Perhaps it is because the nature of the quilt encourages the creative instinct in so many people, some of whom might not otherwise be enticed into artistic design and the learning of the construction and embroidery techniques that make quilt production possible. Or perhaps it is because a quilt is mainly to be enjoyed by those closest to the maker, by family, friends, or an intimate social circle, and the question of approval by a wider public only infrequently arises. Only the bolder quiltmakers submit their creations to be publicly judged, say at a church or local fair, along with the best community apples or pies, as is illustrated by this panel from a nineteenth-century stereo view (p. x). No matter how a quilt is considered, it is that close or even intimate connection between the maker and the relatively few people who will see or benefit from her—and occasionally his—work that stands out. The quilt is most often a personal creative expression, or a series of personal expressions, and its use is usually a personal, limited one also. It draws people together and emerges from the ties sustained by families or communities. The exhibition that this book represents is thus well named: *Comfort and Community: 250 Years of Maine Quilts*.

The Maine State Museum has, at this writing, over 180 Maine quilts, a collection that is still growing. The museum's collection is the largest gathering of Maine quilts in any single institution. We obviously believe that the quilt is one of the key elements of Maine folk art and craft. Even though Maine quilts are not always dramatically different from other New England quilts, as a group they do display identifiable regional distinctions and are, both artistically and sociologically, essential products through which to examine and understand Maine and

PREFACE

its people. History curator Laureen LaBar has long studied Maine quilts. She conceived and organized this exhibition, the first major exhibit of Maine quilts ever produced. It represents five years of episodic consideration and planning and over two years of active development. Her energy, and the assistance of her colleagues and collaborators, has given the museum, and Maine, a way to analyze, classify, interpret, and appreciate Maine quilts that has never existed before. I thank her and her pioneering spirit for making a "royal road" into the subject of Maine quilts, one that I trust will be traveled by many others in the years to come, as they build on what she has founded to advance our understanding of this subject, and our affection for it.

Local Quilt Display, *panel of stereo view by F. W. Fowler, Salisbury, MA, about 1880. Private collection.*

Bernard Fishman, Director, Maine State Museum

INTRODUCTION

by Lynne Zacek Bassett

Dealers in American antiques identify Maine as the last fertile ground in New England for finding great early folk art objects. Two bedcovers of exceptional artistic merit, discovered in the bottom drawers of old chests during the evaluation of historic estates, appear in this book—the Paul Family embroidered wool quilt from South Solon, and the Nanna Bradley Whittier stenciled spread from Mount Vernon. As so often, and so understandably, happens after multiple generations, these masterpieces of American folk art were largely forgotten by the families in which they descended. Both bedcovers now have new homes out of state.

Concerns over fading memories and the loss of a state's quilt heritage to distant collectors sparked the movement to document American quilts. Dealer Bruce Mann of Kentucky, recognizing his role in selling regional quilts to collectors around the country, proposed the idea of documenting Kentucky's quilts to raise the general public's awareness of the beauty and history of these objects.[1] Unfortunately, Mann's untimely death in 1980 meant he was not able to act on his idea, but his friends, including Shelley Zegart (co-founder of the Quilt Alliance), did act, starting in 1980 and catalyzing a grassroots movement that has spread from Kentucky to every state, even jumping the United States borders to other countries, including Canada, England, South Africa, Australia, and others.[2]

State quilt documentation projects across the country have aided in producing an accurate history of American quilts and quiltmakers, revealing the romanticism that colored early quilt historians' understanding of the craft.[3] Each book offers highlights from days of public and local history museum "discovery days," contextualized with research into the quiltmaker and family histories when known, along with overviews of state histories.

Quilts offer a perspective that traditional historical research too often overlooks—the "micro" histories of domestic economies, families, and women. Careful examination of a quilt sometimes shows the work of many hands—the small, even stitches of the experienced matron alongside the comparatively clumsy stitches of the young novice quilter. Who sat together to quilt and what were the dynamics of that gathering? Were these women well known to one another through bonds of family, friends, and neighborhood, or was this a more political gathering brought together by the needs of a church, a reform movement, or a national crisis? Was the quilt intended for a young woman's upcoming nuptials, to raise money for a cause, to express love and remembrance to a departing community member, to make a statement of belief, or to give comfort to an individual? Perhaps the

maker undertook the project to provide emotional as well as physical comfort to herself.

Quilts reveal regional and household economies in their materials. Quilts made of expensive imported worsteds from England were reserved for the wealthy in the colonial period. Middling farmwives of the New Republic desired such luxuries, too, and spun and wove their own twill and tabby wool stuffs that were given a slightly glossy finish by the local cloth dresser. The backs of these quilts are often the most revealing. Were they made of fresh goods (perhaps an inexpensive, but still shiny, calendered worsted called "tammy") or were they frugally pieced of recycled wool sheets, with the old cross-stitched markings turned to the inside? Were the threads used to stitch the layers together homespun worsted, imported silk, or factory-spun cotton? Careful analysis reveals much about the availability of goods and the choices made based on economy, tradition, or personal preference.

With the arrival of the Industrial Revolution at the turn of the nineteenth century, cotton displaced wool as the most common quilting material. The affordable, colorful prints were cut and pieced or appliquéd in myriad combinations. The ubiquity of cotton fabric caused a division of opinion. The arbiters of taste wrote dismissively of cotton patchwork, with comments such as, "It is not worth either candle or gas light,"[4] and "Patchwork quilts of old calico are only seen in inferior chambers . . ."[5] Ignoring such advice, New Englanders earned their reputation as thrifty Yankees in this period with their bountiful production of pieced calico and chintz quilts—but their scrap patchwork was not only stitched for the sake of economy. The scraps were often deeply imbued with meaning and the memory of loved ones whose clothing was carefully cut into the various geometric shapes for piecing. This sentimentality was a reaction to the Industrial Revolution, which upset the Western world, shifting economies from rural agriculture to urban industry. The Romantic Movement of the early nineteenth century offered relief and escape from the challenges and stress of unfamiliar work and environment, from the trauma of friends and family moving to far-off cities or to new territories, and from worries caused by the boom-and-bust economy. Romanticism encouraged emotive displays and religious piety, promoted an idyllic view of history, venerated nature, and celebrated imagination. The new United States, eager to establish its own national culture in literature, music, and the visual arts,

enthusiastically embraced Romanticism, and American women stitched into their quilts the values of the period. They used them as vehicles for their emotion, their piety, and their imagination—and made this textile form uniquely their own.

Antebellum Romanticism inspired the fashion for friendship quilts, in which signatures and verses of friendship, piety, and remembrance were penned directly onto the cloth. The period's interest in reform movements—abolition particularly—led some women to use their quilts also to express their opposition to slavery or to voice their support for a presidential candidate (since they were not able to vote themselves). The Civil War (1861–1865) catalyzed these developments in quiltmaking, spreading the use of the medium to express distinct messages. Women, North and South, stitched their voices into their quilts with urgency and passion. They created quilts to comfort their beloved husbands, brothers, and sons on the battlefield and in the hospitals; they stitched quilts to raise funds for their side in the war; and they stitched quilts to distract and comfort themselves as they worried and grieved.

After the war, the American economy boomed with industry, and products rolled out of the factories, including sewing machines and fancy machine-woven laces, ribbons, and silks. The Gilded Age, with its love of excess and "conspicuous consumption," spawned the crazy quilt—the decorative sofa or table throw made of scraps of randomly shaped silk satins, velvets, and brocades held together with colorful embroidery in multitudinous stitches. Crazy quilts evidenced the maker's creativity, taste, and cognizance of broader fashions in art.[6]

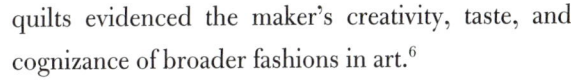

Many quilts of the early twentieth century were inspired by the Colonial Revival. Variations on traditional patchwork and appliqué designs and new designs with old-fashioned-sounding names were produced in fashionable pastel shades—made popular for their attractiveness in the new technology of electric lights.[7] Sadly, in the spirit of traditional home decorating, many old quilts were cut up and used to upholster furniture in the homes of the wealthy.[8]

After World War II (for the United States, 1941–1945), American women made fewer quilts and the art of quilting went into a decline, but the Bicentennial of 1976 revived interest in the possibilities of quilting as an expressive medium, especially for female hobbyists and artists. Many towns in the United States boast a Bicentennial quilt made in celebration of the national event on a local level, with prominent historical events and landmarks represented in appliqué and embroidery. The Quilt Revival inspired not only new practitioners of the craft but also scholarly study of the history of quiltmaking—including the state documentation projects.

The goal of the state quilt documentation projects has been to identify regionalisms in style and to illuminate family, local, and state history. So far, the New England states of Vermont, Connecticut, Rhode Island, and Massachusetts have produced books recording their findings. Although Maine was part of Massachusetts until 1820 (the two-hundredth anniversary of its establishment as a separate state being celebrated in part by the publication of this book), *Massachusetts Quilts: Our Common Wealth* (2009) does not include any discussion of quilts from the Pine Tree State.

This publication from the Maine State Museum is therefore a welcome addition to these other studies of New England's quilt heritage, assisting in the production of an understanding of the region's quilt heritage in comparison to that of states to the west and south. Like the multitudinous scraps of calico and delaine stitched into objects of beauty and utility, the authors have chosen highlights from the nearly one thousand quilts they documented, and organized them into meaningful assemblages with the dominant theme of "community." Starting logically with the earliest quilts known to have been produced in the state, the authors discuss wholecloth wool bed quilts and quilted petticoats (which were simply called "quilts" in the eighteenth century, as they significantly outnumbered quilts for the bed). The embroidered wool quilts of Maine from the early nineteenth century are arguably the most distinctive type in the state. No other state project has turned up any. Another distinctive form of needlework related to quilting techniques that only Maine can offer is that of the Wabanaki silk ribbon appliquéd garments.

The antebellum era brought forth wonderful album quilts in Maine—each block different and made by a different person. Shared fabrics and overlapping names reveal community efforts and important insights into local history. This was also the period of expanding choices in manufactured printed cottons and the explosion of scrap quilts that continued throughout the rest of the nineteenth and into the twentieth centuries.

Maine's commitment to the Union in the Civil War is evident in the patriotic quilts made by women, including that of Octavia Lewis of Jay, Maine. Octavia inked her own poem in the center of her quilt, below her pieced representation of the Stars and Stripes, ending, "The Banner of Union forever must wave." Two distinctive appliqué Civil War–period album quilts, worked on an unusual brown cotton background, hail from Munjoy Hill, a neighborhood of Maine's largest city, Portland. Featuring American flags, shields, and Civil War armament, the quilts also feature symbols of Maine's marine heritage: the Portland Observatory, a sextant, anchor, and mariner's compass.

Maine women followed the trends of the rest of American quiltmakers in the generations after the Civil War by producing hundreds—perhaps thousands—of log cabin and crazy quilts. Charm quilts and postage-stamp quilts were produced by the more competitive late nineteenth- and early twentieth-century quiltmakers. As is true of American quilts in general, regional distinctions diminished in this period with the distribution of quilt patterns through periodicals. Ladies' magazines in the early twentieth century promoted the pastel Colonial Revival quilts, and Maine women of course were enthralled by their attractions. The Bicentennial and Quilt Revival brought out Maine women's individuality again, and this book stands out from the other regional quilt books in including examples from this more recent era.

After attending school in Medford, Massachusetts, Eliza Southgate returned home to Scarborough, Maine, in 1801. She complained in a letter to a friend that

> I left school with a head full of something, tumbled in without order or connection. I returned home with a determination to put it in more order. . . . The greater part of my ideas I was obliged to throw away . . . what remained I pieced as ingeniously as I could into a few patchwork opinions,—they are now almost worn threadbare, and as I am about quilting a few more, I beg you will send me any spare ideas you may chance to have that will answer my turn.[9]

That a quilt metaphor was chosen by Eliza to explain her mind in this early period is not only charming, but prescient. We feel connected to this young Maine woman as we, too, work to piece together the discoveries of this exploration of Maine's quilt history into a dynamic understanding of the quilting heritage of this varied and wonderful state.

The Davis-Dow Quilt
Alumnae, students, and staff of the
Home Institute school
Portland, Maine, May, 1864
Maine State Museum, 2015.11.1
See fig. 4.1

1

TRADITION AND COLONIAL TIES

Early Maine quilts are rare, and documented examples rare, indeed. Quilts are fragile, and documentation gets lost or garbled over the years. As Jane Nylander points out, the realities of life in the 1700s meant life on a frontier with "demanding schedules of daily work in a highly producing household economy, and the stress of supervising and caring for large and complex extended families."[1] Simply put, many women were too busy running their homes to devote much time to quilting. Maine's turbulent early history also contributes to the lack of early quilts. When European explorers and would-be colonists established temporary settlements in the first decade of the 1600s, Maine was already occupied. Native American communities dotted the coast and major riverways, precisely the areas most attractive to Europeans. Largely ignoring Native claims, England, France, and Massachusetts assigned conflicting land grants and charters.[2] By 1675, many early trading sites along the southern and central Maine coast had evolved into villages.[3] Poor relationships between settlers and their understandably disgruntled Indian neighbors resulted in conflict, exacerbated by wars between the French and English. A series of clashes in the late 1600s and early 1700s resulted in abandoned towns along the coast, but as a fragile peace returned, so did Euro-American settlement. After Quebec fell to the British in 1759, and again after the American Revolution, when veterans were awarded land bonuses in the area, Maine's population burgeoned and increasingly moved inland from the coast.[4] The earliest surviving Maine quilts date to this period of increased settlement.

Maine was part of Massachusetts until 1820, and its northern border was not defined until 1842. Despite their location on the frontier, early Maine residents still took pride in possessions.[5] They looked to Boston and to London for cultural inspiration, as most settlers were of British descent or were recent immigrants from Great Britain. These women brought with them British needleworking traditions. Maine's early wholecloth quilts and pieced examples with framed central medallions echo those made in England. Martha Babson Lane Soule's coverlet and quilt, made in Freeport, Maine, in the 1790s, bear embroidery similar to that on bed hangings from a generation or two earlier, such as those owned and probably made by Mary Swett Bulman of York before 1745 (fig. 1.1; see also figs. 1.22 and 1.23).[6]

CHAPTER 1

**Fig. 1.1
Bulman Bed Hangings**
Mary Swett Bulman probable maker
York, Maine, 1725–1730
84 inches high
Old York Museum, 1961.002
The Bulman bed hangings on display in the Emerson-Wilcox House, Old York Museum, around 2005.

Mary Swett Bulman is the presumed maker of this set of embroidered bed hangings, made sometime before her husband's death in 1745. The maker embroidered the words of "Meditation in a Grove," a 1706 poem by Isaac Watt, on the inside of the valances.

Medallion quilts include a central focus, with pieced blocks arranged in frames around it. Maine's medallion quilts are similar to those made elsewhere in New England and the mid-Atlantic states and like them, reference those made in England.[7] Two early dated examples from Maine were made in 1804 and 1805. The 1804 quilt bears an embroidered date and the initials L. R., as well as a solitary number four (fig. 1.2). Unfortunately, nothing else is known about the quilt's history, other than its use and probable origin in Maine. The maker of the quilt was skilled in piecing and in the layout of her design. Over the years the fabrics have faded slightly with washing and exposure to light, but a strong central design is still evident, visually reinforced by a series of frames. The second of these early quilts was made

**Fig. 1.2
Pieced Cotton Medallion Quilt**
Maker unknown, inscribed L ♥ R 4
Maine, 1804
100 x 96 inches
Courtesy of Judy Roche

A quilter with the initials L. R. likely made this 1804 quilt. The number 4 implies that this was her fourth quilt.

by Martha Agry Vaughan of Hallowell, Maine (figs. 1.3 and 1.4).[8] Martha made her quilt top from silk and other clothing fabrics, some of which are quite rare.[9] Consistent with English quilts of the period, it features a central medallion, framed by several bands of patchwork. As in L. R.'s quilt, Martha Vaughan's design includes blocks at the corners of some of the frames. Neither quilt subscribes to today's insistence on precise symmetry in a quilt's layout. Some of Martha's frames include extra rows of half-blocks, and a few blocks meander into the next frame. While Martha was aware of what fashionable quilts should look like, she did not apparently receive any instruction in their construction. Complex silk medallion quilts such as this were generally made using paper piecing. Paper templates kept fabric components the right size and shape, ensuring crisp designs and the success of the quilt. The templates could be removed after construction of the quilt top. Martha's technique was to piece the triangles into blocks without the paper templates. She added the paper afterwards, behind the pieced

CHAPTER 1

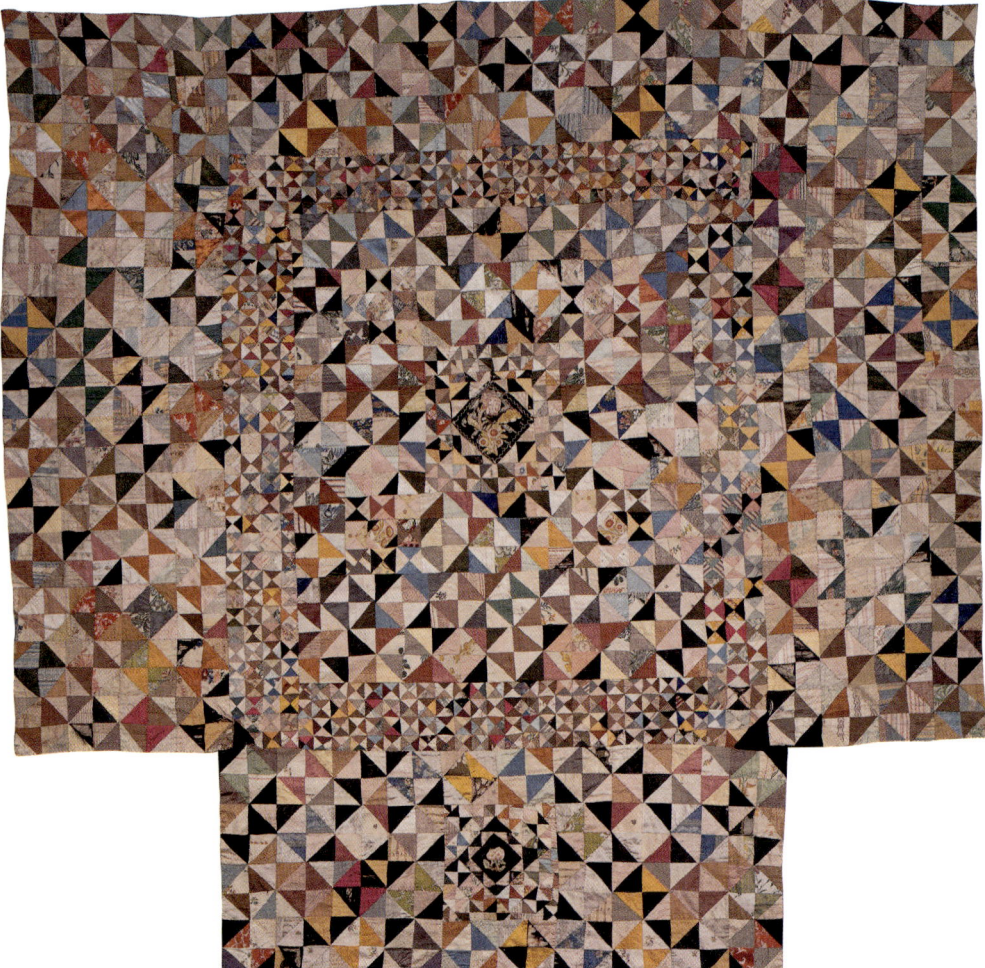

Fig. 1.3
Silk Medallion Quilt
Martha Agry Vaughan
Silk, wool, cotton, linen, and newspaper
Hallowell, Maine, 1795–1815
100 x 104 inches
Courtesy of Winterthur Museum, museum purchase, 1957.48

Martha Agry Vaughan likely made this quilt around the time of her 1805 wedding to William Oliver Vaughan.

top, where it remains.¹⁰ The result is a quilt that is a little irregular and slightly lumpy. This appears to be the result of inexperience, rather than a design choice.

Polly Allen's 1811 quilt top also shows disregard for precise symmetry (figs. 1.5 and 1.6). She was only eleven years old when she pieced and embroidered the quilt top, which may explain the off-center medallion. Judging from the design imperfections in early quilts, it is also possible that the precise symmetry that is valued today was not important to Mainers in the early nineteenth century. In the center of her quilt top Polly embroidered a tree-of-life block, with fanciful foliage and flowers. In an outlined leaf at the top of this block, she added "Polly Allen's / quilt wroght

Fig. 1.4
Detail, Martha Agry Vaughan's Silk Medallion Quilt
Courtesy of Winterthur Museum, 1957.48

Detail of Martha Agry Vaughan's quilt, showing imprecise construction details and variety of materials.

4

**Fig. 1.5
Pieced Cotton
Medallion Top**
Polly Allen
Sedgwick, Maine,
1811
63½ x 63¾ inches
Courtesy of Wilson
Museum, w13176

Polly Allen embroidered the medallion and solid blocks in the central section of her quilt top.

**Fig. 1.6
Medallion Detail,
Polly Allen's Quilt
Top**
Courtesy of Wilson
Museum, w13176

The somewhat childish execution of the embroidery in the medallion of Polly Allen's quilt top reflects the fact that she was eleven years old when she stitched it.

A.D. / 1811. Born Feb 2, 1800. / Sedgwick." The style of embroidery Polly chose was often used to decorate bed hangings and other domestic textiles (see fig. 1.1). She extended the use of embroidery into the first series of one-patch borders that frame her center medallion. Three rows of blocks featuring careful embroidery alternate with block-printed and hand-colored, or penciled, cotton in brown, pink, and blue on a natural ground. The quilt top's embroidery and design, as well as its incomplete status, reflect Polly Allen's British heritage. She lived in a rural area, with many daily chores that may have prevented her from completing this emblem of her affection for stylish, beautiful household goods, similar to those that would have been enjoyed by distant family members still living in England.

CHAPTER 1

As might be expected in a cold climate, wool wholecloth quilts were popular throughout New England. The term wholecloth implies that the quilt top was made from one wide piece of fabric, but several widths of fabric were needed. Grid lines of slightly darker pigment can often be seen on wool wholecloth quilts. This is evidence of calendering, a surface treatment for wool, in which steamed or dampened fabric was pressed between hot rollers, giving the cloth a smooth finish. Fabric was generally folded before passing through the heavy, hot rollers. This resulted in a sharp crease and a slight increase in the amount of pigment caught in the fold (figs. 1.7 and 1.8). The fabric often had glazing applied to the top surface, which added luster to the cloth, at least until it was laundered. Quilters frequently used commercially produced wool for the fronts of their quilts. For the backs, however, they often used locally made fabric, or "homespun," and in some cases reused old household fabric scraps to make the back (see fig. 1.14).

Fig. 1.7
Wool Wholecloth Quilt
A member of the Hussey or Tarbox family
Biddeford, Maine area, ca. 1800–1820
94 x 88 inches
Maine State Museum
74.68.1

Family stories recall that Mary Hussey made this quilt. However, Mary was born on December 7, 1824, so she probably inherited the quilt from the family of her mother, Sally Tarbox, or her father, John Charles Hussey, who was a farmer and a minor town official in Biddeford. A member of her parents' or grandparents' generation likely made the quilt.

**Fig. 1.8
Quilting Design for the Hussey/Tarbox Wholecloth Quilt**
Drawing by Lynne Z. Bassett
Maine State Museum 74.68.1

The quilting pattern chosen by the maker of the Hussey/Tarbox wholecloth quilt is based on a tree-of-life motif.

Family stories often relate that the wool for fabric and batting was raised by the family, and the fabric woven by household members. In many cases this may be accurate. Lynne Bassett points out that eighteenth-century wool wholecloth quilts "tended to be owned by farming families."[11] In the late 1700s or early 1800s, quilts were often a group effort, with neighbors pitching in on one another's quilts at every stage, but especially when quilting. Then as now, space in a home was at a premium. A quilting frame, usually made up of four beams tied at the corners, with chairs to support them, might take up most of a room, so women tried to complete the quilting as soon as possible, often by inviting neighbors and family to help.[12]

Most Maine wool wholecloth quilts are not dated, but those that are date as late as the 1830s (see figs. 1.31 to 1.33). Like Martha Lane Soule, most Maine wholecloth quilt makers in the 1700s and early 1800s embellished their work with baroque floral and vine motifs, related to tree-of-life motifs (see figs. 1.8, 1.18, 1.19, and 1.33). These designs, popular generations earlier, continued to find expression in quilts even after householders' tastes in furnishings and clothing had become more neoclassical. By around 1800, however, the clean lines of the neoclassical style were making inroads into the bedroom, in the quilting patterns of wholecloth quilts. In northern New England, especially in Maine and New Hampshire, women began decorating their wholecloth quilts with grids, within which they quilted elements from the traditional design vocabulary, such as flowers, or feathered motifs (figs. 1.9 and 1.10).[13] In rural areas, however, complex baroque tree-of-life quilting designs continued in popularity until the middle 1800s, long after styles elsewhere had moved on.[14]

A few Maine quilters wanted it all: a wool quilt and a medallion quilt. One such example comes from the Waterville, Maine, area (fig. 1.11). As with many wholecloth quilts, the fabric of the top appears to have been commercially produced, while the backing was likely made within the community or by the quilter. The layout, the piecing, and the quilting are

Fig. 1.9
Wholecloth Quilt
Mrs. Harrington
Biddeford, Maine,
1800–1830
102 x 101 inches
Maine State Museum,
2008.44.1

Mrs. Harrington's given name was lost over the years, though the name of her hometown was not. The fabric on the front of her quilt shows the telltale creases and straight lines of darker pigment left by the calendering process. The pale-yellow backing fabric was probably locally made and dyed.

TRADITION AND COLONIAL TIES

Fig. 1.10
Detail of Harrington Quilt
Maine State Museum, 2008.44.1

Mrs. Harrington decorated her quilt in what was for the time, a modern style, using a grid. The motifs she used within the grid are similar to those used in more baroque, tree-of-life designs.

all high quality. This maker's attention to detail is especially evident in the cut corners of the quilt. When on the bed, the corners would feature a bright red series of arrows with a red ruffle at the top, like a flower on a leafy stem. Ties would have held the corners tight and tidy (fig. 1.12). Rather than using a tree of life sprouting from an

Fig. 1.11
Wool Medallion Quilt
Unknown maker
Waterville, Maine, area, ca. 1800
108 x 92 inches
Courtesy of Waterville Historical Society and Redington Museum, 4028

The maker of this medallion quilt used red and off-white wools to create a bold design that overwhelms its skilled and detailed quilting. She matched thread colors to her background, effectively camouflaging the intricate quilting motifs. A close examination of the quilt reveals baskets trimmed with spirals, holding bouquets of flowers, and a tendril of flowers and leaves in the border. The quilting of the central compass rose features a vase of flowers and is surrounded by still more flowers and feathery foliage.

CHAPTER 1

**Fig. 1.12
Detail, Medallion Quilt**
Courtesy of Waterville Historical Society and Redington Museum, 4028

The quilting on this wool medallion quilt is exceptionally fine. The cut corners of the quilt originally had red ties at each corner to join the side and foot drops when the quilt was on a bed.

abstract plant motif or small vase, the quilting features wide baskets with flowers and vines climbing from them.

The flowers, leaves, and feathers Perlina Chadwick stitched on her wool medallion quilt are also based on the tree-of-life motif, although they are separated even more from the form of the tree and are randomly placed across the surface (fig. 1.13). In contrast to the maker's traditional quilting, the overall design with its bold rectangles of salmon, gold, and pale green on an indigo blue ground would not be out of place in a twenty-first-century art quilt. Some of the fabrics on the front have been calendered and glazed. The piecing and fabric on the back of the quilt, however, is much more humble. It features recycled scraps from several household textiles such as blankets (fig. 1.14). For Perlina Chadwick, as for many quilters, the front of the quilt was what mattered.

Maine women persisted in sewing wholecloth quilts after the style had lost popularity elsewhere in the new nation. In part, this conservatism may have been a reaction to the length and severity of Maine's winters. Thrift may also have played a part. Laborious though it may have been to card and spin the fiber, and dye the wool, and weave the fabric before beginning a quilt, the work could be done by household members at little expense but time. Maine is at the end of the trade road today, but in the late 1700s and early 1800s it was an important player in regional trade, and the sea and rivers were as highways. Even so, relative to consumers in port towns and cities like Hallowell and Falmouth (later Portland), farm wives in rural areas were somewhat removed from access to a wide variety of fabrics.

**Fig. 1.13
Pieced Wool Medallion Quilt, front**
Perlina Chadwick or a member of her family
Clinton or Sebasticook, Maine, ca. 1825
86 x 82¾ inches
Maine State Museum
2004.53.2

The fabrics and design of Perlina Chadwick's quilt suggest it was made after 1820, but the flowers she quilted are similar to the baroque examples that several earlier generations of Maine artisans had used.

**Fig. 1.14
Perlina Chadwick's Wool Medallion Quilt, back**
Maine State Museum
2004.53.2

The back of Perlina Chadwick's quilt is also pieced, but in a strictly utilitarian way, with pieces of several recycled, mismatched blankets and other textiles stitched together. The very small tan patches are modern repairs.

CHAPTER 1

PETTICOATS

In the 1700s, quilting was not only found in bed linens. It was more often present in clothing, especially in petticoats.[15] The term petticoat has changed in meaning over the last three hundred years. In the 1700s it was a public garment, meant to be seen, worn front and center of a woman's skirts. The skirts themselves opened from the waist in an inverted V, or "open robe," to show off the beauty of the petticoat. Quilted silk versions were popular in England and in the mid-Atlantic American colonies, but in New England, whether for warmth or from frugality, women favored woolen petticoats.

English fashion featured decorative quilted petticoats from around 1710 until the late 1700s.[16] England exported silk petticoats, but even in the early 1700s, some Massachusetts women were making their own, in addition to quilted bonnets, hoods, and other garments.[17] This option offered two advantages: lower cost and control over the decoration. The patterns that women quilted into their petticoats show the attention they paid to London fashion. At the same time, motifs demonstrate regional differences in their expression: the flowers in a petticoat or quilt from Maine will be differently composed than one from western Massachusetts, or Rhode Island.[18]

Fig. 1.15
Wool Petticoat
Maker unknown
Southern Maine,
1775–1800
27½ inches, waistband to hem
Courtesy of Brick Store Museum, 3042

The quilting on these two southern Maine petticoats implies that they were made at different times. However, their fabric appears to be from the same source.

Fig. 1.16
Wool Petticoat
Maker unknown
Southern Maine,
1775–1800
39¾ inches, waistband to hem
Courtesy of Maine
Historical Society
1993.300.362

Although the makers of the two petticoats used the same fabric, they decorated the garments differently.

Fig. 1.17
Wool Petticoat, Selvedge Detail
Courtesy of Brick Store Museum, 3042

The makers of both petticoats used the entire width of their fabric. The selvedges are visible at the seams. The selvedges of each petticoat included two blue strands of wool in the warp.

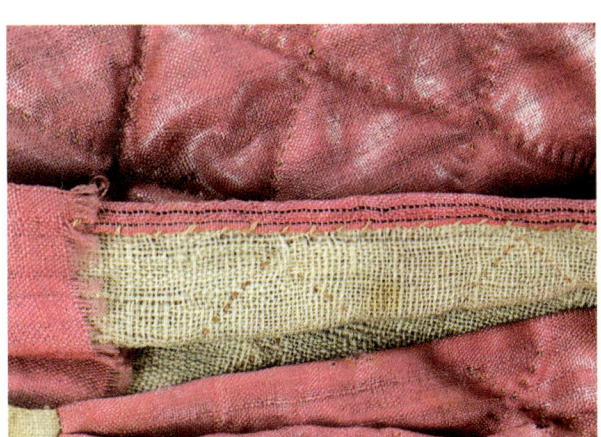

It is difficult to determine in period diaries whether an item being quilted might be a petticoat. Unless a diarist specifically refers to a "bed quilt," a quilt might be either a bed quilt or a petticoat.[19] Martha Ballard of Hallowell noted quilting several times in her diary, generally in the fall, after the garden work was largely done for the year. In the year or two before their weddings, her daughters made several quilts, sometimes inviting friends to help with the quilting and an evening of merriment, and each of the women occasionally quilted at the homes of friends.[20] Martha Ballard called some "bed quilts," but others just "quilts."

Surviving eighteenth-century petticoats from Maine are very rare, indeed, despite their popularity in the day. Two of them from southern Maine appear to have been cut—literally—from the same cloth (figs. 1.15 and 1.16). The glazed wool in bright pink is remarkably similar in both petticoats. A selvage visible in the seams of each garment includes two blue warp threads, an unusual feature

CHAPTER 1

in worsted wool fabrics, but found in cotton yardage in the late 1700s and first decade of the 1800s (fig. 1.17).[21] The British government struggled to promote local cotton production and printing, while at the same time supporting the domestic linen industry. Restricting imports was one solution. Another was to encourage exports. Accordingly, between 1774 and 1811, the government put in place a tax loophole for exported cottons. Provided that printed cloth for export was woven with three blue threads in the selvage, the manufacturer could receive a tax exemption.[22] This measure was specifically for cotton goods, not wool. The threads in the selvedges of the two woolen petticoats from Maine suggests that consumers—or importers—expected to see blue threads as evidence that the goods were produced in Britain for export to the American colonies.

A quilted petticoat is essentially a long, rectangular quilt, gathered along one edge. As for wholecloth quilts, several lengths of fabric were needed. Quilting disguised the seams. The strips were generally used vertically. The resulting seams allowed for slits on either side to accommodate pockets. These were separately sewn garments that were tied to the waist underneath one's clothes. After quilting, the petticoat was gathered to a waistband.

The differences in the motifs on the two pink petticoats provide a clue to their creation: on the Maine Historical Society (MHS) petticoat, the motifs are crowded together, whereas the Brick Store Museum (BSM) example features vines and blossoms with much more negative space between them (figs. 1.18 and 1.19). The motifs are similar in style, but not so closely as to suggest they were designed and laid out by the same person or shop. This suggests that, while British exporters sent many already quilted silk petticoats to the American colonies, these two wool examples were probably locally made and quilted. The fabrics used inside the garments also suggest that they were made locally. The linings of ready-made petticoats featured new fabric. The makers of these petticoats used pieces of worn woolen clothing. The resulting odd shapes of the pieces can reveal the type of garment that was upcycled.[23]

**Fig. 1.18
Quilting Design for Petticoat**
Drawing of Maine Historical Society 1993.300.362 by Laureen LaBar
Courtesy of Maine Historical Society 1993.300.362

The maker of the Maine Historical Society (MHS) petticoat covered the entire surface of the garment with a dense pattern of baroque florals, vines, and feathers.

**Fig. 1.19
Quilting Detail, Brick Store Petticoat**
Courtesy of Brick Store Museum, 3042

The maker of the petticoat now held by the Brick Store Museum (BSM) also quilted baroque flowering vines but focused her efforts on the lower half of the petticoat. On the upper half, which would not be seen for the most part, she stitched crossed diagonal lines over an inch apart.

The quilting on the two petticoats shows the choices women made in striking a balance between budget (or time expended) and fashion. The maker of the petticoat from MHS decorated it with curving, feathery foliage and flowers. Her chosen motifs would not have been out of place on a locally made wholecloth quilt and cover all the available space from hem to waist. In contrast, the quilter of the BSM petticoat focused her creative efforts on the lower, more visible portion of the petticoat, filling the top half with simple crossed diagonal lines. Here, too, the feathered vines, flowers, and background of closely spaced diagonal lines are very similar to those stitched into wholecloth quilts.

The demand for quilted petticoats was on the wane by 1790, with fashion favoring a new silhouette: a high waist and loose, narrow, flowing gown that recalled classical garments. Some women, generally older, more conservative, and less fashion-conscious, would have continued to wear the dresses with woolen petticoats that were fashionable in their youth, but by 1800, few Maine women were making these practical garments.

CUTTING CORNERS

Many Maine quilts appear to have bites taken out of two adjacent corners (fig. 1.20). These have been called T-shaped quilts and the bites have been dubbed cut corners or cut-out corners. None of these labels is completely satisfactory, as the quilts aren't really T-shaped, nor are the corners cut or cut out: the quilts were, in nearly every case, designed without corners. The reason is simple: most beds at the time had bedposts, and tucking a quilt around a post was difficult and resulted in untidy lumps at either side of the foot of the bed. The solution was to omit the two corners all together. The result lay smoothly on the bed, with the drops meeting around the bed posts. In addition to less work making the bed on a daily basis, cut corners would have appealed to a quilter's sense of frugality, as the resulting quilts were slightly smaller in area, requiring less time and fabric in their manufacture.

Not everyone favored the look. One woman changed her mind after the quilt was completed and filled the empty squares at the lower corners with matching fabric. Because she used different fabrics to edge the once-cut corners, the result is more obvious than if she had used matching fabric throughout (fig. 1.21). Less than a third of the bed quilts in the Maine State Museum's collection, and less than 10 percent of the quilts brought to Maine Quilt Heritage gatherings have cut corners. Most such quilts date before 1875. Unlike quilters in other

CHAPTER 1

Fig. 1.20
Trapunto Quilt
Member of the Tucker family
Wiscasset, Maine, 1820s
71 x 54 inches
Courtesy of Wilson Museum, W04620

The three-dimensional designs of this quilt were accomplished by quilting the outline of each motif. The maker then used a heavy needle to gently open a small hole behind each element. She individually filled each leaf, petal, and feather, carefully stuffing soft cotton cordage through the hole and then coaxing the threads together again to close it. Trapunto quilts such as this often featured emblems of the early republic, such as eagles. This maker chose instead the familiar motifs of a basket of flowers within a meandering feather border. She finished the quilt with a hand-knotted fringe around the perimeter.

areas of the country, however, Maine's quilting women continued to use the cut corner into the twentieth century, at least in more rural areas (see figs. 5.32 and 5.33).

Fig. 1.21
Quilt with Replaced Corners
Emma Harmons, probable maker
Saco, Maine, 1830–1840
88 x 94 inches
Maine State Museum, 2015.40.3

After the quilt was completed, someone, probably the maker of the quilt, filled in the cut corners. They can still be seen, highlighted by lighter squares at the lower corners.

CHAPTER 1

REFLECTIONS OF COMMUNITY: AN ISLAND EXPRESSION OF A MAINE DESIGN

Quilts were not the only source of warm bedding in the late 1700s and early 1800s. In other parts of New England, women covered the entire surface of a bedcover with dense wool embroidery. No such bed rugs, as they are now called, with clear Maine provenance are known to have survived, although it is likely that at least a few local families used them. Instead—or in addition—Maine women created embroidered coverlets, such as the example made by Martha Babson Lane Soule of Freeport (figs. 1.22 and 1.23), and one held by the Shelburne Museum, made by Eunice Wentworth of West Lebanon, Maine, or one of her ancestors. A related type of pieced, embroidered bedcover made in the early 1800s appears to have its center of production in Maine. Like the embroidered wool blankets from Vermont, New Hampshire, and western Massachusetts, the Maine examples feature crewelwork embroidery on a wool foundation.[24]

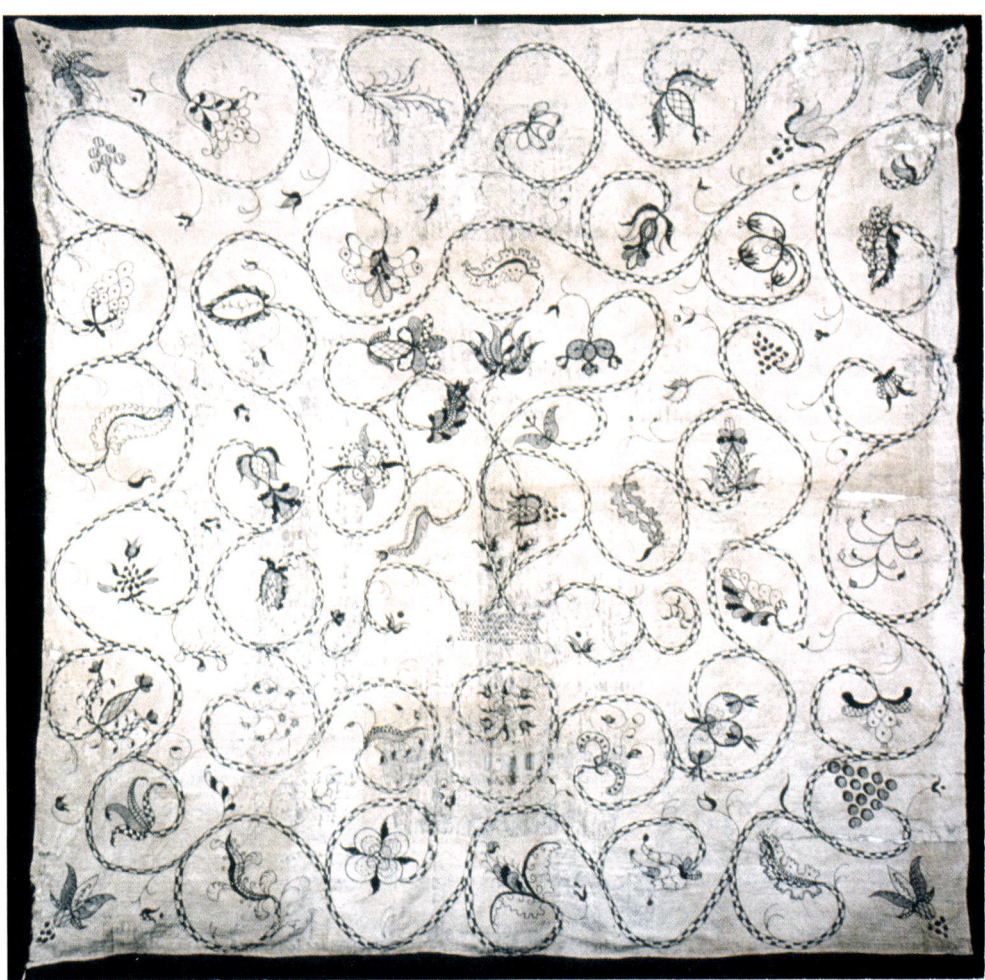

**Fig. 1.22
Embroidered Bedcover**
Martha Babson Lane Soule
Freeport, Maine, 1790–1795, with later additions
84 x 87 inches
Courtesy of National Museum of American History, Kenneth E. Behring Center, SI 88838

According to family tradition, Martha Babson Lane Soule made this coverlet around the time of her 1794 marriage to Moses Soule. Years later, Martha or one of her descendants added a back and batting and quilted it.[25]

TRADITION AND COLONIAL TIES

Fig. 1.23
Embroidered Quilt
Martha Babson Lane Soule
Freeport, Maine,
1790–1795
89 x 91 inches
Courtesy of National Museum of American History, Kenneth E. Behring Center, SI 190856

Martha Babson Lane Soule probably made this quilt in the 1790s. It includes panels cut from embroidered bed hangings, as well as copperplate-engraved textiles dating from 1775–1785. Family tradition states that Martha made the quilt before her 1794 marriage.[26]

However, the Maine bedcovers are pieced, usually in contrasting shades of brown, or brown and dark blue. Although they date to the early 1800s, and as late as 1841, their embroidery motifs still echo those of earlier quilts and bed hangings.[27] As Laurel Thatcher Ulrich observed in a different context, "Though their embroidery was unpolished in comparison with the fine crewelwork made in elite households, it asserted the impulse toward betterment that often lay beneath rural industry."[28]

Janneken Smucker notes a likely relationship between the Vermont embroidered bedcovers and earlier bed rugs from Connecticut, and laments the declining practice of signing and dating the simpler, later bedcovers.[29] Pieced and embroidered wool quilts also lack signatures, making a clear understanding of their source difficult. Where provenance exists, however, it is from Maine, and the area is likely the center of the creation of pieced and embroidered wool quilts. Their inspirational source may not be bed rugs. Rather, the makers of Maine's embroidered bedcovers may have been inspired by the area's unadorned pieced-wool quilts

Fig. 1.24
Pieced Wool Quilt
Member of the Libby family, maker
Scarborough, Maine
1830–1850
87 x 91 inches
Maine State Museum, 2014.2.1

The Libby family used this quilt on a bed, as can be seen from pattern of fading on the quilt. The foot of the bed was in shade, while the side drop, seen on the right of the image, faced the light. The bold colors of the quilt were even more dramatic when the blocks that are now brown were nearly black in color.

(fig. 1.24; see also figs. 1.34 and 1.35).

One example with strong Maine provenance was made in Solon between 1830 and 1835, by a member of the William and Catherine Rice Paul family, likely Catherine herself (figs. 1.25 and 1.26).[30] It is by far the most complex of the group of pieced and embroidered quilts. It is also the most colorful, incorporating black, brown, orange, and green wool, in a combination similar to that

19

CHAPTER 1

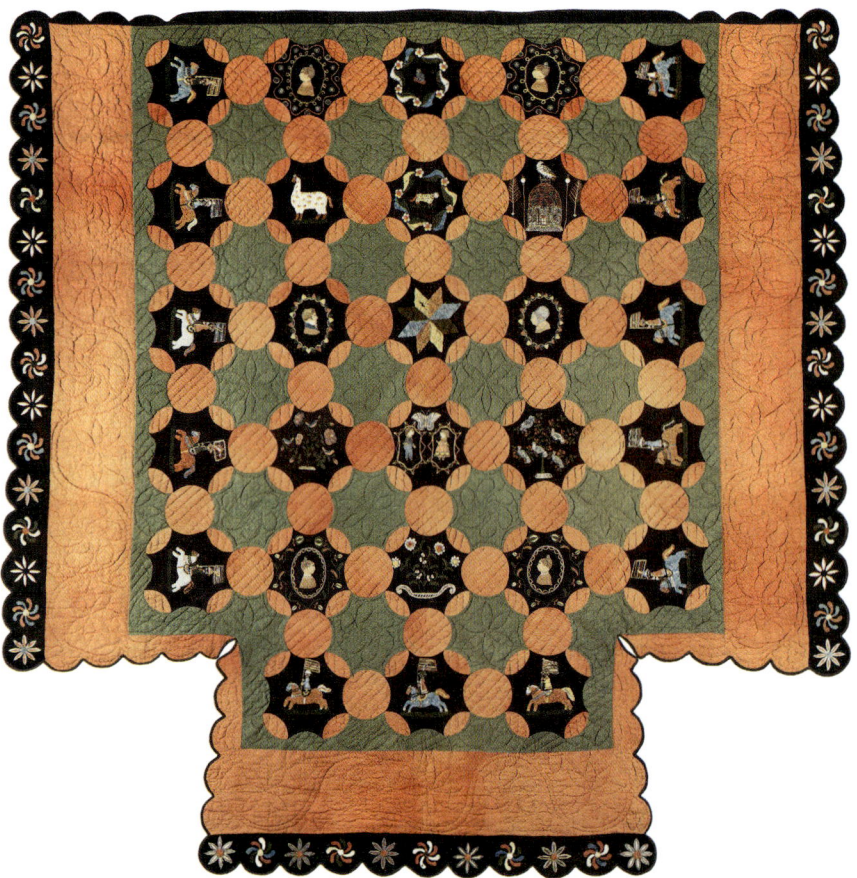

Fig. 1.25
Pieced and Embroidered Wool Quilt
A member of the William and Catherine Rice Paul family, maker
Solon, Maine,
1830–1835
105 x 106 inches
Courtesy of Museum of Fine Arts, a museum purchase with funds donated from the Marshall H. Gould Fund, Joyce and Edward Linde, and an anonymous supporter, 2005.95

According to family lore, Catherine Rice Paul of Solon, Maine, made this complex pieced and embroidered quilt. Many of the seemingly solid blocks are made from several pieces, and the fabrics appear to have been recycled. The quilt's embroidered motifs feature a combination of the everyday and the exotic. The embroidered portraits likely represent family members.

of the Libby family pieced wool quilt (see fig. 1.24). The member of the Paul family who made it probably drafted its pattern herself. The layout of eight-pointed medallions sashed with orange circles and lozenges appears to be unique. The scalloped edges of the quilt echo these curves, as does the quilting in the plain, green blocks. The plain-woven wool on the front of the quilt was likely locally made. Much of the fabric was reused, as seen by the many seams in the seemingly solid wool components. The quilt is alive with scenes of everyday life, patriotism, and the exotic. Some of the many embroidered figures likely represent family members, or like the militiamen riding along both sides, reflected the quilter's life. Other motifs, such as the llama, did not, and were most likely copied from illustrations in books.

Like the maker of the Paul family quilt, Lucy Dyer created a quilt that is a reflection of the community in which she lived (fig. 1.27). Dyer's ancestors came on

Fig. 1.26
Detail, Paul Family Quilt
Courtesy of Museum of Fine Arts, 2005.95

The embroidered beehive-shaped building in this block may represent the local meetinghouse.[31]

20

TRADITION AND COLONIAL TIES

the *Mayflower*, and her family moved from Plymouth, Massachusetts, to North Haven, Maine, around 1800. Euro-Americans settled the island in the 1760s, and the Dyer family arrived not long after Massachusetts awarded the settlers clear title to the land in 1786. Lucy Dyer likely called the island North Haven, but until 1847 it was named North Vinalhaven, at which time it separated from the town of Vinalhaven and became Fox Island. That name hearkened back to 1603, when English explorer Martin Pring dubbed both North and Vinalhaven Islands the Fox Islands. The revived name did not stick, and in 1847, the island was renamed North Haven, a name its inhabitants had been calling it for generations. Fishing was central to life on the island of North Haven, a fact Dyer underscored in the decoration of her quilt, which she made in the early 1800s, not long after the family arrived on North Haven.

The embroidered decoration of Lucy Dyer's quilt is limited to the portion of the quilt that would have covered the surface of the bed. The quilt has cut-out corners, and the side and foot drops are solid and plain, apart from their quilting. The quilt is a one-patch pattern of alternating brown and black wools. The brown fabric was likely woven in the community;

Fig. 1.27
Pieced and Embroidered Wool Quilt
Lucy Dyer, maker
North Haven, Maine,
ca. 1825
99 x 115 inches
Courtesy of North Haven Historical Society and the Denham family
2012.02.01

Lucy Dyer's embroidered fishing schooner and cod set her quilt apart from similar pieced and embroidered wool quilts.

the black broadcloth was suiting material and may have been commercially woven.[32] The yarn Dyer used in her embroidery was probably made on the island as well. Lynne Bassett notes that the colors "orangey-red, pale green, yellow, blue, and dark pink" could all have been achieved using locally available dyestuffs, many of which were from local natural sources.[33]

The central portion of Dyer's quilt included five rows of decorated black blocks on point, and another row of triangular half-squares. There were four whole squares to each row, with half-squares at either side. Most of the blocks are filled with flowers and baskets of flowers. The four blocks at center top, however, speak to

**Fig. 1.28
Detail, Lucy Dyer Quilt**
Courtesy of North Haven Historical Society and the Denham family, 2012.02.01

Lucy Dyer included two blocks with images of cod, the major source of income for her fishing community.

**Fig. 1.29
Detail, Lucy Dyer Quilt**
Courtesy of North Haven Historical Society and the Denham family, 2012.02.01

Fishing schooners would have been an everyday sight on North Haven in the early 1800s. Community members and likely members of Lucy Dyer's family used them to fish for cod. See fig. 3.29 for a later quilt block that includes a fishing schooner.

Dyer's home and community. She embroidered the two outer blocks with cod, the primary catch of North Haven's fishermen. A small bird of prey, perhaps an osprey, hovers above one of the large cod (fig. 1.28). The two blocks in the center of the row feature a fishing schooner and a large, stylized bird of prey (fig. 1.29). As Lynne Bassett points out, the bird's body is in the shape of a shield, so it is likely an eagle.[34] This was a popular image in the art of the early republic, and then as now a symbol of national pride. Dyer had clearly seen cod before: she drew the fish's three dorsal fins and two anal fins. She did not include the barbel under its chin, but did include the diagnostic lateral line from gill to tail. In place of the speckled skin, she embroidered crosses and in one case, concentric lines of color. The fishing boat would have been a daily sight on North Haven Island. Every family that lived on the island was tied to fishing in some way, as fishermen or as tradesmen who supported or supplied or profited from fishermen. In four small squares of fabric, Lucy Dyer told the world who she was: an American, from a Maine fishing community.

Quilts like those made by Lucy Dyer and the unknown member of the Paul family are very rare, made in a relatively small area for a short period of time. Janneken Smucker suspects that, elsewhere in New England, embroidered bedcovers were a reaction to the lack of available woolen fabrics during the 1807 Embargo and the War of 1812. The disruption to shipping before and during the war strongly impacted New England, providing short-term hardship

**Fig. 1.30
Embroidered Wool Strip Quilt**
Maker unknown
Likely Maine, or Massachusetts,
1800–1830
92½ x 85 inches
Courtesy of Winterthur Museum, gift of Henry Francis Du Pont, 1955.739.1

The maker of this strip quilt used recycled woolen clothing for at least some of the quilt top. She probably lived in what would become the state of Maine.

for those whose livelihoods depended on trade directly or indirectly, but also offering strong impetus for local manufacturing.[35] Some embroidered wool quilts, such as one at Winterthur (fig. 1.30), include recycled woolen fabric. Whether this transformation of an old pair of woolen breeches into a bed quilt was a reaction to war scarcity or simply Yankee thrift cannot be known, but this and other pieced embroidered wool quilts offer clues to daily life in rural Maine in the early 1800s.

☙

Compared to the number of Maine quilts from the late 1800s, those from the 1700s and first decades of the 1800s are relatively rare. However, each one provides evidence of lives lived, of women and families making a life on a frontier. Some of the women led comfortable lives in Maine's large coastal towns and made silk quilts that recalled British examples. These ladies may have had access to imported silk petticoats and wore wool petticoats seasonally, for warmth, rather than for fashion. The petticoats of rural women, like their quilts, tended to be made from wool, though their quilting shows the same British design vocabulary. Farm wives and daughters might not have had as much access to imported commercial fabrics as their city relations did, but revolution was in the air: three revolutions, the American, the industrial, and a revolution in textile printing.

CHAPTER 1

GALLERY

Fig. 1.31
Wool Wholecloth Quilt
Rachel Chapman maker or recipient
Possibly mid-coast Maine, 1838
105 x 113 inches
Maine State Museum 70.110.1

Rachel Chapman, who may have lived in the mid-coast region of Maine, quilted her name at the center top of her quilt in such a way that it could be seen right-side-up to someone lying in bed, under the covers. Below her name she quilted the date: "October 2the 1838" [sic]. Did she quilt all but the day designation first, assuming a –th suffix was the most common, and therefore the most likely, or did she simply forget to add a number 1 before the 2, in which case the date would read "October 12the?" Either way, Rachel was proud enough of her accomplishment that she wished whoever used the quilt to see her signature. Her pride was justified. The quilt is well made, and the complex decorative quilting is skillfully designed and executed. Because she used red thread to quilt her designs, the designs are more visible on the back of the quilt than on the front. They include flowers, hearts, fans, and feathers around a tree-of-life motif that grows out of a large heart. Rachel's quilt designs recall the curves and foliage popular in the mid- to late 1700s. The spoked half-circles at the top of the quilt and the stitching of the binding are similar to examples found on quilts made in Great Britain. Rachel may have been an immigrant, or the daughter of one, or taught by one. And judging by her quilting patterns, her tastes were conservative. Rachel could have been middle-aged or elderly, still quilting designs that were popular in her youth. It is also possible that Rachel was not the quilt's creator, but its recipient, and that an older relative made the quilt for her, perhaps to commemorate a life event such as a marriage or a move away from her home community. Whatever the details of its creation, the quilt was treasured and little used, and remains in excellent condition today.

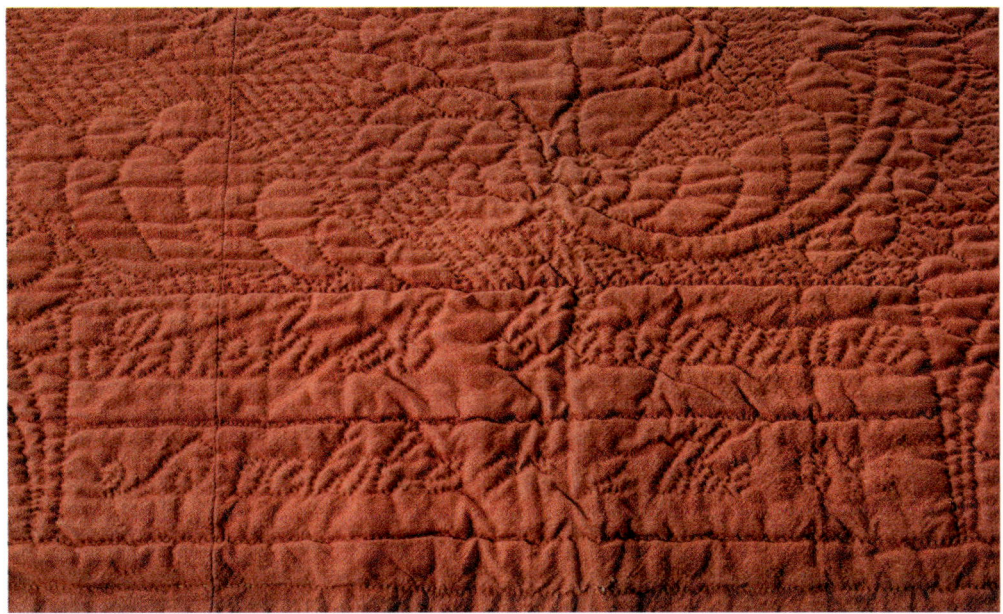

Fig. 1.32
Detail of Rachel Chapman's Quilt
Maine State Museum 70.110.1

Rachel Chapman's name and the date "October 2the 1838" appear at the center of the top of the quilt. When the quilt is hanging, the words appear upside down, but when it was on the bed, those lying under it would have read the writing right-side up.

CHAPTER 1

Fig. 1.33
Quilting Design of Rachel Chapman's Quilt
Drawing of Maine State Museum 70.110.1 by Laureen LaBar

Rachel Chapman quilted a complex tree of life on her quilt. Not shown in the drawing, diagonal rows of quilting help the primary pattern stand out.

TRADITION AND COLONIAL TIES

Fig. 1.34
Pieced Wool Quilt
Maker unknown
Isle au Haut, Maine, 1800–1825
101½ inches x 114½ inches
Maine State Museum, 80.152.21

The maker of this bold woolen quilt from Isle au Haut, the outermost large island in Penobscot Bay, reused fabrics, much as other quilters did. The fishermen of Isle au Haut and their families dressed in bright colors, it seems.

CHAPTER 1

Fig. 1.35
Pieced Wool Quilt
Rachel Calderwood Carver, maker
North Haven, Maine, ca. 1835
90 x 90 inches
Courtesy of North Haven Historical Society, 005.5.1

Rachel Calderwood Carver of North Haven made this quilt not long after Lucy Dyer made her embroidered wool quilt (see figs. 1.27 to 1.29).

Fig. 1.36
Pieced and Embroidered Wool Quilt
Delphos Turner, maker
Palermo, Maine, 1818
70½ x 109 inches
Courtesy of Maine Historical Society 2002.098.001

Delphos Turner of Palermo made this quilt in 1818, signing and dating it in embroidery and adding her birth date, July 1, 1800.

CHAPTER 1

Fig. 1.37
Pieced and Embroidered Wool Quilt
Unknown maker
Likely Maine, ca. 1820
97½ x 98½ inches
Courtesy of New England Quilt Museum, 1991.2

The maker of this quilt is not known, but likely lived in what would become the state of Maine. The floral designs are similar to those of Lucy Dyer's quilt, as well as that of other Maine quilts of the time.

Fig. 1.38
Pieced and Embroidered Wool Quilt
Maker unknown
Likely Maine, possibly Massachusetts, 1800–1840 with later additions
75 x 65½ inches
Courtesy of Winterthur Museum, bequest of Henry Frances du Pont, 1969.562

The wool yarn used to embellish this quilt reveals some of its history. Designs on the darker brown blocks and black, embroidered half-blocks at the margins feature woolen thread that was not produced until years after the quilt was first made. The maker of the original, central part of the quilt used commercial two-ply crewel wool, as well as single-ply, home-spun wool yarn in her embroidery.[36]

2

A TIME OF REVOLUTION

Two revolutions, the American and the industrial, shaped Maine in the late 1700s and early 1800s. A third, a revolution in textile printing and dying technologies, affected the lives of Mainers more indirectly, but period quilts reveal the changes in consumer goods that it brought about. Settlement in Maine increased rapidly after the American Revolution. As Alexander Hamilton pointed out in 1791, manufacturing requires a certain population density for it to succeed, and by 1820, enough people had moved to Maine that its faltering manufacturing sector began to take off.[1] In 1815, for example, even the hamlet of Damariscotta Mills included a fulling mill for finishing wool fabric, two sawmills, two grist mills, a potash manufactory, and a distillery, in addition to its seasonal alewife processing facilities.[2]

The changes brought about by these political and industrial revolutions transformed Maine physically and culturally. The shifts were as obvious as the new upriver settlements and as subtle as changes in the fabrics that residents made and purchased, and by extension, changes in their quilts. Although the majority of households did not have looms, families in a neighborhood often cooperated, participating in the many steps involved in textile manufacture.[3] But "the whole spectrum of imported textile choices was too large and the pressure of fashion too great to be satisfied by the limited range of local products."[4] As Paul Rivard points out, people wanted fashionable printed fabrics, and those were not made locally. Fabrics available for purchase in Maine were part of a global economy, as they are today. In 1790, a well-to-do Maine housewife might order English or French fabrics for her bed curtains. Her printed cotton dress and quilting fabrics were imported, as were her better-quality wool and linen, and silk of any kind. By 1810, Maine weavers were able to purchase cotton thread made by one of the three mills operating in Maine, as well as from mills in southern New England.[5] And by the time of statehood in 1820, most towns in southern Maine had carding mills and fulling mills, which considerably sped production of spinning, weaving, and finishing wool, and preparing batts for quilts.[6]

Entrepreneurs had long built sawmills along Maine's rivers, but these required few laborers. It took many years for the right combination of technology, water power, industrial know-how, and capital to coincide with a large enough workforce and market to greatly enlarge

A TIME OF REVOLUTION

Maine's industrial economy. Gradually in the first decades of the 1800s, optimistic investors established mills for wool and cotton production, changing Maine's economic, physical, and demographic landscape. In 1820 Brunswick's Maine Cotton and Woolen Manufacturing Company produced 100,000 yards of sheeting.[7] Even so, Rivard notes that "some two-thirds of cotton cloth was still being woven on handlooms at the time of Maine Statehood," much of it stripes and plaids that did not require printed decoration.[8] Printed textiles were still imported from Europe, or increasingly, from elsewhere in New England. In 1827 a printworks began operation in Springvale, Maine, the first in an increasing number of such mills in the state.[9]

Printing technology was undergoing its own revolution in the late 1700s and early 1800s. For generations, block printing had been the norm. A skilled carver cut designs in wooden blocks that corresponded to the location of one of the dyes needed in the print pattern. Every color in the print required its own block. Careful block placement was critical, and registration marks—usually small dots or lines—can often be found on the fabric, showing where the

Fig. 2.1
Detail, Pieced-Cotton Medallion Top
Polly Allen
Sedgwick, Maine,
1811
63½ x 63¾ inches
Courtesy of Wilson Museum, W13176

The block-printed fabric in the left corner has been over-painted with dye, a technique called penciling. This is especially evident in the upper right-hand sample. Quickly brushing dye—in this case, blue over yellow—gave the print another color faster and more cheaply than adding an extra print block.

CHAPTER 2

printer aligned successive blocks. Additional colors could be added to block-printed textiles by painting or "penciling" dyes, for example, adding yellow to blue-printed foliage or blue to yellow-printed foliage to turn the leaves green (fig. 2.1). Whether printed or penciled, each color required substantial time and a skilled workforce, which added to the cost of the fabric.

In the mid-eighteenth century, after years of experimentation, fashion and technology coincided in the form of copperplate printing. Printers had been using intaglio printing—transferring pigment to paper via engraved plates—since the early 1600s, but in 1756 London textile printers began to apply mordants to affix dyes to fabric in this way.[10] The engraved copper plates could measure up to 36 inches square. The resulting fabrics, though monochromatic, were richly detailed and subtly shaded. The subject matter ranged from whimsical botanicals,

Fig. 2.2
Copperplate-printed Wholecloth Quilt
Maker unknown
Maine, 1770–1790
72½ x 62 inches
Courtesy of Wilson Museum, w13234

Copperplate printers often produced on fabric images that were popular prints on paper. Bucolic scenes like this one were suitable for fabrics that would be used as bed hangings, or in other home settings.

34

Fig. 2.3
Pieced Cotton Quilt
Unknown maker
Maine use history,
1815–1830
99½ x 109½ inches
Courtesy of Wilson
Museum, w04509

The maker of this quilt used fabrics made with every type of print technology of the period: block printing, copperplate engraved printing, and cylinder printing. The drops to either side and the foot of the bed are made from a cylinder-printed column-print pattern. The short repeat creates a strong diagonal. The quilter made the outer border from alternating triangles of block-printed and cylinder-printed fabrics. The central print was first produced in 1795 and probably represents recycled bed hangings. The cylinder-printed fabrics were created in the early 1800s.

birds and fruits, to political scenes, interpretations of popular prints (figs. 2.2 and 2.3), or a juxtaposition of all of them, with a vaguely Chinese gazebo thrown in for good measure. In figure 2.3, the central print, which would have covered the top of the bed, was made from a copperplate-printed fabric called "The Deserted Village" that was manufactured around 1795. The print was based on a poem written by Oliver Goldsmith in 1770. The poem laments the passing of village life as aristocrats take over small farms, forcing families into life in the city, a theme that continued to resonate a generation after Goldsmith wrote the verses. Copperplate printing was used for handkerchiefs, as well as for furnishing fabrics. Several Maine quilts incorporate the latter. In some cases, a quilt may have been made from bed curtains that had hung for some time and had faded, or were no longer as fashionable as they had once been (see figs. 2.3 and 2.26).

Copperplate printing was extremely popular, but like block printing, it was time-consuming to produce. By the 1780s, printers in Great Britain had developed an improved technique: by using engraved metal cylinders, they could print fabric mechanically and much faster than with the laborious system of aligning wooden blocks or copper plates. Furthermore, by the

**Fig. 2.4
Detail, Pieced Cotton Quilt**
Courtesy of Wilson Museum, w04509

The busy border of the quilt (top) is less complex in construction than in surface pattern. The maker used alternating triangles of block-printed fabric in blue and red, and cylinder-printed floral fabrics. The floral fabric has been penciled with blue to make green leaves. Also shown in this image: the cylinder-printed column print (lower right) and copperplate-printed central panel (lower left).

1780s, multiple colors could be printed in one pass of the fabric.[11] The cylinders were as wide as the fabric (about 21–25 inches). Their circumference resulted in shorter design repeats than those on copperplate-engraved fabric. Repeats in the collection of the Winterthur Museum range from 10 1/16 inches to 23 1/2 inches.[12] For several decades the textile industry used all three printing techniques (figs. 2.3 to 2.6), but gradually cylinder printing became the norm.

Customers may not have been wholly aware of the textile revolution in which they were partaking. They would, however, have appreciated the gradual cost decrease and the simultaneous growth in print complexity. And after the supply uncertainties they had endured during the War of 1812, they would have relished the sheer increase in the volume of fabric that became available over the next twenty years.

The War of 1812 affected Maine economically as well as politically. Trade with Europe was curtailed, so some shipowners sought opportunity in smuggling, and others in privateering.[13] In 1814, the British took control of Maine east of the Penobscot River and raided Biddeford Pool. The District of Maine was still part of Massachusetts, but that government refused to come to the area's aid, an act (or rather, an omission) that contributed to Maine's vote to become an independent state five years later.[14] "The rhetoric of the Revolution and the War of 1812 emphasized home production, not only because it was an essential component of the nation's economy, but because images of industrious, self-sacrificing, and patriotic women domesticated and softened the often harsh realities of political conflict, economic uncertainty, and war."[15] After the war, laws against the export of British textile machinery relaxed, which provided a boost to American industry, and the variety of printed cottons available to Maine

A TIME OF REVOLUTION

Fig. 2.5
Medallion Quilt with Engraved Copperplate Printing
Unknown maker
Maine, possibly Troy or East Troy, 1770–1800
100 inches x 86 inches
Maine State Museum
2012.45.1

At first glance, this quilt appears upside down. However, a family member stitched a label on the quilt that places the border-free edge at the head of the quilt. The maker of the quilt may have intended for the design to appear right-way-up to someone lying in bed. The maker included dark brown block-printed and lighter brown copperplate-printed fabrics.

Fig. 2.6
Label Detail, Medallion Quilt with Engraved Copperplate Printing
Maine State Museum
2012.45.1

A century or more after the manufacture of this quilt, Walter Knight, probably a descendent of the maker, entered the "ancient" quilt in a fair, winning a prize. He lived in East Troy, Maine, and while the quilt might have been made there, the town was not settled by Euro-Americans until 1801, well after the quilt's fabrics were made. The maker might have brought old fabrics with her to make the quilt, but it is more likely that she or a descendant brought the quilt to Troy.

quilters, even in the hinterland, gradually increased.[16] By the 1830s, quilters reveled in their access to so many colorful fabrics, often combining scores of different prints in one quilt (figs. 2.7, 2.29–2.31).

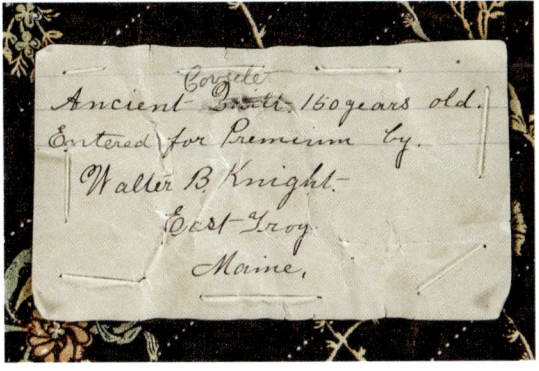

CHAPTER 2

Fig. 2.7
Pieced Star Quilt
Maker unknown
Probably Maine,
ca. 1840
77 x 72 inches
Courtesy of Sue Clark
Rivers

Today this eight-pointed star is called the Star of LeMoyne or Eastern Star. Its maker used over a dozen different fabrics to make the stars.

☙

Politics changed Maine's population after the American Revolution, and the Industrial Revolution changed its demographics, as textile mills drew girls from the country and immigrants from abroad. Gradually even rural farm families wove less fabric at home, instead buying it from the local textile mills that bought their flocks' fleeces. The number of surviving Maine quilts increases dramatically after 1800. This is likely due to the growth of Maine's population and its increased stability after decades of war, as well as to the revolution in production and printing techniques that allowed Maine's women increased access to more affordable fabrics.

Stenciled Bedcovers

By Lynne Bassett

During the first half of the nineteenth century, and especially from about 1820 to 1840, Americans reveled in new and inexpensive textiles, wallpapers, and paints made possible by the water-powered technologies of the Industrial Revolution. The "Fancy" fashion called for layers of pattern and color, with interior walls and trims painted in multiple hues, and furnishings of faux-grained furniture, boldly patterned chintz, painted tin, colorful ceramics, and sparkling pressed glass.[17] Among the arts that contributed to this aesthetic was stenciling, which was employed for multiple surfaces within a home, and even used on costume accessories such as purses and collars. Probably the most familiar form of this decorative technique is stenciled walls, including those decorated by the famed artist, inventor, and publisher Rufus Porter (1792–1884), and his nephew, Jonathan D. Poor (1803–1845), whose legacy is preserved at Maine State Museum and at the Rufus Porter Museum in Bridgton, Maine.[18]

Women also picked up the stenciling brush (called a "stub" for its short bristles) and embellished not only walls but also textile surfaces. Many women may have learned the skill as girls at a female academy, which would have offered a variety of fancywork techniques along with an academic curriculum of English, French, geography, history, and arithmetic. A number of books offered instruction, as well, including widely circulated texts such as Lydia Maria Child's *The Girl's Own Book* (first published in 1833 and frequently reissued). Rufus Porter published instructions for stenciling in *A Select Collection of Approved, Genuine, Secret, and Modern Receipts, for the Preparation and Execution of Various Valuable and Curious Arts, as Practised by the Best Artists of the Present Age*. Fortunately, his instructions were more succinct than his book title:

Take a sheet of pasteboard and paint thereon with a pencil, any flower or figure that would be elegant for a border or carpet figure; then with small gouges and chisels, or a sharp penknife, cut out the figure completely, that it be represented by holes cut through the paper. Lay this paper or pasteboard on the ground intended to receive the figure . . . and with a stiff, smooth brush, paint with a quick vibration over the whole figure.— Then take up the paper and you will have the entire figure on the ground.[19]

Other published instructions of the time recommended a rubbing motion to apply the paint. A close examination of stenciled surfaces often reveals which school of thought the stenciler followed.

The coloring matter used for stenciling could be dyes (such as indigo, cochineal, or saffron) or pigments (such as the mineral ferric ferrocyanide, also known as Prussian blue). In any case, preparing the materials was laborious, requiring care not only in following the recipe for each color, but for handling materials including hydrochloric acid, sulfuric acid, chloride of ammonia, and others.[20] The colors used on stenciled bedcovers are generally limited to three or four, unlike the more complex schoolgirl theorem paintings—perhaps reflecting the onerous job of grinding and mixing a large amount of coloring matter. Gum tragacanth, produced from the sticky sap of various Asian and East European shrubs, was generally used to control the spread of the coloring matter on a textile.

Stenciled bedcovers are often cited as being "rare," but at least sixty are known.[21] They were particularly popular in the northeastern United States, with only three identified so far as falling outside the region of New England and New York.[22] The sophisticated adaptation of common stenciling motifs on Nanna Bradley Whittier's spread suggests a broad familiarity with this decorative technique in Maine (fig. 2.8). Schoolgirl theorems commonly depict similar baskets of fruit, and the floral vines and trees were also popular motifs on stenciled walls and on other stenciled bedcovers—but the fantastic representation of an undulating grapevine sets this spread apart. Emanating from a large blue pitcher at the bottom center, the vines are espaliered to form a grid, with bird-laden trees and the baskets of fruit stenciled within the interstices. The composition is colorful, balanced, whimsical, and expertly executed. It is made of three strips of cotton sheeting, seamed rather than butted. The straight-grain binding of pink and white gingham is an unusual finish, as other stenciled spreads are typically hemmed.

This masterpiece of American folk art was found by an auctioneer, folded in a dresser drawer during an estate evaluation.[23] Two old notes accompanied it—one written in nineteenth-century script with the names of Nanna Bradley Whittier and Nathaniel Whittier, and the other note stating that Nanna was the bedcover's maker. Nanna (1793–1841) and Nathaniel (1794–1822) had two sons before Nathaniel's death at just twenty-eight years of age. Nanna did not remarry. One son, Hiram Thing Whittier, died as an adolescent. Fortunately, Nanna was surrounded by family in Mount Vernon and Vienna, with in-laws, parents, brothers, and sisters all nearby.[24] The exuberance of this stenciled bedcover belies the grief that Nanna endured in the decade during which it was likely produced. Perhaps it was a project to distract her—folded up and put away in the chest when she was done, leaving it to be discovered, bright and unfaded, 180 years later.

**Fig. 2.8
Stenciled Bedcover**
Nanna Bradley Whittier (1793–1841)
Mount Vernon, Maine. 1820–1830
102 x 96 inches
Private collection.
Photo courtesy of Olde Hope Antiques

Nanna Bradley Whittier's masterful design of a leafy vine forming a grid is a unique feature among stenciled bedcovers.

A TIME OF REVOLUTION

Fig. 2.9
Stenciled Bedcover
Emily Morton (1810–1879), maker
Thorndike, Maine, 1826
103 x 104 inches
Courtesy of Colonial Williamsburg Foundation, bequest of Mrs. Jason R. (Grace H.) Westerfield, 1974.609.28

Sixteen-year-old Emily Morton employed a motif commonly found on various types of early nineteenth-century bedcovers—a vessel filled with flowers. However, her design of a bowl set upon a tripod candlestand is particularly whimsical and charming.

Another documented Maine stenciled bedcover, made in 1826 by sixteen-year-old Emily Morton of Thorndike (in Waldo County), also features a design of flowering branches growing from a central pot, though the plant is smaller and sits on a pedestal base resembling a candlestand (fig. 2.9).[25] The plant grows with the uncontrolled vigor of a weed. Several inner borders of small pots and sprays of flowers surround this central motif; birds sit atop the largest pots. Interestingly, the large flowerpots on one side differ from those on the other side. Delicate floral sprays compose the outer border. Emily carefully considered the placement of her motifs along the bottom drop, spacing three flowerpots evenly, and calculated her borders to wrap around the edges of the cut-out corners smoothly. Perhaps she had learned from her miscalculation on the spread's left side, where she added some filling from the border design to make up for the difference in the smaller-sized pots. The spread is constructed of three widths of cotton cloth and is finished with hemming.

Quilting Beyond the Bed

By Lynne Bassett

Not all quilting was intended for bedcovers. Surviving garments and notations in women's diaries and other period documents clearly indicate that a variety of garments were quilted as well—including petticoats, coat linings, pelisses, bonnets, and even shoes. Sarah Bowman Winter (1793–1828) of Bath kept warm when the cold winds blew in off the ocean in this quilted pelisse (a dress-like coat that opens down the length of the center front) of sage green silk woven with a floral pattern (figs. 2.10 to 2.12). Wool wadding provides the insulating layer.

The daughter of Dr. Nathaniel Bowman, Sarah (1793–1828) was named for her mother. She married Samuel Winter (1789–1835) and gave birth to seven children before dying at only thirty-five years of age. The pelisse descended in the line of her eldest daughter, Marcia Bowman Anderson of Windham, until it was donated to the Maine Historical Society. A portrait of Sarah Bowman Winter from the early 1820s shows her to have been a young woman with dark eyes and a fashionable hairstyle with brunette curls clustered around her temples and a tortoiseshell comb tucked into the loops of hair on the top of her head.[26] Her clothing, too, was stylish for this period of transition from the Neoclassical to the Romantic Era. The portrait shows a stiffly starched, sheer muslin collar

**Fig. 2.10
Silk Pelisse**
Worn by Sarah Bowman Winter (1793–1828) Bath, Maine. ca. 1820–25
54 inches high
Courtesy of Maine Historical Society, 1992.297.2

The removable cape collar of this quilted pelisse provided extra warmth, if necessary. A common cold-weather garment in the early nineteenth century, the pelisse provided a modicum of comfort when worn over a fashionable sheer cotton dress.

A TIME OF REVOLUTION

**Fig. 2.11
Silk Pelisse, back**
Courtesy of Maine
Historical Society,
1992.297.2

Simple lines of vertical quilting and a horizontal chevron border keep the insulating layer of wool batting inside the pelisse from shifting.

**Fig. 2.12
Silk Pelisse, detail,
back and cape collar**
Courtesy of Maine
Historical Society,
1992.297.2

The pelisse is made of an imported sage green silk woven with a delicate floral pattern.

edged with ruffle falling gracefully from a high, rounded fold, emphasizing the sloped shoulder line. The waistline of the dress is high—just under the bust.

Sarah Winter's pelisse is constructed with a similarly high waistline and dates from the same period as the portrait. The pelisse is exactly what a young woman would have worn over a fashionable dress of sheer muslin (also called "cambric" in the period) if she had to venture outside. In her reminiscence of this period, Sarah Anna Emery of Salem, Massachusetts (another New England port city), wrote:

The usual outdoors garment for . . . the younger [ladies], silk pelisses in fancy colors were fashionable. . . . White dresses were worn entirely by young ladies when in full dress, and usually on Sundays. However cold the weather or wet the walking a white cambric, with a green, blue, or lilac silk pelisse, a straw bonnet trimmed to match, white silk stockings and kid slippers of the same hue of the pelisse, or cork soled morocco walking shoes, with a sable muff and tippet, was the street dress of a young lady of ton.[27]

Winter's pelisse has a removable cape collar, which would have provided extra warmth and protection from damp weather if necessary. The sleeves are extra-long, gathered at the shoulders and tapering to a narrow wrist. When they were pushed up to the proper arm's length, they would have puffed a bit, anticipating the large leg-o'-mutton shape that would be fashionable by the end of the decade. The quilting of the elegant patterned silk is simple—just vertical lines throughout the body, with a band of parallel sideways V's forming a border around the bottom. The shoulder cape is quilted in echoed lines following the contour of the cape. Plain, tan-colored cotton forms the lining.

Sarah Bowman Winter certainly had at least a bonnet trimmed to match her pelisse, as noted above by the fashion-conscious Sarah Anna Emery. She may even have quilted a bonnet to match.[28] Quilted bonnets and hoods were very common cold-weather garments for New England women prior to the twentieth century. They could be elegant, like the golden brown mid-nineteenth-century bonnet with a pleated ruffle edging and sapphire blue silk lining (fig. 2.13)—or simply warm, like the plain black silk hood, which was probably actually intended to be a lining under a more fashionable bonnet (fig. 2.14).

Quilted covers for bonnets are also a form that survives, as seen in the black Quaker bonnet with its golden tan silk cover (fig. 2.15). (Quaker bonnets retained the straight, closely fitted brim that was fashionable in the early nineteenth century for decades after it fell out of style for the general population, as part of the "plain" Quaker philosophy.) The warmest style of quilted bonnet or hood was the "prodigiously hot" pumpkin hood, as described by colonial revival historian Alice Morse Earle.[29] Wadded thickly with wool and gathered over a line of cording between lines of puffs, this type of head covering does, indeed, look like a pumpkin (fig. 2.16). The addition of pretty silk ribbon bows does little to reduce its bulky appearance.

The difference between a quilted hood and a quilted bonnet is debatable. The terms are largely interchangeable, though typically a hood is a soft head cover with a neck skirt, while a bonnet has a stiffer structure and may not cover the neck. In the period, people would have certainly recognized the difference between a fashionable quilted bonnet and a utilitarian quilted hood. Harriet Beecher Stowe, in *Poganuc People*, a reminiscence of her childhood in the early nineteenth century, associated hoods with "prudent old house mothers."[30] That would probably be the case with the quilted hood pieced of two not-quite-alike blue-gray silks (2.17). The quilted head covering made with changeable pink/gray silk, on the other hand, has an undeniable elegance due to its shimmery luster, which combined with its stiffer construction would seem to place it in the "bonnet" category (2.18).

Fig. 2.14
Plain, Black Silk Bonnet Lining
(opposite, top left)
Used in the Richmond, Maine, area, nineteenth century
12 inches high
Maine State Museum, 77.15.3

This plain silk bonnet was not likely used alone, but as a warm lining for another bonnet.

Fig. 2.15
Quilted Bonnet Cover
(opposite, top right)
Worn by Deborah Robbins Wing
Manchester, Maine, ca. 1845
11 inches high
Maine State Museum, 70.91.2

Like bonnet liners, quilted bonnet covers added warmth. Unlike bonnet liners, covers showed, so the silk tended to be brighter and the form more stylish.

Fig. 2.13
Quilted Bonnet
Used in Gardiner Maine, ca. 1850–1860
11¾ inches high
Maine State Museum 69.44.60

The stiffened brim and elegant pleated ruffle mark this garment as a quilted bonnet, rather than a less fashionable hood. The rows of thick batting encircling the head would have been welcome protection against winter's cold.

Fig. 2.16
Pumpkin Hood
(middle left)
Used in Maine
1830–1860
17 inches high
Courtesy of Maine
Historical Society
1998.1.90.2

Stuffed with warm wool, pumpkin hoods protected the wearer from the coldest winter winds.

Fig. 2.17
Quilted Hood
(middle right)
Sarah Hodge Barrett Hubbard, probable wearer
Hallowell, Maine, 1850–1875
11½ x 10 x 8½ inches
Maine State Museum, 80.157.153

This quilted hood was found in the home of Governor John Hubbard and his wife, Sarah. The couple had two daughters, but this was probably worn by Mrs. Hubbard.

Fig. 2.18
Quilted Bonnet
(bottom)
Maker unknown
Worn in Maine, ca 1825–1850
13 inches high
Courtesy of Maine
Historical Society
1993.300.1054

The warp and weft of this silk bonnet were different colored threads. The resulting fabric shimmers as it is moved.

CHAPTER 2

REFLECTION OF COMMUNITY: WABANAKI SILK-RIBBON APPLIQUÉ

In the late 1700s and early 1800s, as Euro-American settlement expanded into new areas of Maine, its indigenous population was squeezed onto increasingly small tracts of land. Many Natives living west of the Kennebec moved away, but east and north, settlement pressures were less, and Native Americans remained on their homelands, albeit in more constrained settlement areas. Today Maine is home to four tribes: the Penobscot, Passamaquoddy, Maliseet, and Micmac. Together they form the Wabanaki Confederacy. In the first half of the 1800s, Wabanaki artists crafted exquisitely detailed, wearable textile art. The technique, appliqué, was familiar to any non-Native quilter in Maine, but Wabanaki expression of the art was wholly different from Euro-American appliqué, reflecting the difference between the two communities. Its materials were silk on wool, and the execution was finer than that found on most mainstream quilts. Embellished with glass beads, Wabanaki appliqué work was part of a visual language of identity.

In any culture, the primary purposes of clothing are shelter—protection from the cold or wet—and a means of adherence to cultural norms of modesty. Its secondary purpose is communication. Dress worn by social classes is generally different, as is that worn by men and women. Clothing of any era and any source sends messages to other members of the group. For example, one might not wear gardening clothes to, say, be part of a wedding party. The two outfits send very different messages to viewers. The first is comfortable, casual, and likely dirty. The second is likely to be dressier, more fashionable, festive or formal, and will, at the beginning of the wedding at least, be clean. Viewers can easily distinguish the two ensembles and gauge the type of setting in which they might be worn and the role the wearer plays in the activities. The same is true of clothing in the 1820s or 1840s. While today's time traveler might not understand the nuances of bystanders' clothing in Bangor, Maine, in 1835, the local residents would have recognized at a glance the difference between a well-cut suit and that worn by a laborer, and the difference between the day dress of a well-off woman and the clothing of a servant. Wabanaki artists took this communication potential a step further, creating intricate designs on clothing that were not only beautiful, but stated the identity of the wearer to those who understood the visual code.[31] The clothing "instantly communicated messages of community affiliation. . . . To non-Natives, the overall [perceived] exoticism of these garments likely masked messages of tribal identity. To other Wabanakis . . . the motifs appliquéd and beaded on each garment would have communicated the wearer's place in a complex social world."[32]

As early as the 1780s, some Wabanaki men were wearing clothing that was indistinguishable from that worn by the general (Euro-American) public.[33] By the 1860s, few Wabanaki men wore traditional leggings, although women continued to do so for a few more decades, probably because leggings, shorter skirts, and a wrap, called a matchcoat, were more practical and comfortable than prevailing fashions.[34] On special occasions,

A TIME OF REVOLUTION

however, Wabanaki men wore beaded coats, sashes, and collars, and women wore peaked caps, a custom that persisted into the early 1900s.[35] The styles of regalia evolved over the twentieth century, and today Wabanaki artists are again making ribbon-appliqué regalia (see figs. 8.39 to 8.41).

In the 1800s, Wabanaki women traditionally wore peaked caps, decorated hats that came to a point behind the crown of the head. Those worn by Penobscot, Passamaquoddy, and Maliseet women had a curved edge (fig. 2.19), while those worn by Micmac women were cut at a right angle in the front (fig. 2.20). Silk-ribbon appliqué work also adorned men's regalia,

Fig. 2.19
Penobscot Peaked Cap
Worn, and likely made by Molly Molasses
Indian Island Maine, 1790s
Back seam 15½ inches
Maine State Museum
2014.17.1

Marie or Mary Balasee Nicola was popularly known as Molly Molasses. She was a powerful woman in her own right and was the partner of John Neptune, the lieutenant governor of the Penobscot Nation.

such as coat cuffs, collars, and leggings (see figs. 2.23 and 2.24). A pair of Passamaquoddy cradleboard wrappers has survived (fig. 2.21). An 1817 watercolor portrait of a Passamaquoddy woman named Denny Soccabeson shows her at a table in an English garrison during the War of 1812 (fig. 2.22).[36] Soccabeson was the daughter of Governor Francis Joseph Neptune, and her clothing proclaims her status: her peaked cap and blouse are richly appliquéd; her skirt and leggings are trimmed as well; and she is wearing a gold cross on a necklace, silver ear bobs, and two silver brooches, which were political as well as status symbols.[37] The baby at her feet is bundled into a cradleboard with decorated wrappers like those in figure 2.21.

Fig. 2.20
Micmac Peaked Cap
Maker unknown
Made for Lady Mary Louisa Lambton
Canada, probably 1838, possibly 1847–1854
Back seam 14¾ inches
Courtesy of New York State Historical Association, T0041

Lady Mary Louisa Lambton acquired this Micmac woman's peaked cap when she was in Canada, either in 1838, or when her husband, Lord Elgin, was governor general of Canada. It may have been a presentation piece, given by representatives of a Micmac/ Mi'kmaq community.[38]

Fig. 2.21
Passamaquoddy Cradleboard Wrappers
Maker unknown
Eastern Maine or western New Brunswick, 1790–1820
6 x 46¼ inches and 7 x 52 inches
Maine State Museum, 84.127.1

Wabanaki mothers carried their babies in cradleboards, wrapping them in for safety much as Euro-American mothers swaddled their infants. These decorative cradleboard wrappers of silk-ribbon appliqué on wool broadcloth date to the turn of the nineteenth century.

Fig. 2.22
Watercolor Portrait of Denny Soccabeson
Lt. Alexander Henry Charles Villars
Eastport, Maine, September 18th, 1817
7¾ x 5¾ inches
Maine State Museum photograph. Courtesy of Colonial Williamsburg Foundation, 1994.300.1

During the War of 1812, the British seized the eastern half of Maine. British lieutenant Alexander Villars painted "Denn—daughter of Frances Joseph [Neptune]—Governor of Passamaquoddy" when she visited the British fort, possibly with her father and husband. She brought her baby with her, swaddled in a cradleboard. Cradleboard wrappers cushioned the child, and ties held baby and wrappers in place. Denny wears a peaked cap embellished with silk-ribbon appliqué similar to that worn by Molly Molasses (see fig. 2.19), as well as a jacket, skirt, and leggings. Her jewelry displays her status within the community.

Silk-ribbon appliqué is delicate, exacting work. Jennifer Neptune, a noted Penobscot artisan, recently recreated a chief's collar similar to that worn by Francis Stanislaus (fig. 2.23), for Penobscot elder Charles Shay, a descendent of the collar's original owner (see fig. 8.11). The early nineteenth-century collar is now in the collection of the Smithsonian and is too fragile to be worn (fig. 2.24). Neptune, a skilled needleworker, labored over three hundred hours to make the new collar. And unlike the ancestor who made the original, Neptune had the advantage of commercial ribbons in very narrow widths, not to mention electric lighting and

Fig. 2.23
Francis Stanislaus in His Regalia
Photographer unknown
1891
Courtesy of Maine Historic Preservation Commission

The regalia that Francis Stanislaus wore when he posed for a photo shoot in 1891 was much older than he was. It had probably been worn by two or even three generations before him. The panels around his waist are very similar to those in fig. 2.25. They may originally have been worn on the front of a coat.

Fig. 2.24
Penobscot Chief's Collar
Possibly made by Ada Sockbeson, or a member of the Nicola-Neptune family
Indian Island, Maine, ca. 1800
22¼ x 19.5 inches
Courtesy of National Museum of the American Indian, Smithsonian Institution 00 8479

In the late 1700s or very early 1800s, a Penobscot woman spent over 300 hours making this intricate collar embellished with glass beads and fine silk-ribbon appliqué. The wearer would have been a man of standing in the community. He probably also had a decorated coat and leggings that he wore on important occasions, like those shown in figures 2.23 and 2.25.

Fig. 2.25
Ribbon Appliqué and Beadwork Panels
Maker unknown
Indian Island, Maine, early 1800s
Each 21 x 5¾ inches
Maine State Museum, 2011.51.2

These panels were probably once worn along the center front seams of a Penobscot man's chief's coat. Their silk-ribbon appliqué work is nearly identical to pieces worn by Francis Stanislaus. They were probably made by the same individual and worn by a member of Stanislaus's extended family.

magnifiers. She estimates that the original would have required more than five hundred hours of an artist's time.[39] It is no wonder that Frances Stanislaus and his relations found new ways to wear their precious collar, cuffs, and other components after the original garments wore out or became otherwise unusable (fig. 2.25).

The patterns of appliqué and beadwork crafted into Wabanaki garments communicated a wearer's status, as well as their tribal affiliation. Native Americans in Maine, the Canadian Maritimes, and Quebec would have been able to read the garments' visual vocabulary, whereas a non-Native might not. Upon seeing a man wearing a richly decorated coat, someone who had few interactions with Wabanakis might see an Indian who was an important man. To members of the four Wabanaki tribes, and those who attended diplomatic or cultural events with them, the tribal identity of the wearer and his status in the group could be read instantly.[40]

Wabanaki artists used commercially available raw materials: wool broadcloth, silk, and glass beads, and crafted them into communication devices worn within the community. In so doing, they transformed European goods into uniquely Native American works of art and identity. Wabanaki artistic expression mirrored the differences between Maine's indigenous and Euro-American communities: though the materials and techniques were common to both groups, the results of their artistry were as different as their makers' worlds.

CHAPTER 2

GALLERY

Fig. 2.26
Copperplate-Printed Wholecloth Quilt
Maker unknown
Possibly Augusta, Maine, area, 1775–1800
95 inches x 87 inches
Maine State Museum, 69.163.1

Nothing is known about the maker or owners of this quilt. The people who bought it at an Augusta, Maine, area yard sale were told that it was part of the furnishings sent to Maine from France as part of a plot to save Marie Antoinette from the guillotine by sending her to rural New England. Stories have circulated for years that a Maine ship's captain was thwarted in his attempt to bring Antoinette to freedom. However, it is much more likely that this quilt was made as part of a set of bed furnishings or made from bed hangings.

Fig. 2.27
Libby Family Cotton Quilt with a Ruffle Fall
Unknown maker from the Libby family
Scarborough, Maine, 1830s, with eighteenth-century fabric
93 inches x 107 inches
Maine State Museum, 94.25.1

The condition of this quilt is nearly pristine. It was apparently treasured by the first generations to own it, after which either its family history or by then unfashionable colors caused family members to stow it in a trunk and leave it there. Purchased at a Libby family estate sale in the 1990s, the quilt was made by a member of that prominent Scarborough, Maine, family. Its maker used fabrics manufactured by two very different processes, decades and continents apart. Two of the three fabrics feature cylinder printing, where a series of metal cylinders engraved or etched with patterns carry the various colors of pigment, allowing the fabric to be impressed with multiple colors in one pass of the fabric through the machine. The printed fabric was then glazed, to give its colors extra punch. The patterns and bright colors of the cottons date the quilt to the 1830s. The third fabric was one the family had treasured for several generations. One hundred or more years after the quilt was made, the family recalled that it was fabric from the wedding gown of Hannah Libby. Hannah was an honored name in the family, and several Libby women were named Hannah. One of them was born in 1731. This Hannah Libby married John Fogg in Scarborough on January 18, 1751. She may have worn the gown that her family so treasured.

Fig. 2.28
Detail, Libby Family Quilt
Maine State Museum, 94.25.1

The lighter-colored fabric the Libby family quilter used in her quilt was produced in England or France around 1750. It is block printed. The two brighter fabrics were cylinder printed, probably in the United States, in the 1830s.

CHAPTER 2

Fig. 2.29
Flying Geese Quilt
Unknown maker
Maine, 1830s
101 x 95 inches
Courtesy of Sue Clark Rivers

By the 1830s, cotton was plentiful and cheap enough that some quilters used scores of fabrics, some reused, but many new.

Fig. 2.30
Detail, Flying Geese Quilt
Courtesy of Sue Clark Rivers

The construction of this quilt shows some of the variety of fabrics used, but also illustrates the somewhat casual approach to quilt construction common in the 1800s.

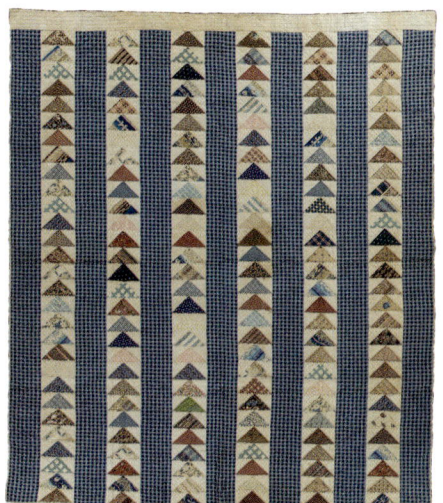

Fig. 2.31
Flying Geese Quilt
Unknown maker
Maine, 1840s
84 x 75 inches
Courtesy of Sue Clark Rivers

The blue color that dominates this quilt became very popular around 1840. German chemists developed the color, called Prussian blue, in the early 1700s. It was not until the late 1830s that textile production and dye chemistry combined with fashion to make Prussian blue fabrics a fad.

A TIME OF REVOLUTION

Fig. 2.32
Diagonal Strip Quilt with Uneven Nine-Patch Quilt
Made for the Leavitt family
Waterboro, Maine, 1835–1845
109 x 104 inches
Maine State Museum, 2019.40.1

In 2019, nonagenarian William Frey Taylor recalled his grandmother telling him that this family quilt was made by the Waterboro town clerk. The town had six town clerks in the period between 1835 and 1845, and all of them were men. It is possible, but improbable, that one of them made it. More likely, it was made by a family member of one of the town clerks. The quilt descended in the family for over 175 years before a family member donated it to the Maine State Museum. At least some of the bold fabrics used in the quilt were recycled, probably from a woman's dress. The fabric shows patterns of wear and fading that predate its use in the quilt. Many of the fabrics remain bright. The quilt's maker used several colors of quilting thread, white for the light bands, and blue and brown as well as white for the colored strips. Strip quilts were fairly common in the second quarter of the 1800s in Maine. The diagonal layout of this example is very unusual.

Fig. 2.33
Star Quilt
Signed by Betsy Merrill
Cumberland, Maine, 1834
99 x 101 inches
Courtesy of the Blanchard family

Betsy Merrill of Cumberland, Maine, signed the reverse side of this star quilt. While it is smudged, the date appears to be 1834, and the fabrics are consistent with that date.

CHAPTER 2

Fig. 2.34
Flying Geese Strip Quilt with Harrison Print
Unknown maker
Waterville, Maine, area, ca. 1840
101 x 94 inches
Maine State Museum 2012.44.1

Although light damage has badly drained a third of this quilt of color, the overall design of strips of pink and brown flying geese, alternating with a pink print fabric, can still be seen. The pink fabric was produced around the time of the presidential campaign of William Henry Harrison in 1840 and bears motifs associated with him, namely a log cabin and a barrel of hard cider. Despite Harrison growing up in a well-connected family, his campaign used these hardscrabble images to imply that he was a man of the people. His short presidency included several superlatives: he was the oldest man elected president, a record that stood until Ronald Reagan's election; at nearly two hours in length and over 8,000 words, his inaugural speech was the longest ever; and by dying of a fever 31 days into his presidency, he was the first American president to die in office; his term was also the shortest. This sad fact may have added to the popularity of the printed fabric used in this quilt, making it a memorial print, and not just one used to support a presidential candidate.

Fig. 2.35
Detail, Flying Geese and Harrison Print
Maine State Museum 2012.44.1

The Harrison print featured a group of log cabins. The barrel outside the closest of these bears the words "HARD CIDER." This bucolic political scene alternates with bands of leaves and flowers, with an eagle and banner above a portrait that reads "HARRISON AND REFORM."

ANTEBELLUM ALBUM QUILTS

"An Album gift
Each piece a flame
High in your memory
A place would claim."

Huldah E. Blanchard, Bark Messenger quilt, 1850, Cumberland Center

In the 1840s, a quilting fad spread from the mid-Atlantic states throughout the country.[1] Album quilts, also called friendship quilts, in which many quilters contributed blocks, were immensely popular and as varied as the quilters who made them. Some quilting groups in the mid-Atlantic region exclusively favored blocks of chintz motifs. They stitched pre-printed chintz panels to a white background, or cut individual flowers, leaves, birds, and other elements and combined them into new compositions. This was not a new idea; it had been popular a few generations earlier, as women sought to create their own *palampore*, or tree of life.[2] In Baltimore, Maryland, another trend developed: professional designers created complex appliqué patterns and inspired women to make similar creations. In Maine and elsewhere in New England, however, album quilts were an amateur affair. Some quilt groups used one block pattern for a unified look, despite the variety of prints used in the quilt (fig. 3.1).

But many Maine album quilts from the 1840s and 1850s include an assortment of pieced and appliquéd blocks. Each quilter contributed one or more blocks in the pattern and construction method(s)

Fig. 3.1
Album Quilt
Friends and family members of May Philbrick Gardner, 30 inscribed names
Dennysville, Maine, 1848
85 x 86 inches
Maine State Museum, 2001.82.1

Thirty friends and family members of May Philbrick Gardner inscribed album blocks on this quilt. According to her granddaughter, May's mother or mother-in-law gave her the quilt.

CHAPTER 3

Fig. 3.2
The Colesworthy Album Quilt
Probably the Ladies' Sewing Circle of the Falmouth Congregational Church;
48 inscribed names
Falmouth, Maine, 1857
98 x 98 inches
Maine State Museum, 97.29.1

A group of women from Falmouth, Maine, made this quilt for Joseph Colesworthy when he turned twenty-one and moved to Portland. Although the two towns are only eight miles apart, Colesworthy was striking out on his own, away from his home community.

of her choice, and the women coordinating the quilting effort put the blocks together with varying degrees of regard for overall composition (figs. 3.2 and 3.3). Album quilts were community efforts, regardless of the techniques involved.

In the twenty years before the Civil War, Maine communities were in flux, as they had been throughout the state's relatively brief history. The border between Maine and Canada was finally defined in 1842. By 1840, Maine's population had reached the half million mark, and by 1850, the pattern of settlement in the state was firmly established. Hornsby's map of 1850 population centers can be laid over a 2020 map of Maine towns, and with the exception of a few late nineteenth-century communities, the two maps look much the same.[3] Maine's cities, mill towns, and rural hamlets of 1840 to 1860 saw many changes, as individuals and families moved, seeking better economic situations. New textile mills in Massachusetts and Maine were making cotton cheaper and easier to obtain. New loom designs made woolen mills profitable, and entrepreneurs built them along small rivers throughout southern Maine.[4]

ANTEBELLUM ALBUM QUILTS

Fig. 3.3
Libby-Freeman Album Quilt
Various makers; 29 inscribed names
Gray, West Gray, New Gloucester, Maine, 1852
96 x 97 inches
Courtesy of Maine Historical Society, 2002.318

This album quilt from the Gray-New Gloucester area is similar to that of other quilts from southern Maine in the years leading up to the Civil War. Its blocks are a mix of colors and patterns. Its makers used pieced and appliqué techniques, with a smattering of embroidery. Some of the blocks, such as those above the right cut corner, have interior borders, a feature often seen on antebellum Maine quilts.

These mills tended to be much smaller than cotton mills. Unlike most cotton mills, which employed hundreds of employees, many early woolen mills employed fewer than twenty local people.[5] In 1843, Maine had 175 fulling mills and woolen mills, employing 532 people. By contrast, its six cotton "manufactories" and three dyeing and print works employed 1,414.[6] While cotton mills employed more women, men constituted most of the workers in woolen mills.[7]

By 1830, Massachusetts mills in just the three towns of Taunton, Lowell, and Fall River were producing over twenty million yards of calico a year, and each mill introduced hundreds of new patterns each year.[8] The dramatic increase in cotton production was consistent across New England and grew with the decades as new mills were established. Merchants accordingly stocked more fabric in their shops. In March 1842, a buyer for Thomas Wilson O'Brien's store in Portland bought in Boston twenty-one lots of fancy prints, in quantities ranging from 32 yards to 132 yards, as well as "eight bales of brown cotton." It was the first of three buying trips that year for O'Brien's staff.[9]

Industrialization was growing in Maine. In 1855, the *Maine Register* listed eighty different manufacturing categories, ranging from axes to yarn.[10] Many of these manufacturers, such as dyers and spool makers, supported the growing textile industry. In 1850, 17 percent of Maine's manufacturing workforce worked in textile mills, most in cotton mills. This was second only to the lumber industry (21 percent).[11] New mills needed new workers, and new workers needed lodging. As Paul Rivard has observed, "There were no commuters in the age of the horse."[12] Towns grew, accordingly. Mills in Lowell, Massachusetts, initially employed young women, known as "mill girls." In the 1830s and 1840s, thousands of New England farm girls moved to Lowell and other mill towns, to seek the modest wages mill work promised. The hours were long and the work was hard, but farmers' children were used to both. At other factories, entire families worked in the mills. By 1850, new immigrants began to replace local girls and families at the factories.[13] Both trends in mill work transformed Maine communities. Rural Maine lost workers, while towns like Biddeford and Saco, and later Auburn, expanded rapidly as textile mills were established and grew. Like Maine itself, Biddeford was changing rapidly. In 1820, it was a community of 1,738 souls. By 1850, the town had a population more than three times that, with eleven textile factories that employed 3,000 men, women, and children, and produced over thirty million yards of cotton fabric each year.[14]

CHAPTER 3

At the same time, the country was steadily advancing toward Civil War, with its attendant uncertainties of cotton supplies for mills, the potential of trade (and hence employment) interruptions, and the lack of labor as men went to war.

Community groups such as ladies' societies were a stable presence in these turbulent years. And many of these groups made album quilts. Many such quilts from the 1840s and 1850s include inscriptions providing the reason for the quilts' construction, or clues to it. Even with inscriptions, the reason for a quilt's construction is not always obvious. Ministers and their wives, who were called or sent to new churches every few years, were often the recipients of quilts, as were newlyweds. Other life events could spark the creation of a quilt, such as that made for Joseph Colesworthy when he moved from Falmouth, Maine, all the way to Portland (a distance of eight miles) at age twenty-one, to start his professional life (see fig. 3.2). Mainers were on the move in the second quarter of the 1800s. Some families moved to the new communities within the state that were springing up farther upriver, centered on mill industries or logging. Others moved west, to the promise of farmland that had fewer rocks and more frost-free days. Many families were involved in seafaring trades, and Maine mariners took goods around the world. Opportunity for advancement could mean that an aspiring officer and his family moved to a new community. The recipient of the 1850 Bark Messenger quilt is not yet known, but an inscription, "The Bark Messenger, laden with friendship, bound for Wellfleet," suggests that the gift was for community members moving from Cumberland, Maine, to Massachusetts (see fig. 3.11).

It is no surprise that some of Maine's outstanding album quilts come from towns with strong shipbuilding and maritime trades. Mariners left for months or years at a time with the possibility that they might not return. Their wives and daughters found support in one another and in their churches. As Lynne Bassett observed, "Friendship quilts were the product of a highly religious and sentimental society that romanticized friendship, death, nature, and the home," the very aspects of their lives that women could count on.[15] Album quilts, carrying the goodwill of many members of a community, are tangible reminders of the fluid communities in which they were sewn and the bonds of friendship that travelers carried with them. The names they carry can also provide clues into the nature of the community that made the quilts.

Inscribed Quilts

by Pamela Weeks

Inscribed quilts represent a variety of friendship, presentation, donation, and fundraising functions.[16] Because the texts of some quilts were obviously penned by one person, I prefer to use "inscribed quilt" instead of "signature quilt" as a general

Fig. 3.4
Stencils
Maker unknown
Maine, mid-to late 1800s
Each 1 x 2.25 inches
Maine State Museum,
79.117.7 (top);
76.38.4 (bottom)

For decades, brass stencils were used to mark one's name on a wide variety of objects, including quilt blocks.

Fig. 3.5
Detail, Stenciled Album Block
Angie S. Glidden
Embden, Maine, late 1800s
9 x 9 inches
Maine State Museum,
89.82.46

This quilt block was made in the last quarter of the 1800s. Quilters were using stencils in the same way forty and fifty years earlier.

descriptive term. Every block in a true signature (or autograph) quilt is inscribed by the individual maker, and therefore the handwriting varies across the quilt.[17] The general body of inscribed quilts typically includes such data as complete or partial names, relationships, place names, and dates. Some quilts also contain personal messages, dedications, Bible verses, riddles, proverbs and aphorisms, line drawings, and/or literary quotations. The information may be written in ink, stenciled, embroidered, or stamped (figs. 3.4 and 3.5). Some of the quilts were inscribed by many different individuals; in others, the handwriting indicates the work of a single person.

Certain inscribed quilts may be classified as *friendship* quilts. In some cases, a group of friends agree to make a number of blocks to share, so that each participant receives blocks from everyone in the group. Alternatively, an individual may issue a request for quilt blocks of specified size, colors, and/or pattern. Whether the quilts resulting from these blocks are then completed individually or with the help of the group, each becomes a document of the circle of friends. Without written evidence to support this arrangement, however, it is nearly impossible to identify friendship quilts, and the more general term album quilt is used.

Inscribed quilts frequently represent the work of a group for a particular purpose. In some cases, the blocks are signed by the individuals who made them; in others, individuals make blocks which are then signed by others. Some inscribed quilts are *presentation* quilts, created as a gift for a particular recipient. Within the private sphere of friends and/or family, many presentation quilts were made for a prospective bride, or for a leave-taking. In the public sphere, others were made by church congregations to honor ministers or their wives, by students and their parents in gratitude to teachers, or by various self-defined communities, whether local or dispersed, as a token of respect for a prominent person.[18]

Another group of inscribed quilts includes those that functioned as *fundraisers* for various groups and causes. Typically the sponsoring group collected donations from individuals whose names were then inscribed on the quilt.[19] The resulting quilt was often auctioned or raffled to raise additional funds, and then it might be presented to a significant individual, taking on a secondary presentation function. The majority of fundraising quilts that I documented feature hundreds of names, and the majority of the inscriptions are executed by one person with excellent penmanship.

Potholder Quilts

by Pamela Weeks

On August 13, 1848, Persis Sibley Andrews wrote the following in her diary:
I have at last made my square to Mrs. Davis Album Quilt & it is really beautiful. It contains all the work I have done in the week beside family cares (my baby has not been well) & is only one foot square quilted & bound. I do not approve of this way of making a quilt for the Ministers wife, but I have a great deal of esteem & admiration for the lady & beside wishing to be remembered by her I wish to see the variety quilt finished as it wanted only half a dozen of the required 70 before I made mine.[20]

Louisa Griffin Davis was the wife of the second minister of the Paris Hill, Maine, Baptist Church.[21] The seventy signers of the quilt blocks were parishioners of this church and included women and one man from all levels of Paris Hill and South Paris society (fig. 3.6 and 3.7). There are several family groups—sisters, a brother, mothers, cousins, and neighbors. The signers included the wives of physicians and lawyers; a woman who later served as a nurse during the Civil War; and the mother, sisters, and first and second wives, Sarah Jane Emery and Ellen Vest Emery, of Hannibal Hamlin, President Abraham Lincoln's first-term vice-president.[22] Although many signature quilts survive from this period as documents of family and community relationships, Persis Andrews's diary entry is the earliest known reference to a particular construction technique practiced almost exclusively in New England.

Potholder quilts, made by joining a number of individually finished blocks, are an example of a technique practiced in New England during the mid-nineteenth century. Many extant examples are signed and dated, documenting their functions as friend-

ANTEBELLUM ALBUM QUILTS

Fig. 3.6
Friendship Quilt
Various makers; 72 inscribed names
Paris Hill, Maine, 1848
101 x 101 inches
Courtesy of Hamlin Memorial Library and Museum

Parishioners of the Baptist Church of Paris Hill, Maine, made this album quilt for Louisa Griffin Davis, the minister's wife. Most unusually, one of the quilters, Persis Sibley Andrews, mentioned the quilt in her diary.

Fig. 3.7
Paris Hill Friendship Quilt, detail
Courtesy of Hamlin Memorial Library and Museum

Persis Sibley Andrews's block in the 1848 Friendship quilt made for Louisa Griffin Davis.

ship, presentation, and fundraising quilts. "They are a New England thing," stated Stephanie Hatch, one of the collectors interviewed for this research, and Maine is well represented in the inventory of these unusual quilts.[23]

I purchased a quilt at auction in 1999, and looked first to find the name and date, "Sarah A. Leavitt, December 16, 1847," embroidered in cross-stitch across the top. Then I examined the rest of the quilt, which was composed of eight-pointed star blocks set on point, and I discovered that each block was individually bound with dark blue silk, and that the blocks were closely whip-

63

CHAPTER 3

**Fig. 3.8
Oak Leaf and Reel
Potholder Quilt**
Susan Batchelder
Bath, Maine, 1850s
75 x 65 inches
Maine State Museum,
2011.29.1

While many potholder quilts were also album quilts, this example, given to the Maine State Museum by quilt collector and historian Stephanie Hatch, was made by one individual.

**Fig. 3.9
Detail, Oak Leaf and Reel Potholder Quilt**
Maine State Museum,
2011.29.1

The whipstitched seams between the completed blocks are visible on the reverse side of Susan Batchelder's Oak Leaf and Reel pattern potholder quilt.

stitched together on the back. It seemed that the maker had finished each block like an elegant eleven-inch-square potholder, then joined them to make a quilt. I chose to reference the technique with the term "potholder," and it emerged as a recognizable and useful descriptor.

Shortly after acquiring this quilt I showed it to a number of experienced quilt researchers. They were familiar with other "quilt-as-you-go" techniques, but they had never seen this particular method of construction. Four other quilt researchers and collectors whom I met at about this time were familiar with the technique. Deb Grana of Albany, New York, and Stephanie Hatch of Boxford, Massachusetts, collect potholder quilts, among other styles (figs. 3.8 and 3.9). Cyndi Black of Litchfield, Maine, and Wendy Reed of Bath, Maine, coordinate the Maine Quilt Heritage Project, which has documented nearly 3,000 quilts since 1987. Wendy Reed prefers to make her quilts using the potholder technique (see figs. 8.3 and 8.22 to 8.24). These women shared their collections and knowledge and encouraged me to undertake this research. My search for other examples of potholder quilts included an examination of published sources and online collections. I contacted curators of national and regional museums with large quilt collections and I searched major historical museums in New England, as well as a number of local museums in Maine and Massachusetts.

I searched needlework and quilting literature for descriptions of the technique. The January 1835 issue of *Godey's Ladies Book* suggests that making "kettle holders" of quilted patchwork and binding them with tape is a good exercise for children learning to sew, but there is no suggestion that one should make many of these and sew them together to make a quilt.[24] In the 1877 edition of *The Ladies' Guide to Needle Work*, S. Annie Frost states:

> It is a great improvement upon the huge and unwieldy quilting-frames of the days of our grandmothers, to make the patchwork for a quilt in bound squares. Each one is lined, first with wadding, then with calico quilted neatly, and bound with strips of calico. These squares being then sewed together, the quilt is complete. Album quilts made in this way, with the name of the giver neatly written upon a small square of white in the centre of each piece are much more acceptable than when they must all be quilted together in a huge frame.[25]

Potholder quilts are a sub-category of quilt-as-you-go. With other quilt-as-you-go methods, each unit is pieced, appliquéd, or left as one piece, then layered and quilted individually. The raw edges are left unfinished and the blocks or sections are joined to make a quilt in a multitude of techniques. The blocks of potholder quilts are not only layered and quilted individually, but the edges are finished before the blocks are joined. Construction-wise, each potholder block could stand alone as a finished one-block quilt. As there are no raw edges, the finished blocks are tightly whipstitched together from the back, not seamed, to form a larger quilt (see fig. 3.9). The predominant method for finishing potholder quilt blocks is to apply binding. Some are finished with a "knife-edge," in which the edges of the two fabric layers are turned under, with the raw edges tucked inside the layers, and held with a running stitch or an invisible ladder stitch.

Many books refer to other "quilt-as-you-go" methods, a term that refers to the construction of small units that are then joined to make a larger quilt. There are several ways in which to do this, but very few recommend individually finished blocks. In a 1971 book on machine quilting, Robbie and Tony Fanning describe three quilt-as-you-go methods. "Finish-as-you-go," described as "making quilted 'pillows' with finished edges which, when joined, make a whole quilt," is the only one using individually finished blocks. Further, the Fannings state that this is not a new idea, "having been around since the Civil War."

To anyone who has participated in the creation of a group quilt, whether for presentation or fundraising, the advantage of potholder construction becomes immediately obvious. Instead of sewing unfinished blocks together to make a top, then layering, quilting, and binding them together, potholder blocks can simply be sewn together to complete the quilt. Generally, potholder blocks typically contain little or no batting, and although most are quilted, the quilting is very light compared with traditionally made quilts. The stability resulting from the construction of the relatively small, individually finished units makes heavy quilting unnecessary. Within particular quilts, the quilting designs and the amount of quilting vary among the blocks. Many are quilted to pattern, following the lines of the patchwork or appliqué, and the quilting is seldom an important decorative element. Most are hand-quilted but several contain blocks that are machine-quilted.

The earliest quilt in my sample is dated 1837, and the latest, circa 1950. Of the quilts for which the geographic provenance is known, three-quarters are attributed to New England, and the majority of these to Maine or Massachusetts. This is no surprise to Stephanie Hatch, who localizes the technique to coastal Maine, centered in the area surrounding Wiscasset.[26] Folk art collector Robert Bishop, who was raised in this area of Maine, wrote in 1982: "In Friendship Album quilts from Maine, individual blocks were usually pieced or appliquéd, stuffed, and then quilted before all the blocks were sewn into a full-size quilt."[27] Today, Wendy Reed of Bath is at the center of a modest revival of the technique, and Maine may again become the center for this practical art of sewing potholder quilts.

THE QUILTS OF "SHE" STREET

To judge from published histories, women played no role in the life of Cumberland, Maine, apart from marrying notable men and bearing notable sons.[28] Yes, the occasional wife had to captain her husband's cargo ship when her spouse died suddenly on a voyage, but overall, the histories suggest that that women's participation in the history of the town was so minor as not to bear mention.[29] And yet, one resident recalled in his memoirs that North Yarmouth (now Main) Street was called "SHE Street, [author's emphasis], so named in old days from the fact that at times there were almost no men on it—all widows and unmarried women," and, he might have added, women whose husbands were away at sea, as the writer's own father often was.[30]

Cumberland incorporated in 1821, when the town fathers carved it from North Yarmouth. Until 2007, the town included Chebeague Island, in Casco Bay. This recent split reflects the gradual decline in importance of the sea to the economy of Cumberland. Through the late 1800s, many of the men of Cumberland Center were involved in maritime trades as captains, seamen, brokers, traders, and shipbuilders. Several of the town's shipyards produced large ships for global trade. The *Dakotah*, made in the Spear Yard, could carry 1054 tons of cargo. Spear's clipper ship, the *Grapeshot*, built in 1853, had a 345-ton capacity. Unfortunately, within a few years its primary cargo was slaves.[31] Shipbuilding in Maine peaked in 1855 when the 396 vessels built in the state that year accounted over for one-third of the tonnage of all the ships built in the country. After the economic Panic of 1857 and the gradual increase in demand for iron ships, local shipyards closed or shifted production to smaller craft that operated along the coasts and rivers of the United States, rather than across oceans.[32]

Maine's state seal features a farmer and a mariner flanking a shield, and the two industries had comparable representation in the town of Cumberland in the mid-1800s.[33] Even today the town is home to several prosperous farms, and in the 1800s, many mariners retired to a quiet life on a family farm. Town histories read like lists of ship captains, and many more townsmen filled less prestigious posts at sea. Whether captains, mates, cooks, or cabin boys, the town's mariners were absent from home for months—and for those involved in global trade, for years—at a time. Cumberland's wives, the women of She Street, all but absent from the annals of the town, ran households and farms, kept the books, and supported the churches, schools, and libraries. They supported one another as well. Between 1793 and 1893 fifty-seven Cumberland men were lost at sea.[34] Most women of Cumberland would have experienced the death of a seagoing family member or neighbor. The help of women's family, friends, and church members would have been central to recovery from such calamity.

Like many New England towns in the early 1800s, Cumberland was caught up in waves of religious fervor. In 1831, a year of revivals, the present Cumberland Center Congregational Church was built in the heart of the town (fig. 3.10).[35] This church was the center of town life, and the spiritual home for many of the town's ship captains, although their wives' and daughters' names appear on the church rolls more often than theirs. Several captains' female family members joined the church during the great revivals of 1831. Many participated in the church's Ladies' Sewing Circle and were involved in the construction of nine quilts that the group made between 1843 and circa 1855. A generation later, the ladies of the Cumberland Center Congregational Church (C4), led by Abbie Thomes and Mary Osgood, made at least two more quilts. One now resides in the collection of the Cumberland Historical Society (see fig. 3.35).

**Fig. 3.10
Cumberland Center Congregational Church**
Photographer unknown
Cumberland Center, Maine, ca. 1905
Courtesy of Prince Memorial Library, 2009.0155

The Cumberland Center Congregational Church, as it appeared around 1905, with stables for parishioners' horses behind it to the left, and the village schoolhouse in the background on the right.

CHAPTER 3

Fig. 3.11
The Bark Messenger Quilt
Ladies' Sewing Circle of the Cumberland Center Congregational Church; 64 inscribed names
Cumberland Center, Maine, 1850
99 x 108 inches
Maine State Museum, 2011.36.1

The largest of the quilts produced by the Ladies' Sewing Circle of the Cumberland Center Congregational Church, the Bark Messenger includes sixty-four inscribed names. Some of the individuals, such as the young twins depicted on one square, did not make the block that bears their names. Rather, they were likely included in the quilt as important members of the recipient's social circle.

Fig. 3.12
The Merrill Quilt
Ladies' Sewing Circle of the Cumberland Center Congregational Church; 28 inscribed names
Cumberland Center, Maine, 1851
84 x 82½ inches
Private collection

This quilt may have been given to Lucy Louville Merrill around the time her daughter Emma was born.

CHAPTER 3

Fig. 3.13
The Captain Wilson Quilt
Ladies' Sewing Circle of the Cumberland Center Congregational Church; 39 inscribed names
Cumberland Center, Maine, 1851
88 x 62 inches
Courtesy of Cumberland Historical Society, 91.7

Captain John Wilson is the only man to whom the Ladies' Sewing Circle of the Cumberland Center Congregational Church is known to have given a quilt. He and his wife, Margaret Cummings Wilson, lived across the street from the church and the village school. The house embroidered near the center of the quilt depicts their home.

Fig. 3.14
The Jane Blanchard Quilt
Ladies' Sewing Circle of the Cumberland Center Congregational Church; 39 inscribed names
Cumberland Center, Maine, 1850
89 x 82 inches
Courtesy of Maine Historical Society, 3646a

Family history recalls that this was a quilt given to Jane Blanchard when she married Warren Porter. However, the two were married twenty years before the quilt was made. Unlike most of the quilts in this group, this example is not made using the potholder method. The couple settled in New Hampshire, Porter's home state.

Fig. 3.15
The Ladies' Sewing Circle Quilt
Ladies' Sewing Circle of the Cumberland Center Congregational Church; 28 inscribed names
Cumberland Center, Maine, 1852
90 x 84 inches
Quilts, Inc., 2010.06. Photograph by Mike McCormick, M3 Photographic, Houston, Texas.

Mrs. H. B. Merrill attached a signed paper label to the back of this quilt, stating that it was "Made by the Ladies' Sewing Circle. Cumberland Center. 1852." She signed one block of the quilt, as well. There were two H. B. Merrills living in Cumberland Center in the 1850s: Henrietta Buxton Merrill, and Hanna E. Blanchard Merrill.

CHAPTER 3

The location of eight of the nine mid-century C4 quilts is known, and the quilts have been examined.³⁶ Comparison of names on the quilts showed that five had the highest number of common makers. The Bark Messenger of 1850 is one of these core quilts (fig. 3.11).

This is not surprising: with ninety-seven blocks, it has the largest number of associated names (sixty-four), and so the greatest likelihood of matches. An 1851 quilt in private hands made for a member of the Merrill family (fig. 3.12); a quilt made for Captain John Wilson in 1851, now at the Cumberland Historical Society (fig. 3.13); and an 1850 quilt at the Maine Historical Society associated with Jane Blanchard (fig. 3.14) also have many makers in common. The last quilt in the group bears a label stating that the "Ladies' Sewing Circle" (LSC) made it in 1851. This quilt sold at auction in 2010 and is now in private hands (fig 3.15). The

Fig. 3.16
The Lyre Quilt
Ladies' Sewing Circle of the Cumberland Center Congregational Church; nine inscribed names
Cumberland Center, Maine, ca. 1850
83 x 76½ inches
Courtesy of Historic New England. Gift of Miss Lola B. Tomlinson, 1968.6

The motifs and inscriptions of the Lyre quilt suggest it was given in condolence to a friend or family member who had lost a loved one.

Fig. 3.17
The Compass Rose Quilt
Ladies' Sewing Circle of the Cumberland Center Congregational Church; 34 inscribed names
Cumberland Center, Maine, 1849
82 x 82 inches
Courtesy of David Hupert, Labors of Love; photo courtesy of Jane Lury.

Researchers have named this quilt after its center block. The recipient of the Compass Rose quilt is unknown at this time.

Fig. 3.18
The Comet Quilt
Ladies' Sewing Circle of the Cumberland Center Congregational Church; 17 inscribed names
Cumberland Center, Maine, 1849
80 x 76 inches
Courtesy of the Blanchard Family

The Comet quilt, so named because two comets appear on it, was made for the February 1849 wedding of Lucy Sweetser and Davis Merrill, and has descended in the family. Maria Mitchell of Nantucket discovered a new comet on October 1, 1847. It is not known if comets in general held importance for the couple, or if the then-recent discovery of a comet was significant to them in some way.

CHAPTER 3

Fig. 3.19
The Craig Quilt
Ladies' Sewing Circle of the Cumberland Center Congregational Church; various makers
Cumberland Center, Maine, possibly 1843–1844; likely ca. 1850
Dimensions not known
Private collection; location unknown

If correct, the dates associated with the Craig quilt make it the earliest of the C4 quilts. Its location is currently unknown.

Fig. 3.20
The Sweetser Quilt
Ladies' Sewing Circle of the Cumberland Center Congregational Church; nine inscribed names
Cumberland Center, Maine, ca. 1850
76 x 64 inches
Courtesy of the Sweetser family

The Sweetser quilt is undated and has few signatures or inscriptions. It was most likely made between 1849 and 1855.

authors have photographs of most of the individual blocks of the LSC quilt, but not all. Even so, it has at least thirteen makers in common with the other C4 quilts.

These five core quilts feature the highest number of common makers within the C4 group. The core quilts share many attributes as well: they are constructed on point; they have fabrics, motifs, and blocks in common; and four are made of individually bound and quilted blocks sewn together, a construction method now called the potholder technique. The organizers of three of the quilts, the Blanchard, Merrill, and LSC, appear to have asked quilters to use light, neutral fabrics for the backgrounds of their blocks, while the makers of the Captain Wilson and the Bark Messenger had no such limitations. The colors of the Captain Wilson quilt are still especially vivid. The remaining quilts in the group include: the undated Lyre quilt (fig. 3.16); the 1849 Compass Rose (fig. 3.17); the 1849 Comet (fig. 3.18); the 1843–44 Craig (fig. 3.19); and the undated Sweetser family quilt (fig. 3.20).

Not surprisingly for a town with strong seagoing roots, at least five of the nine quilts include blocks with a nautical theme. The Compass Rose includes its namesake, as well as a fouled anchor. In addition to the ship of its titular block, the Bark Messenger also includes a fouled anchor (fig. 3.21), as do the LSC, the Compass Rose, and the Craig quilts. The Blanchard quilt includes a plain anchor. As the Captain Wilson quilt was made for a ship's captain, it is not surprising that it includes multiple nautical images: an anchor and a fouled anchor, a

Fig. 3.21
Detail, Bark Messenger Quilt
Maine State Museum, 2011.36.1

Detail of the Bark Messenger quilt showing blocks with its namesake ship and fouled anchor, with its green chain around its shaft.

ship's pennant with the name of Wilson's ship (the *Marcia*), a lighthouse, and two ships (fig 3.22). The LSC quilt includes one appliqué block in the upper right with four motifs that could be interpreted as stylized sextants, as well as an embroidered anchor. Three quilts, the Comet, the Sweetser, and the Merrill quilt, contain no nautical images. The Comet was made in honor of an 1849 marriage. Family tradition states that the Merrill quilt was made for Mary Ellen Wyman Merrill. While her quilt contains no overt nautical references, her husband, Louville Merrill, went on to serve in the U.S. Navy during the Civil War. The creative rationale for the Sweetser quilt is unknown, but it may also have been made for a woman, or for a member of a farming family with few nautical connections.

Fig. 3.22
Detail, Captain Wilson Quilt
Courtesy of Cumberland Historical Society, 91.7

As might be expected in a quilt made for a ship's captain, the Captain Wilson quilt includes several blocks with nautical references. It also includes a three-dimensional, silk cigar framed by laurel leaves for Wilson, an avid cigar smoker (see fig. 3.13).

A fouled anchor—one whose cable has become twisted around its stock—has multiple meanings. It is used by both the U.S. and British navies, and can indicate an individual's ability to overcome adversity, as a fouled anchor is one that is difficult to raise from the sea floor. In addition to its obvious association with ships and mariners, an anchor can symbolize religious faith and hope in Christ, the anchor of the soul.[37] Fitting for quilts made by members of a church, other religious motifs appear on C4 quilts, including the bible on the LSC and Captain Wilson quilts (3.23; also see fig 3.22), a cross on the Compass Rose, and an embroidered church on the Merrill. A grapevine on the Bark Messenger may refer to Jesus's statement "I am the vine and you are the branches."[38] The later Thomes-Osgood quilt also includes nautical and religious themes, with blocks featuring a fouled anchor, two crosses, and an olive branch (see figure 3.35). The messages embedded in such motifs would have been well known to the makers and viewers of these quilts.

Fig. 3.23
Detail, Ladies' Sewing Circle Quilt
Quilts, Inc., 2010.06
Photo courtesy of Pamela Weeks

The message inked below the bible on the LSC quilt reads: "Should storms of sorrow thee assail, / And heart should sink, and courage fail, / Then to the Book of Life repair, / And find relief from every care. / M. W. Rideout"

Far fewer patriotic symbols appear on C4 quilts: an eagle was embroidered onto a block of the Merrill quilt, and a flag block appears on the Captain Wilson quilt. Most blocks on the C4 quilts have little symbolism other than that associated with flowers, or bear motifs implying abundance, such as fruits and the occasional cornucopia. Of all the C4 quilts now known, two include blocks that reflect the agrarian nature of the town. Three such blocks are on the Bark Messenger, and one, featuring a horse, is on the Comet. Bark Messenger block 55 features a bull or steer,

**Fig. 3.24
Detail, Bark
Messenger Quilt**
Maine State Museum,
2011.36.1

*Bark Messenger block
with an agricultural
theme and the inscribed
name Solomon L.
Blanchard.*

**Fig. 3.25
Detail, Bark
Messenger Quilt**
Maine State Museum,
2011.36.1

*This whimsical
block from the Bark
Messenger features
a sheep under a
gargantuan pear bough,
with the inscribed name
William Blanchard.*

**Fig. 3.26
Detail, Bark
Messenger Quilt**
Maine State Museum,
2011.36.1

*The inscription under
the horse on this Bark
Messenger block bears
the name Asaph Buxton.*

a plow, and a yoke, all made from blue fabric with outlined white ovals, appliquéd on a red print ground (fig. 3.24). A second block on the quilt contains a sheep beneath a highly-stylized branch with two leaves and two pears, the latter of which are the same size as the sheep (fig. 3.25). The sheep and branch of pears are made from the same fabric as the bull, plow and yoke, and both animals stand on a thin rectangle of brown fabric. Together this suggests that the two blocks share a common maker. The sheep block bears the name William Blanchard, and the bull and plow, Solomon L. Blanchard. A third block in the Bark Messenger depicts a horse and is inscribed Asaph Buxton (fig. 3.26). The rectangle of ground on which it stands is made from the same fabric as that of the sheep in William Blanchard's block. All three blocks may have been designed or stitched by the same hand. However, the handwriting on Asaph and Solomon's blocks is the same, but that on William's is different. The 1850 census data lists a Solomon Blanchard and a William Blanchard owning farms and livestock. The names William and Solomon were given to Blanchards in several generations. Those referred to on the Bark Messenger quilt appear to be William M. Blanchard and Solomon Loring Blanchard, who were first cousins, once removed. Asaph Buxton married Sarah P. Blanchard on March 15, 1831.[39] Sarah was William's second cousin and Solomon's second cousin, once removed. Solomon's father, also named Solomon, was a ship's captain who died the year his son was born. The Solomon whose name appears on this block and his wife Hulda Prince Blanchard, who also contributed to the Bark Messenger quilt, died of fever twelve days apart, in September 1853.[40] The quilt thus became a memorial quilt as well as a presentation quilt for its recipient.

CHAPTER 3

Including the Thomes/Osgood 1870s quilt, and not the Craig quilt, for which no names are available, two hundred twenty-six names appear on the C4 quilts. Of these, twelve are male family members (ten husbands, two sons), and at least two are very young daughters (twins). Many blocks were inscribed, not signed. While this generally prevents identification of the maker of a particular block, it also suggests that the featured individual was important to the community of Cumberland Center.

Looking at the list of available names, a distinct subset of women appears to have been central to the manufacture of the quilts or to the community of quiltmakers and quilt recipients. The names of forty women are found on two or more of the five core quilts, along with the names of some of their husbands.[41] Twenty-one of the forty names appear on at least three quilts. Just two members of the church sewing group, Mary Jane Pittee Sweetser and Mary Ann Weston, contributed their names, and likely their work, to all five core quilts. Saba Gray Blanchard's and Lucy Weston Humphrey's names appear on four quilts; neither is present on the yet-documented blocks of the LSC quilt. Saba Blanchard, Sweetser, and Weston also contributed to other quilts in the C4 group. Mary Jane Pittee Sweetser's name appears on seven of the eight mid-century C4 quilts for which inscriptions are known and on the 1870s Thomes-Osgood quilt, as well. She is missing only from the Sweetser family quilt, which includes very

Fig. 3.27
The Poland Corner Methodist Church Quilt
Women of the Poland Corner Methodist Church; 37 inscribed names
Cumberland, Maine, 1857
100 x 76½ inches
Courtesy of Cumberland Historical Society, 97.9

The quilt made by the Poland Corner Methodist Church ladies was made in a different manner and style than the examples made by the Ladies' Sewing Circle of the Cumberland Center Congregational Church. Even without looking at the names, one might suspect that it was made by a completely different group of women.

few names. That quilt includes several blocks with common design elements and fabrics and was likely the work of a very small group of women. Three other women involved in this mid-century constellation of quilts also signed the later Thomes-Osgood quilt.

In 1857, the church ladies of the Poland Corner Methodist Church in Cumberland Center made a quilt (fig.3.27). The Methodist and Congregational churches are situated less than three miles apart. Despite their proximity, none of the women from the Congregational Church appear to have participated in the quilt's manufacture. No C4 names are present on the Poland Corner quilt. In this case, differences in religious belief might explain why neighborliness did not extend to participation in the generation of a quilt made at a Methodist church as opposed to a Congregational church. However, only seven of the 226 names appearing on C4 quilts have been found on a sample of fourteen other Cumberland County quilts from the third quarter of the 1800s. Of the seven, only one name, that of Jane Merrill, is present on more than one of the C4 quilts. Her name appears on the Bark Messenger and the Captain Wilson quilts, the quilts with the largest number of names in the group. It appears again in 1871 on a quilt from West Falmouth, a town adjacent to Cumberland. Generally speaking, those whose names appear on quilts from other Cumberland County communities appear to have been on the periphery of the C4 sewing circle.

It appears that the busy thimbles of Cumberland Center's Congregational Church Ladies' Sewing Circle made quilts for members of their church community only, and the group included quilters or inscribed names of importance to a quilt's recipient. Family tradition says that the Comet quilt was made for the 1849 marriage of Lucy Sweetser and Davis Merrill. The Bark Messenger quilt's central inscription implies that it was made for someone leaving the community: "The Bark Messenger laden with friendship, bound for Wellfleet." The occasion for the construction of other quilts, such as that given to Mary Ellen Wyman Merrill, may never be known.

In the five years from 1849 to 1854, the Congregational Church ladies of Cumberland Center made at least nine quilts for members of their small community, and then stopped. Six of the quilts were made between 1849 and 1851, and one in 1852. No other quilts have been found dating between 1855 and 1870, and only two after that, including the Thomes-Osgood quilt. Reasons for discontinuing the manufacture of the quilts are not known, but the possibilities are many. Making two quilts a year is an ambitious exercise, and without the energy of a determined and capable organizer or team, success is not assured. Any number of minor events could have derailed the process: the health of organizers may have been compromised; quilters might have had to give their attention to raising children or assisting family members; a community need could have arisen, shifting the energy and direction of the group. Events such as the September 1853 deaths of Solomon and Huldah Blanchard, for example, may have required the attention of many family members and neighbors in this small quilting community. It is unlikely that the group of nine quilts represents the entire production of the Ladies' Sewing Circle. As more quilts come to light, we may better understand the community, the quilts, the reasons they were made, and the events that caused the group to cease manufacture.

CHAPTER 3

Reflections of Community: Two Cape Elizabeth Album Quilts

Debra Grana and Laureen LaBar

In 1845 a group of women from Willard Point in Cape Elizabeth decided to make an album quilt, an effort that they completed a year later (fig. 3.28). The quilt offers a glimpse into a thriving community of fishermen and farmers, sailors and master

**Fig. 3.28
Cape Elizabeth Album Quilt**
Various makers; 41 inscribed names
Cape Elizabeth, Maine, 1845–1846
65 x 55½ inches
Maine State Museum, 2018.47.1

Only one block of the 1845–1846 Cape Elizabeth quilt hints that its makers came from a neighborhood of skilled laborers, farmers, and families who made their living from the sea.

**Fig. 3.29
Detail, Cape Elizabeth Album Quilt**
Maine State Museum, 2018.47.1

The realistically depicted fishing vessel on the Cape Elizabeth quilt, sewn by a friend or family member of George Loveitt, is strikingly like that on Lucy Dyer's quilt (see fig. 1.29). However, its colorful appliqué fish are highly stylized.

mariners, and masons and brickmakers, among other occupations. The makers of the quilt were neighbors, friends, and kinswomen: the surnames Loveitt, Sawyer, Willard, Woodbury, Jordan, Davis, Simonton, and Boothby appear over and over within the intertwined family histories of Cape Elizabeth. Many current streets are named for these families, providing evidence of where they lived and worked in the 1800s.

Several of the blocks were made by family members: Achsah J. Stanford Fickett and Reliance H. Anderson were linked by tragedy as well as by family ties. Achsah was married to Captain Ezekiel Fickett. She died on April 16, 1847, not long after the quilt was completed. In 1848, Capt. Fickett married Reliance, a local widow. Reliance also made a block for the quilt. Sisters-in-law Susan S. Cobb Woodbury, Elizabeth Willard Woodbury, and Martha A. Woodbury Loveitt all contributed to the quilt. Susan and Elizabeth were married to Martha's brothers.[42]

One block on the quilt stands out for its whimsy and artistry: rendered in appliqué and embroidery, a two-masted fishing boat sails along, towing its boat while fish swim below (fig. 3.29). The block is inscribed with the name George Loveitt. Loveitt

CHAPTER 3

is listed as a fisherman on the 1850 and 1860 census records.[43] He was undoubtedly related to one or more of the Jedediah Loveitts in the area, one of whom owned Commercial Wharf and was a prominent fish dealer in Portland.[44] George Loveitt's wife, Lavinia, may have made this block. The depiction of the fishing vessel is remarkably similar to that on Lucy Dyer's North Haven quilt (see fig. 1.27). This reinforces the idea that Lucy Dyer and the maker of the Loveitt block were documenting familiar fishing vessels.

**Fig. 3.30
Breakwater Lighthouse Quilt**
Various makers; 34 inscribed names
Cape Elizabeth, Maine, 1854–1860
88 x 68 inches
Maine State Museum, 2020.18.1

Although fewer than ten years separate them, this later Cape Elizabeth quilt was made by different people than the example in the collection of the Maine State Museum. The two groups appear to have some relatives in common, and further research may reveal more connections between the two groups.

Fig. 3.31
Detail, Breakwater Lighthouse Quilt
Maine State Museum, 2020.18.1

Angela Emery Lee's block on the Breakwater Lighthouse quilt featured a branch of red roses. Angela Emery married Richard Lee in 1854. She signed the quilt with her married name, thus providing a clue to the date of the quilt. The block next to it includes Masonic symbols. Unfortunately, the name inscribed on that block is illegible.

Fig. 3.32
Detail, Breakwater Lighthouse Quilt
Maine State Museum, 2020.18.1

The Breakwater Lighthouse quilt gets its name from this appliquéd depiction of the light. The initials inscribed on the block correspond to those of its second lighthouse keeper. Next to it, Valera Jane Smart also appliquéd a red flower block for the Breakwater Lighthouse quilt. Valera Jane Smart married John Murch in 1859. She signed her block with her maiden name, providing another clue to the age of the quilt.

About ten years later, members of the Cape Elizabeth community made another album quilt (fig. 3.30). The blocks are undated. However, two life events provide clues to its construction. Angela Emery married Richard Lee Jr., on March 13, 1854. Her married name appears on her quilt block, and that inscribed with her husband's name features a circle of hearts (fig. 3.31; see also fig. 3.30). Valera Jane Smart married John Murch on August 28, 1859. Her maiden name is on her quilt block (fig. 3.32). Together these wedding dates imply that the quilt was made between the spring of 1854 and the fall of 1859. Quilts take time to make, however, and some blocks are finished earlier than others. Clues on another block might move the completion date later. That block is decorated with an image of the Portland Breakwater Lighthouse (see fig. 3.32). The half-mile long breakwater was completed in 1837. Officials constructed a wooden lighthouse at the end of it in 1855 (fig 3.33). William Lee Willard of Cape Elizabeth was the second keeper of the lighthouse. He served from June 1857 until his death in February 1860, of a tumor.[45] He was twenty-six years old. His older brother, Benjamin F. Willard Jr., took over care of the lighthouse until a new keeper could be found.[46] In 1861, Benjamin and his wife Hannah Ann Stanley Emery Willard had a baby whom they named after Benjamin's deceased brother. Hannah might well have made the block on the quilt that features the Portland Breakwater Lighthouse with the initials WLW upon it (see fig. 3.32). It is also possible that Hannah or someone else made a block for William while he was alive. Many album quilts include blocks inscribed with the names of men who are important to the social circle involved in a quilt's creation and presentation. Or did Hannah sew the block after the death of her brother-in-law? That, too, is possible, as William died only some five months after the November 1855 wedding of Hannah and Benjamin, providing a tentative end date for the quilt's manufacture.

The Civil War erupted about the time that the quilt was being completed. The families involved with both quilts were deeply involved in activities in Casco Bay, and some were directly involved in its defense. Valera Smart's father, Captain Reuben Staples Smart, was the designer of Fort Gorges. Construction of the fort began on Hog Island Ledge in 1858 and was underway through the Civil War. It was completed in 1877.[47] One of the masons on the project was John Murch, who married Valera Smart not long after construction on Fort Gorges began. Their daughter, Annie, was born at the fort in March 1863. Just two months later, early in the morning on June 26, 1863, Murch noticed unusual activity in the harbor and alerted authorities, who gave chase.[48] Having kidnapped two local fishermen who could act as pilots and guide them around Casco Bay's many ledges, Confederates had stolen the revenue cutter *Caleb Cushing*. When escape by sea looked impossible, the Confederates set fire to the ship and abandoned it. The *Caleb Cushing*'s powder magazine exploded. Miraculously, no one was injured, though the pilots were afraid they might be mistaken for spies and shot by enthusiastic pursuers.[49] This was one of only two Confederate attacks on Maine during the war, neither of which was successful.

More research on the two Cape Elizabeth quilts remains to be done. To date, one link to the two quilts has been found: Ebenezer Willard, whose name appears on the earlier quilt, was Benjamin Willard's uncle. Both Benjamin Willard and his wife Hannah have blocks on the later quilt, in addition to the lighthouse block. One of the blocks on the later quilt features Masonic motifs. It is inscribed with a faded name that might be T. Mitchell. It is not yet known whether church affiliation or some other social organization linked the makers. Investigation into the relationships between the families involved in both quilts, and the further roles they played in the life of Casco Bay, its communities, and its life before and during the Civil War may result in a better understanding of that complex time in Maine history.

Fig. 3.33
The First Breakwater Lighthouse
Photographer unknown
Cape Elizabeth, pre-1874
Courtesy of the United States Coast Guard and Maine Historic Preservation Commission

Eighteen years after the Portland breakwater was built, officials added a wooden lighthouse. It was in use from 1855 until it was replaced with a cast-iron lighthouse in 1874.

☙

Not every quilt in the years leading up to the Civil War was an album quilt made by committee. Individuals continued to make quilts for themselves and family members, capitalizing on the variety of affordable, brightly colored fabrics available (see figs. 3.37 to 3.40). Many quilters belonged to church ladies' groups, as did many others for whom sewing was of little interest. Album quilts attracted accomplished quilters, but even those with little skill or desire to sew might occasionally make an album block.

Church ladies' groups made album quilts and fostered social action. Americans granted women an important role in alleviating society's problems, and ladies' groups were an important source of willing workers for causes such as temperance, relief of the poor, and the abolition of slavery. Lynne Bassett observed that "armed with moral authority and religious fervor, women in particular (as sanctified protectors of the home), set out to eradicate social ills."[50] As Lori Ginzburg put it, "Middle- and upper-middle-class women of the antebellum era shared a language that described their benevolent work as Christian, their means as fundamentally moral, and their mandate as uniquely female."[51] In an 1836 speech to the Ladies' Benevolence Society in East Cambridge, Massachusetts, the Rev. C. Gayton Pickman remarked, "It is to female influence and exertion that many of our best schemes of charity are due."[52] By the late 1840s, reform-minded women began to depend less on moral suasion and more on political action.[53] Charity took many forms, and temperance was a popular early cause. Maine became the first "dry" state in 1851, and with minor lapses remained so until the nationwide end of prohibition in 1933.[54] Portland mayor Neal Dow was a staunch booster of temperance, and he had the support of thousands of Maine women. The events that they organized, such as hosting speakers and holding fundraising events, taught them skills that served them well as the country descended into war in 1861.

CHAPTER 3

GALLERY

Fig. 3.34
Potholder Album Quilt
Thomes-Osgood Album Quilt
Various makers; eight inscribed names
Dresden, Maine, ca. 1840
78½ x 67 inches
Maine State Museum, 70.109.1

This potholder quilt was likely made by parishioners of the same small church, including members of the Houdlette family and their friends and neighbors. It was said to have been made for a circuit preacher, sometime around 1840.

Fig. 3.35
Thomes-Osgood Album Quilt
Ladies' Sewing Circle of the Cumberland Center Congregational Church; 50 inscribed names
Cumberland Center, Maine, 1870s
83 x 82 inches
Courtesy of Cumberland Historical Society, 91.10

Twenty years after the Cumberland Center Congregational Church Ladies' Sewing Circle sewed their last known quilt, the group made at least two more examples. Four women who were involved with the earlier quilts took part as well: Saba Blanchard, Lucy J. Merrill, Mary Merrill, and Mary Jane Sweetser.

CHAPTER 3

Fig. 3.36
Falmouth Album Quilt
Various makers: 57 inscribed names
Falmouth, Maine, 1846
107½ x 110½ inches
Courtesy of Brick Store Museum, 3155

Like the Cumberland Center quilts made a few years later, this quilt from Falmouth was made using the potholder technique and was constructed on point.

ANTEBELLUM ALBUM QUILTS

Fig. 3.38
Detail, Serene Wight Quilt
Courtesy of the Knight family collection of Yarmouth, Maine

Serene Wight's pieced baskets with their appliquéd handles are filled with a variety of fruits including these appliquéd pears.

Fig. 3.37
Serene Wight Baskets and Poinsettias Quilt
Made by Serene Lane Wight
Otisfield, Maine, 1840–1850
88 x 89 inches
Courtesy of the Knight family collection of Yarmouth, Maine

A tag that has remained with this family quilt reads "Made by Mrs. [Frank] Knight's great-grandmother between 1840–1850 in OtisField, Maine." Mrs. Wight's masterful folk-art design included several types of fruits in baskets, along with a variety of poinsettia flowers.

Fig. 3.39
Detail, Serene Wight Quilt
Courtesy of the Knight family collection of Yarmouth, Maine

Serene Wight embroidered the cherries and strawberries in the baskets on her quilt.

CHAPTER 3

Fig. 3.40
Laurel Leaves Quilt
Mrs. Powers
Possibly the Presque Isle, Maine, area, 1850–1860
93 x 76 inches
Courtesy of Shelburne Museum, gift of Miss Edith H. Porter, 1954-423. Photography by Andy Duback

The identity of the quilt maker is not completely known. Her name may have been Powers, and she likely lived in the Presque Isle area of northern Maine. The pattern is uncommon, and the quilt's lack of provenance prevents an understanding of how the design made its way to northern Maine.

COMMUNITY AND UNION IN THE CIVIL WAR

"If our State has won imperishable renown from the exploits of her sons on the battlefield, she has gained also a bright record for the noble, self-sacrificing spirit displayed by her daughters."

Henry Worcester, 1866[1]

In the years leading up to the Civil War, many Mainers voiced their opposition to slavery. Before Massachusetts abolished the practice in 1783, a few Mainers had owned slaves. In 1820 Maine was accepted into the Union as a free state, to balance Missouri's status as a slave state. However, while there had been no slave ownership in Maine in many years, in some parts of the state the economy depended indirectly on slave labor. Maine salt cod was shipped to the Caribbean to feed slaves. And, like textile factories elsewhere in the North, Maine cotton mills used slave-grown cotton. The 1790 invention of the cotton gin made rapid processing of raw cotton possible, and the nascent cotton industry required more of it every year. The South reacted by expanding plantation—that is, slave—labor. The booming mills that used this slave-grown cotton were the sources of the fabric Maine women sewed into clothing and quilts. Enough Mainers were complicit in slavery, however indirectly, that declaring oneself to be an abolitionist could be a daring act, rejecting as it did one's neighbors' source of income. It was mostly for economic reasons that some Mainers opposed the Civil War, leading Sarah "Say" White of Skowhegan to worry in 1863 that the "copperheads," as they were called, might be plentiful enough to be able to elect a governor.[2]

After the attack on Fort Sumter and the declaration of war in April 1861, however, Mainers rallied to the cause, raising fourteen regiments of infantry and one of cavalry by the close of the year.[3] In groups and as individuals, Maine women used the needle to express their support for the Union and for its soldiers. Women who in the 1840s and 1850s sewed album quilts, or met to promote temperance, formed Ladies' Aid Societies that made bandages, knit socks, and organized fundraisers for supplies for the troops. Many groups and individual Maine women made quilts for wounded soldiers, or to auction at fundraisers. These quilts were made in commemoration, in expression of solidarity, or in support of wounded soldiers,

CHAPTER 4

and many had patriotic themes. Ladies' groups in many towns contributed to the war effort through several organizations, as well as through private channels. U.S. Sanitary Commission records show that ninety-seven Maine communities large and small sent donations of goods, food, and/or money.[4] In March 1863, the Soldiers' Aid Society of Saco sent two boxes of goods for Maine soldiers including:

> 20 pairs cotton drawers, 27 pairs woolen drawers, 125 cotton shirts, 82 woolen shirts, 20 pairs slippers, 94 pairs woolen socks, 5 pairs mittens, 11 vests, 8 pairs pants, 5 coats, 5 bed sacks, 1 blanket, 7 quilts and comforters, sheets, pillowcases, lint [for bandages], soap, sugar, dried apples, books, pamphlets, newspapers and dressing gowns.[5]

A woman could produce some items for soldiers, such as bandages, shirts, or socks, in odd moments at home. Quiltmaking, however, was more frequently a group effort during the Civil War. Women from cities and hamlets made quilts for wounded soldiers or to raise funds for the war effort. The meetings quilting entailed were social events as well as work sessions, offering opportunities to share news or offer support or condolence to friends while one planned or sewed. For women, the costs of war included the short-term loss of a spouse's income—a soldier's wages were seldom enough to support a family—as well as the potential for widowhood or long-term care for a wounded husband who could no longer work. The year 1864 was a difficult one. The war was three years old, and casualties were brutally high. In Portland that year, neighbors in the working-class neighborhood of Munjoy Hill made quilts that emphasized Maine's maritime contributions to the war (see figs. 4.10 and 4.11). A group of young Portland women and their former teachers also made a patriotic quilt in 1864. It was emblazoned with stars and featured a shield decorated with the stars and stripes (figs. 4.1 to 4.3). The makers inscribed every block with patriotic inscriptions, many intended to encourage the soldier who might ultimately receive the quilt. Also in 1864, Octavia Lewis of Jay, Maine, made a quilt for herself with a proudly patriotic poem in its center medallion (fig. 4.4). Did it reflect confidence in Union victory, or was it a reminder to bear up under the pressure of uncertainty and loss?

In March 1865, the Ladies' Beneficent Association of North New Sharon, a group formed by the ladies of the First Free Will Baptist Church Society, met "in the afternoon and made patchwork for the soldiers."[6] That quilt likely went to a hospital shortly thereafter, perhaps on April 20, when the group's minutes recorded:

> Met with Mrs Sedgly packed a box of articles for the soldiers which were as follows
>   4 quilts
>   3 towels
>   14 pillows
>   3 handkirchiefs
>   5 pairs of socks
>   Some bandages[7]

COMMUNITY AND UNION IN THE CIVIL WAR

Fig. 4.1
The Davis-Dow Quilt
Alumnae, students, and staff of the Home Institute school; 26 inscribed names
Portland, Maine, May 1864
81 x 71 inches
Maine State Museum, 2015.11.1[8]

Students and former students of Portland's Home Institute school made this quilt and may have raffled or auctioned it to raise money for the Union cause. Three of the young women who made this quilt signed several blocks. The primary makers were Carrie Davis and Cornelia Dow, who lived in the same Portland neighborhood. The latter was the daughter of brigadier general and former Portland mayor Neal Dow. Most of those who signed quilt blocks were from Portland, but also from Richmond, Maine; Boston; Saint John, New Brunswick; and Matanzas, Cuba.

The Davis-Dow quilt was made using the potholder method. The quilt's organizers apparently distributed the red and blue stars, as well as fabric for the front and binding. The result is much more visually organized than most album quilts (see chapter 3).

CHAPTER 4

Fig. 4.2
Detail, Davis-Dow Quilt
Block by Carrie Davis
Maine State Museum, 2015.11.1,
photo courtesy James D. Julia, Inc.

Carrie Davis crafted the central shield block in the quilt. Every square of the Davis-Dow quilt includes inscriptions. Some were puns ("While our fingers guide the needles / Our thoughts are intense [tents]"); some were sweet ("Dream what thou wilt / Beneath this quilt, / My blessing is still yours"). Most of the messages were earnest wishes for soldiers that the quilters found in published sources, including the fourth stanza of "A National Jubilee" by Caroline A. Mason, that first appeared in the Hudson Weekly Star *on May 5, 1864, the month the quilt was made, and a quote from "The Cumberland," written in 1863 by Henry Wadsworth Longfellow, whose childhood home was near that of Davis and Dow.*

Fig. 4.3
Detail, Davis-Dow Quilt
Block by Helen D. Chapman
Maine State Museum, 2015.11.1

Helen D. Chapman's block stands out from the others, with its five patriotic sketches of an anchor and line, a banner, a flag, crossed muskets, and a laurel wreath, each with an inspirational quote.

Fig. 4.4
Octavia Lewis Civil War Quilt
Mary Octavia Lewis
Jay, Maine, 1864
82 inches x 83 inches
Maine State Museum 85.92.1

In 1864, during some of the bleakest days of the Civil War, forty-two-year-old Mary Octavia Lewis of Jay expressed her ardent hopes for the Union in a quilt. Above the appliquéd flag, she inked "Union & Liberty" and an American eagle. Below it, to the right of the ribbon she used as a flagstaff, she penned a poem:

The Banner of Union – uplifted in glee
To and fro waves on the land and at sea
The Banner star-spangled which Washington gave
The Banner of Union forever must wave
M. Octavia Lewis
1864

Octavia Lewis was married with three sons when she made her quilt; a fourth son had died at age five in 1855. Little else is known of her life. Lewis died in Jay in 1890, at age 69. Her husband, John, lived another twelve years after Octavia's death. They are buried beside their young son, in Jay.

CHAPTER 4

The record book was used from December 1859 to August 1870. Unfortunately, the minutes of the Ladies' Beneficent Association rarely discussed what occurred at their meetings. They generally noted where the meeting was held, and who read the paper aloud or said a prayer. A few records noted Society contributions to the church's remodeling efforts. These two, however, were the only entries that addressed the Civil War and the only ones that addressed quilting. The group made an album quilt for Jenny Furber, one of their members (fig. 4.5). Unfortunately, the secretaries of the Ladies' Beneficent Association did not record whether their March 16, 1865, quilting meeting was unique, or if the group regularly gathered to quilt for soldiers, friends, and family.

Quilts also commemorated the War. Frances Berry Orbeton of Rockland sewed a quilt for her brother-in-law Brigadier General Davis Tillson after his return home (figs. 4.6 and 4.7). The fabrics she used were all symbolic of his service—his uniform, and two souvenirs: a Confederate flag and part of a Confederate uniform (figs. 4.8 and 4.9). The quilt was a visual

Fig. 4.5
Jenny Furber's Album Quilt
Ladies' Beneficent Association of the First Free Will Baptist Church Society
New Sharon, Maine, ca. 1860
90 x 92 inches
Courtesy of Sandra Stubbs

Jenny Furber of New Sharon, Maine, was a member of the First Free Will Baptist Church and its Ladies' Beneficent Association. According to family lore, the group made the quilt for Furber around the time of the Civil War.

COMMUNITY AND UNION IN THE CIVIL WAR

Fig. 4.6
Brigadier General Davis Tillson
Carte de visite, D. M. Schlere, photographer
Nashville, TN, 1863–1865
4 x 2½ inches
Courtesy of Maine State Archives, Neg. 1069, Container 206642

Davis Tillson lost part of a leg as a result of an accident during his first year as a cadet at West Point, after which he resigned from the school. Despite this, he fought in the Civil War, rising in rank from captain of artillery to brigadier general and brevet major general, and a commander in the field. In early 1864 Tillson recruited the First U.S. Colored Heavy Artillery unit and led them for the remainder of the war. In late 1865, after the close of the Civil War, General Tillson sought to resign his post but was instead appointed to work with the Freedmen's Bureau, in Augusta, Georgia.

Fig. 4.7
Frances Berry Orbeton
John F. Singhi, photographer
Rockland, Maine, ca 1890
6 x 4 inches
Courtesy of Rockland Historical Society

Frances Berry Achorn was born on Valentine's Day, 1824. Sometime before 1846 she married Isaac Orbeton, a farmer, and the two settled on a farm in their hometown of Rockland. Frances's sister Margaret married Davis Tillson, also of Rockland. The sisters appear to have remained close, because Frances made a quilt for her brother-in-law after his return from the Civil War.

CHAPTER 4

**Fig. 4.8
The Orbeton-Tillson Quilt**
Frances Berry Orbeton
Rockland, Maine, ca 1870
79 x 74 inches
Courtesy of Rockland Historical Society

Not long after the close of the Civil War, General Tillson's sister-in-law, Frances Orbeton, made him a quilt from several souvenirs the General brought back from the war. She used pieces of a Confederate uniform and one of Tillson's uniforms as well as part of a Confederate flag or banner.

**Fig. 4.9
Detail, Orbeton-Tillson Quilt**
Courtesy of Rockland Historical Society

Several of the fragments of the Confederate banner Frances Orbeton used in the quilt once had letters sewn to them. Orbeton removed them and turned the fabric so that it faced the inside of the quilt. This did not fully disguise the banner, as the stitch holes around the lettering highlight the letters, as can be seen in the four navy blue corners of this nine-patch block.

reminder of the glories and terrors of his service, as well as of a sister-in-law's affection and relief at his safe return. It became a visible memento and a more practical tribute than keeping souvenirs in a trunk, and certainly more attractive.

The Civil War Quilts of Munjoy Hill

by Pamela Weeks

The eastern part of the peninsula on which sits the city of Portland, Maine, rises 160 feet above sea level and is named Munjoy Hill, for George Munjoy. The wealthy English emigrant moved from Boston to a homestead on the waterfront at the foot of the hill in 1659 and remained there until 1679 when Indians attacked the settlement, killing, capturing, or driving away the inhabitants, and succeeded for a short period in stopping further development of the territory.[9] The Indian Wars, which had begun in 1675, lasted for more than fifty years, with the final peace treaty taking place at a great diplomatic meeting in the fields of Munjoy Hill in 1727.[10]

Most of the early settlement stayed at the waterfront in the eighteenth century and Munjoy Hill remained as open agricultural fields well into the early nineteenth century, with streets and housing for laborers being added as the city grew.[11] As the population expanded east, churches, meeting houses, and commercial and industrial enterprises increased in number. The Portland Company was incorporated on the waterfront at the base of Munjoy Hill in 1846 for the "manufacture of steam engines, all the equipment of a railroad and other works in wood and iron," and operated until 1978.[12] Some of the buildings still stand on Fore Street at the foot of Munjoy Hill. The Portland Company produced 600 steam locomotives, 160 merchant and naval vessels, and railcars, many of which were commissioned for use in the Civil War. Later, the company manufactured Knox automobiles.

The Portland Observatory, organized by Captain Lemuel Moody and built in 1807, towers over the neighborhood and has a prominent place in the history of the city. It was built to observe shipping, and flag signals were devised to alert the merchants in the harbor as to which ships were approaching. This gave them time to organize wharf space and arrange for the sale of the cargo. Ships under sail could be seen up to thirty miles offshore, and if the wind was light, or changed, it could take a day or more from the first sighting for the ship to make port.

Two potholder quilts with similar characteristics and motifs were made in Portland, probably for fundraising for the Civil War cause and probably by the same group of women (figs. 4.10 and 4.11). In both quilts the background fabrics for the appliquéd or embroidered motifs are brown cambric, a fabric used to line clothing, and the blocks in both quilts are bound in red. Both quilts have many machine-quilted blocks

CHAPTER 4

Fig. 4.10
Munjoy Hill Civil War Quilt
The Ladies' Aid Society of Portland
Munjoy Hill, Portland, Maine, 1864
86.5 x 68.5 inches
Courtesy of Brick Store Museum, 2543. Photograph by C. A. Smith

The larger of the two known Civil War quilts made on Munjoy Hill in 1864, this example shares with its smaller counterpart several motifs including the Portland Observatory, cannons, a pile of cannonballs, a mortar shooting a ball, a side-wheeler ship, an eagle, shield, book with clasps (likely a bible or photograph album), and a fouled anchor.

Fig. 4.11
Munjoy Hill Civil War Quilt
The Ladies' Aid Society of Portland
Munjoy Hill, Portland, Maine, 1864
58.5 x 80.5 inches
Courtesy of Mystic Seaport Museum, 1968.24

The quilt blocks on this quilt are smaller than those of the example held by the Brick Store Museum. Despite this, several of the motifs appear to have been made from the same pattern on both quilts. The makers incorporated patriotic symbols as well as blocks depicting the tools of a sailor, a draftsman, or a soldier. Portland's most prominent landmark, the Observatory, played a defensive role during the Civil War. The side-wheeled ship depicted on both quilts likely represents a gunboat made at the Portland Company at the foot of Munjoy Hill.

and both have duplicate blocks including a depiction of a paddle wheel steamboat, the type of cannons and other weapons produced at the Portland Company, and a rendition of the Portland Observatory.

The first quilt, which is in the collection of the Brick Store Museum in Kennebunk, Maine, is attributed by the donor to the Ladies' Aid Society of Portland (see fig. 4.10).[13] This quilt contains twenty blocks that are embroidered, pieced, or appliquéd with Union shields, flags, and military ordnance and equipment. The blocks are inscribed with names, dates, and addresses, including Atlantic and St. Lawrence

Streets on Munjoy Hill. The second quilt is in the collection of Mystic Seaport Museum in Mystic, Connecticut (see fig. 4.11), and is made of thirty-five blocks that are slightly smaller than those on the Brick Store quilt.[14] The two quilts have many motifs in common, but the Mystic quilt also contains a number of Masonic symbols, such as a trowel and a triangle with crossed keys.

The combined number of distinct signers in the two quilts is thirty-three for the total of fifty-five blocks in the two quilts, as several women signed multiple blocks. There are four blocks in each quilt made by the same women, all related—mothers, daughters, aunts, and nieces. Abbie J. Sargent Randall signed the greatest number of blocks in the Mystic Seaport Museum quilt, and the research on this maker has been confusing and interesting. Brothers Joseph P. and John F. Randall married sisters Abbie J. and Elmira Sargent. Their brother Isaac married Abba Jenny Redlon, which sets up the mystery of which A. J. Randall was the maker of the several blocks signed with this name. Elmira Sargent Randall did not contribute a block. The relationships of the family members who made blocks center around Joseph P. and Abbie J. Sargent Randall, and include her mother, several members of her mother's family, and several women related by marriage to Joseph and his brothers. All three brothers served in the Civil War in different units.[15]

The 1860 census for Portland includes several of the other signers of both the Portland, Munjoy Hill, Civil War quilts. Their husbands are listed as machinists, and it is possible that they were employees of the Portland Company, as the Munjoy Hill neighborhood rises directly above where the machine shops once stood. There are no details in the depictions of the double-ended, side-wheel steamships that would let us conclude the makers had a particular ship in mind. The Civil War side-wheel gunboats *Agawam* and *Potoosuc* had steam engines built at the Portland Company. Both were commissioned in 1863, in the summer before the quilts were made. They were shallow-draft ships, with rudders at the bow and stern, allowing them to operate in either direction without having to turn around in the narrow rivers for which they were intended. They were used to carry troops and to transport the wounded in the war.[16]

We are left to wonder if the makers of the two quilts were, in their fundraising efforts, honoring their male relations who worked in the Portland Company, the service of their family members fighting in the war, or in general their Munjoy Hill neighborhood and their pride in the products of their city.

☙

Most of Maine's surviving Civil War quilts were sewn by hand. In the 1850s, after several false starts and much legal wrangling, inventors and manufacturers produced sewing machines designed for home use.[17] Making clothing by hand sewing took many hours: an estimated fourteen hours for a man's shirt and upwards of six for a simple dress—and dresses in the 1850s and 1860s were not necessarily simple.[18] Sewing machines dramatically reduced the time spent on these tasks. Many women continued to piece and quilt by hand, however. Perhaps some women saw the relatively short seams needed in quilting too simple to bother sewing on a machine. Sewing by machine also made piecing a more solitary task. While it was technically possible to transport sewing machines from place to place, their weight would have made it impractical. Although sewing machines saved many hours of time per garment, they were initially too expensive for many Maine families. At the close of the war, a return to relative prosperity and savvy marketing techniques on the part of manufacturers ensured that sewing machines were well represented in Maine homes as well as those elsewhere.

GALLERY

Fig. 4.12
Belfast Flag Quilt
The First Church of Belfast Ladies' Volunteer Aid Society
Belfast, Maine, 1864
61.5 x 91.5 inches
Courtesy of Belfast Historical Society, 110001

The Ladies Volunteer Aid Society of the First Church of Belfast made this quilt between June 17 and July 7, 1864. Many of the blocks include inscriptions, most of a comical nature ("A popular Union drink / – Meade"). Mrs. John H. Quimby, whose handwriting was best, was given the job of inscribing them all. Dubbing themselves the U.S.G. Society, presumably in honor of General Grant, they celebrated the quilt's completion at the home of former U.S. Congressman Nehemiah Abbot—a party to which young men were invited.[19]

The quilt was sent to the Armory Square Hospital in Washington, D.C. There it was deemed better to hang it on the wall to inspire all the soldiers, rather than give it to one to use as bedding. After the war it traveled west with one of the hospital administrators, ending up in Montana. In 2011, it found its way back to its home town.[20]

Fig. 4.13
Detail, Belfast Flag Quilt
Courtesy of Belfast Historical Society, 110001

While some of the inscribed blocks on the Belfast flag quilt were inspirational ("For God and our Country / you are marching along"), the quilt's makers were fond of puns. Many blocks, such as this one, were meant to be humorous. It reads "Good Maine ham / well cured. and smok- / ed in many battles / Gen Burnham."

CHAPTER 4

**Fig. 4.14
Portland Flag Quilt**
Made by members of the Jewett, Fox, and Wilder families, and their friends
Portland, Maine, 1862
76 x 99 inches
Courtesy of Maine Historical Society, 2017.129

Just two years before the ladies of Belfast, Maine, worked together to make a flag quilt, several Portland, Maine, families and friends made one of their own. The piecing of the quilt was sewn by hand, but the makers used a sewing machine to quilt the flag. Judging from inscriptions such as "May the sweetest of dreams this quilt impart / And deeds of valor inspire the heart / Of the brave soldier who e're thou art," written by Mrs. W. H. Stephenson, the group intended their quilt to be used by a soldier, probably one recovering from wounds or sickness.

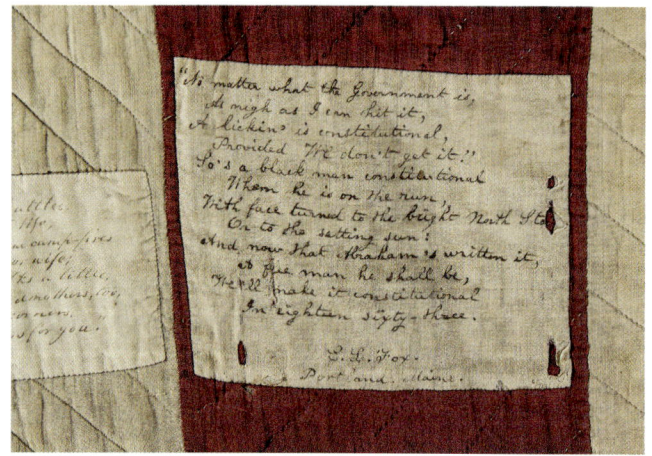

**Fig. 4.15
Detail, Portland Flag Quilt**
Courtesy of Maine Historical Society, 2017.129

Individuals penned their own messages on the quilt, some on the white stripes, but many on the red stripes, as well. Mrs. Stephenson's patch was attached to the quilt before it was quilted. These two, however, were added after the quilting was complete. B. L. Fox's verse anticipates the Emancipation Proclamation: "now that Abraham's written it, / A fine man he [an escaped slave] will be, / We'll make it constitutional / In eighteen sixty-three." Abraham Lincoln wrote a preliminary Emancipation Proclamation in September 1862. It is likely that the flag quilt had not yet been sent away and that B. L. Fox refers to that document.

5

COTTONS GALORE

For many women, sewing machines were the most ubiquitous evidence of the Industrial Revolution that was transforming not only Maine, but the rest of the United States as well. Maine's economy before the Civil War had been dominated by the farm, the forest, and the sea. Farming, lumbering, fishing, and the maritime trades continued to be important throughout the 1800s. But Maine's rivers and streams were the key to its industrial prosperity after 1850. Water powered the eighty-plus industries listed in the 1855 Maine register.[1] Many of these were small, labor-intensive enterprises that "sheltered Maine's largely rural population against the winds of modernism, while newer industries—textiles, paper, and tourism among them—smoothed the transition to the industrial age," as historian Richard Judd put it.[2]

More mills meant a more urban population. Whether Mainers worked at the textile or paper mill, at a shoe factory, or at a business that supported Maine's many industries or their workers, the home was no longer the center of the family economy for many people. After the Civil War, employment of immigrants overtook that of young women at cotton mills. Both parents from many immigrant families worked at Maine mills, and children were often expected to work as well, once they were old enough to do so.[3] Maine remained a largely rural state, but overall, as Jane Nylander, historian on New England domestic life, writes, "the years 1760 to 1860 encompassed the transformation of New England households from a time of mutual production to an idealized domesticity."[4]

As American society adapted to the changes brought by the industrial age, expectations for women changed as well. Middle- and upper-class women were already held to high moral ideals. With the increased pace of work and urban life brought on by industrialization, notions of home became romanticized as well. "The ideal New England home was perceived in the late nineteenth century as warm, welcoming, comfortable, and unchanging—a stable center—which formed a counterpoint to the surging forces of change in contemporary society."[5]

For nearly thirty years after the Civil War, Maine's rural population declined, as families moved west, seeking better opportunities. The population loss was partially offset by immigrants, who came to work in Maine's mills and forests, or built railroads and labored in quarries. Even before the potato famine of the 1840s, Irish immigrants had moved to Maine, as had

Englishmen and Scots. In 1790, 78 percent of Mainers were of English descent, while Scots, Scots-Irish, and Irish made up 17 percent of the state's Euro-American residents.[6] By 1850, the state was well established, and 95 percent of Mainers had been born within its boundaries.[7] That year, 17 percent of manufacturing jobs were in the textile industry. By the 1870s, cotton manufacture was Maine's largest industry, and wool the third.[8] In 1880, the industry employed 31 percent of the state's industrial workers, with 16,611 employed.[9] Many of these workers were immigrants from French-speaking Canada. The output was astonishing: the mills in Saco produced upward of 10,000 yards of cotton fabric per worker per year.[10] Scores of other cotton mills around New England churned out cottons at a comparable rate, and demand rose to meet the supply.

Not only was the production rate astonishing, so were the colors. In Britain in 1856, eighteen-year-old chemistry assistant William Perkin was trying to manufacture artificial quinine out of the by-products of coal tar (itself a by-product of making gas from coal). Instead of finding a cure for malaria, Perkin created a dye that produced a delicate purple color, mauve.[11] The color was widely popular among the rich and powerful, prompting a race for discovery of new dyestuffs between chemists in Britain and Germany. Many of these artificial dyes turned out not to be colorfast, or not appropriate for cottons, but between the late 1850s and the 1880s, invented dyes produced exciting new shades of color.[12]

Maine quilters took full advantage of the abundance of printed cottons in a riot of new colors and responded with a burst of creativity. New patterns, like log cabin (fig. 5.1), capitalized on the range of new fabrics. Other quilters used their large fabric stashes and swapped fabrics with friends to make charm quilts, in which no two fabrics were the same (fig. 5.2), or

**Fig. 5.1
Log Cabin Quilt, Barn Raising Variation**
Made by Frances Isabel Ward Sawyer Norridgewock, Maine, 1890s
87½ x 86 inches
Maine State Museum, 86.43.1

Log cabin quilts became popular in the third quarter of the 1800s. The pieces were sewn onto a foundation. The close proximity of so many seam allowances added to the thickness of the quilt top, making it difficult to quilt. As a result, most log cabin quilts lack batting and are tied, not quilted, to the backing fabric.

COTTONS GALORE

Fig. 5.2
Charm Quilt
Made by Josephine Snow Files
Benton, Maine, 1890–1910
99 x 81 inches
Maine State Museum, 76.71.33

While a charm quilt may have been the work of one woman, it was in a way a group effort as well. Fabric was relatively inexpensive in the late 1800s. Even so, most women lacked the variety of fabrics necessary to make a quilt in which no two prints were the same. Indeed, Josephine Files's charm quilt suggests that she may have had even more fabrics at her disposal during its construction; presumably some of the fabric swatches she owned would not have been appropriate for the subtle shading of the rows of diamonds she created.

Fig. 5.3
Postage Stamp Triangle Quilt
Made by a member of the Muriel Brown Taylor family
Possibly Readfield, Maine, ca. 1900
83 x 83 inches
Maine State Museum, 2003.54.1

With its 11,448 pieces, this postage stamp quilt is not a charm quilt. Although its maker used many fabrics more than once, it still contains dozens of prints. Quilts like this, with its blocks measuring about three quarters of an inch square, have been dubbed postage stamp quilts for the obvious correlation in size between the quilt blocks and a stamp.

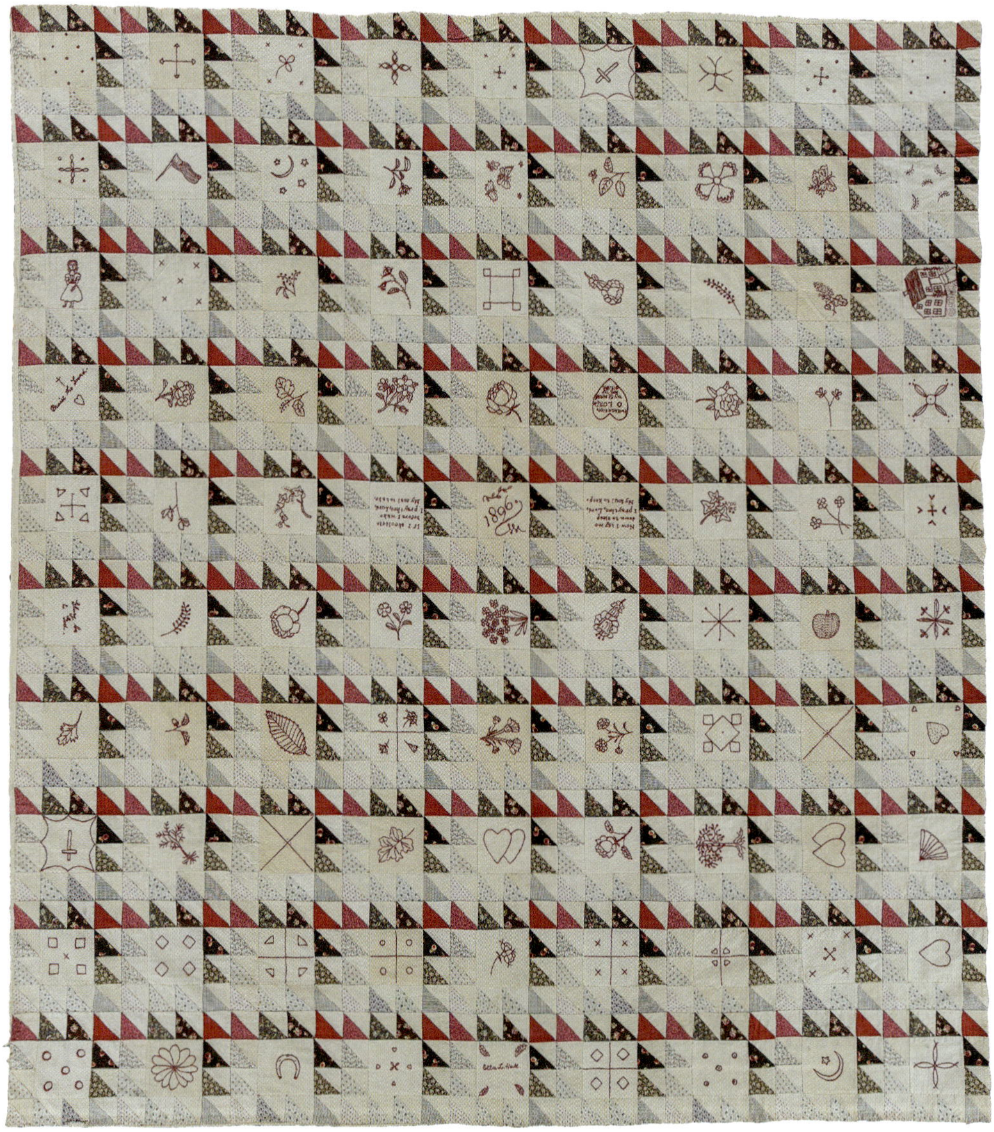

CHAPTER 5

Fig. 5.4
Birds Flying in the Air, Redwork Quilt
Etta Hall
Winterport, Maine
1896
72 x 74 inches
Maine State Museum,
97.125.10

Etta Hall of Winterport was only ten years old when she made this complex quilt. She was an only child. Three older siblings had died before she was born. Hall used red outline embroidery in the white squares in the middle of each block, adding a layer of complexity to the design.

Fig. 5.5
Detail, Etta Hall's Quilt
Maine State Museum, 97.125.10

Etta Hall embroidered a wide range of motifs in the ninety blocks of her Birds Flying in the Air Quilt. They included birds, plants and flowers, abstract designs, the prayer of childhood "Now I lay me down to sleep," religious motifs, and the date of the quilt. She also included figures that may have been more personal, such as a house. A pencil outline of similar structure may be seen behind another embroidered design. The girl embroidered here may represent a self-portrait.

Fig. 5.6
Delectable Mountains Quilt
Attributed to Ellen Alvena Stone Patterson
Industry, Maine, ca. 1870
88 x 83 inches
Maine State Museum, 80.96.3

Little is known of Ellen Stone Patterson's life. The pattern she chose for her quilt, Delectable Mountains, and the name of her hometown, Industry, Maine, speak to the pervasive and comforting presence of religion in daily life in the 1800s. Everything from towns to quilt patterns was named for religious aspirations and values, perhaps to inspire neighbors and family toward the rewards of heaven. In 1882, when Ellen died, her husband, Asa Patterson, "completely overwhelmed by his bereavement," broke up the home and moved to Nebraska, where he died seven years later. Their son, George, was nine years old at the time of his mother's death.[13]

Fig. 5.7
Delectable Mountains Quilt
Made by Ellen A. Tolman
Matinicus Island, Maine, 1875
89 x 90 inches
Maine State Museum, 2005.109.1

Like Christian, the pilgrim in Pilgrim's Progress, *Ellen Tolman Wallace's life held difficulties and sorrows. Her Delectable Mountains quilt may have helped her remember the promised rewards of heaven.*

made what are today called postage stamp quilts, because of the small sizes of each piece in the block (fig 5.3).

Embroidered red-and-white quilts and coverlets, on the other hand, used a limited palette to express their makers' values by means of outlined images of daily life and of the imagined past. Some quilters combined their redwork embroidery with colored frames or incorporated it into the negative spaces in patchwork (figs. 5.4 and 5.5). Local groups continued to make album quilts and fundraising quilts, but the new generation executed them differently, often using red embroidery on white ground. Those who made friendship quilts generally preferred to use one style of block, rather than the exuberance (or chaos, depending on the point of view) of the many-patterned blocks of the album quilts of the 1840s (see fig. 5.20).

Some of the many new patterns that developed in the late 1800s were symbolic of one's faith. *The Pilgrim's Progress from This World to That Which Is to Come*, a Christian allegorical novel written by John Bunyan, was published in 1678. It remained popular well into the 1800s, as evidenced by its presence in *Little Women*, wherein the March girls recall reading and reenacting scenes from the book.[14] *Pilgrim's Progress* also inspired a quilt pattern called Delectable Mountains (figs. 5.6 and 5.7). This was a land described in *Pilgrim's Progress*, "with a pleasant prospect on every side," but full of dangers, the eighth stage in the protagonist's pilgrimage toward the Celestial City.[15] The name of the block expressed the hope of salvation held by most Americans. For some it may have also expressed the hope of happiness in a new homeland for themselves or for friends and family members who had moved away from Maine.

Ellen Tolman made her Delectable Mountains quilt when she was still a teenager (see fig 5.7). She was born on the island of Matinicus in 1860 and married assistant lighthouse keeper Thaddeus Wallace in 1882. Ten years later, the couple moved to St. George when Thaddeus was promoted to keeper of the Tenant's Harbor Light. Their son, Burton Tolman Wallace, was born in the home attached to the lighthouse. When Thaddeus died in 1898, Ellen served as keeper until a new one could be found, despite the challenges of keeping a lighthouse while raising a three-year-old son as a single parent. Afterwards, she and Burton returned to her family's home on Matinicus.[16] In *The Pilgrim's Progress*, Christian the pilgrim has many travails on his wandering progress toward paradise. If in her youth Ellen Tolman Wallace made her Delectable Mountains quilt as a reminder that one could pass through troubles and achieve the goal of heaven, perhaps her quilt was an emotional as well as a physical comfort to her amidst her own travails.

A few quilters chose not to follow strict patterns, but to design their own quilts, or modify patterns that they found. In 1868 Anne Drain Cotter of Alexander, Maine, chose leaves from her houseplants and trees in her yard to serve as patterns for sections of her bold appliqué quilt (figs. 5.8 to 5.10). An unknown maker created a red-and-white quilt in a style that recalls Hawaiian quilts (fig. 5.11). The quilt is difficult to date precisely, because the white background and red twill fabrics were made for many decades. The maker may have been inspired

Fig. 5.8
Appliqué Quilt
Made by Anne Drain Cotter
Alexander, Maine, 1868
84.5 x 79 inches
Maine State Museum, 97.77.1

Anne Drain Cotter's daughter recalled her mother choosing leaves from the trees in their yard to use as patterns in a quilt that she created not long after the close of the Civil War. Anne Cotter bought the fabric for the quilt in New Brunswick. The family lived in Alexander, Maine, and the nearest large town, St. Stephen, was over the Canadian border, twenty-five miles away.

Fig. 5.9
Detail, Anne Cotter's Appliqué Quilt
Maine State Museum, 97.77.1

Anne Cotter's quilt combined the natural with the fanciful. She included lifelike plants and birds, as well as nine blocks of her own design. These she made by folding fabric into quarters and cutting out a pattern, much as paper snowflakes are made. She then sewed the symmetrical motif onto a white foundation. In the wide vertical sashing between the blocks, Cotter placed a potted plant with leaves and cherries below it, and another abstract appliqué wedged in between two others below that. She also included three stylized suns, a moon, and several stars.

CHAPTER 5

Fig. 5.10
Digital Restoration of Anne Cotter's Appliqué Quilt
Maine State Museum, 97.77.1; digital correction by Mike Taylor

Most of the greens in the quilt have faded to tan. This digital restoration imagines what the quilt would have looked like originally. The green of the leaves is based on the color of the few original leaves that have not faded. They were cut from furnishing fabric, likely scraps left over from a set of curtains.

Fig. 5.11
Appliqué Antlers Quilt
Maker unknown
Maine use history, 1875–1900
71 x 65 inches
Courtesy of Judy Roche

The unknown maker of this red-and-white appliqué quilt combined images of birds, floral swags, and what resemble moose antlers into a striking and fanciful composition. Coincidentally, the quilt's owner has a boot scraper that greatly resembles the designs the birds stand upon, adding to the whimsy of the quilt for those who have seen both.

by a Hawaiian quilt she had seen or heard about, or she may have decided to translate local expressions of folded-and-cut paper templates on a very large scale. This end result is reminiscent of moose antlers.

REFLECTIONS OF COMMUNITY: FUNDRAISING QUILTS IN THE LATE 1800s

Aiding soldiers during the Civil War had been good training for women who wanted to contribute to society and ease its ills. Ladies' groups continued to work for causes such as temperance, church missions, the education of freed blacks, and for women's suffrage (or against it), and local churches and charities often needed to raise funds for specific projects (fig. 5.12). A time-honored way to raise extra money from quilts was for the winner to return the quilt to the group to be raffled or auctioned again. But there was never any guarantee that a quilt would raise this second wave of revenue. Some members of the new generation of quilters saw a way to make it a certainty: they solicited donations in advance, asking members of the larger community to pay for the privilege of having their name on a quilt. The makers then embroidered or inked the names of the donors on the quilt before it was raffled or auctioned. Patterns often included zones that indicated the amount given by each individual, with central placement indicating greater generosity. Some fundraising quilts included hundreds of donors. Three of the 100 fundraising quilts Dorothy Cozart examined in the 1980s included over 1,000 names, though most had between 150 and 500.[17]

Fig. 5.12
Quilts for Sale in Alameda Hall, Bath
J. C. Higgins and Son, photographers
Bath, Maine, ca. 1889
5 x 8¼ inches
Courtesy of Maine Maritime Museum, 79.143.420.1, collection PC-003

The Alameda Hall in Bath was built in 1883. Originally used for roller skating, it also hosted political rallies, high school graduations, dances, and fundraising fairs. This fundraiser sold food as well as handworks of all kinds, including hooked rugs and quilts. The event may have raised funds for a local Grange.[18]

CHAPTER 5

Nearly all of the quilts Cozart examined were made by church groups. Two quilts in the Maine State Museum collection are unusual in this respect: they were made by groups of women associated with the Grand Army of the Republic (the GAR). This was a fraternal organization of Union veterans of the Civil War. In Maine, each regiment hosted its own reunions and participated in state-wide reunions and meetings, as well as occasional anniversary gatherings at battlefields. Some of the more active regiments built meeting houses. The veterans of Maine's Fifth Infantry regiment built a memorial hall on Peaks Island in honor of their fallen comrades. It served as a reunion site and a vacation destination for its members and their families. The building has survived and is now a museum. GAR members in many

Fig. 5.13
Fan Fundraising Quilt
Members of the Women's Relief Corps
Biddeford Maine, 1898
80½ x 67¼ inches
Maine State Museum, 2017.68.1

The fan pattern was an ideal pattern for a fundraising quilt. The body of the fan became solid rather than pieced, and groups could divide it into any number of vanes for donors' names.

Fig. 5.14
Fan Fundraising Quilt
Members of the Women's Relief Corps
Waterville, Maine, 1900
69 x 66 inches
Maine State Museum, 93.68.1

The Women's Relief Corps of Waterville made their fan fundraising quilt just two years after their sister corps in Biddeford made theirs. Rather than asking donors to sign the quilt and be committed from the beginning to a certain number of donations, the Waterville group embroidered the names, with one person writing them on the foundation fabric beforehand. They may have based this decision on the experiences their Biddeford counterparts encountered.

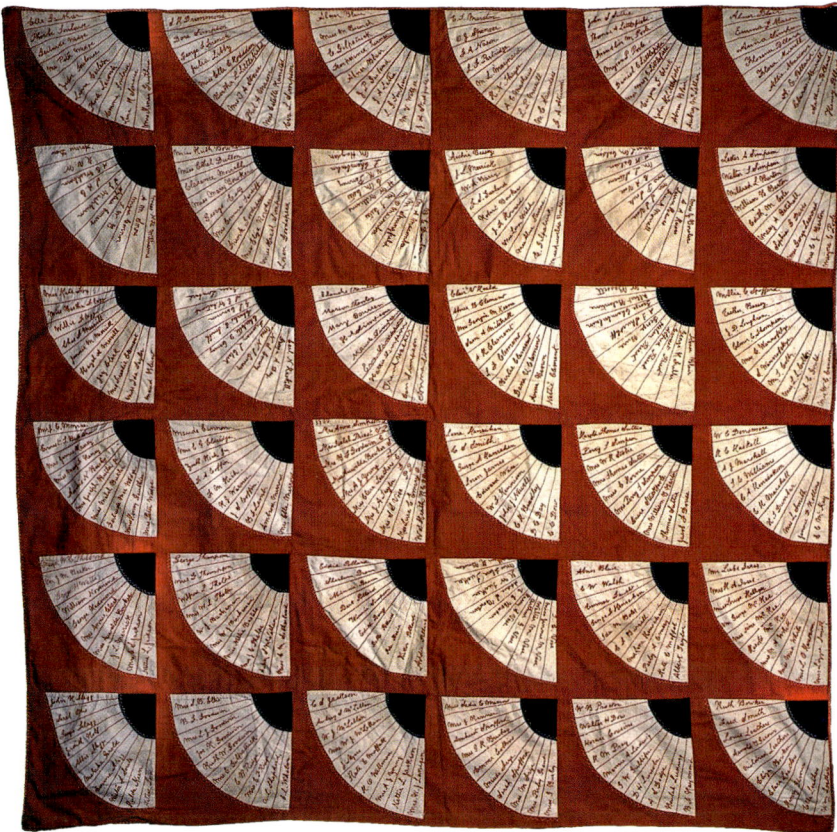

Fig. 5.15
Detail, Waterville Fan Fundraising Quilt
Maine State Museum, 93.68.1

Detail of the Waterville fundraising quilt, showing the embroidered, inscribed names.

communities built local meeting houses. The GAR hall in Pembroke was handed down to the American Legion when the last Civil War veterans were too elderly to care for it, and it is still in use. Local meetinghouses like this served veterans from a variety of regiments.

The GAR was an advocacy group as well as a place where veterans could share experiences and memories. It lobbied for veterans' pensions and helped those who needed assistance in applying. It served as a mutual aid society for its members, as well as lobbying at state and national levels. Many of Maine's politicians in the late 1800s were Civil War veterans, and the GAR was a strong political force in-state and nationally. And behind the power, the lobbying, and the reunions was a beneficent army of women, raising money, organizing, cooking, and supporting one another: the Women's Relief Corps, or WRC. This group acted as the auxiliary wing of the GAR.

Because GAR and WRC members attended both local and regimental gatherings, individuals from different communities came together who might not otherwise have met. In 1898, Waterville, Maine, was a mill city with a sizable French-Canadian immigrant population and a well-defined city center along the river. Likewise, Biddeford was a booming textile mill town, with a population half again as large as Waterville. The two towns are about 95 miles apart. Despite their distance, it appears that at least some residents of the two towns forged relationships through their involvement with the GAR and WRC. Evidence for this can be found in two fundraising quilts made by WRC members in Waterville and Biddeford, made just two years apart, in 1898 and 1900 (figs. 5.13 and 5.14).

Women in the two communities used the same block in the same colors for their quilts: each white fan had a navy blue center and was set on a bright red ground. Further, both set off the outside margin of the blue and inside margin of the red with white embroidery in a rail fence stitch. The two groups executed the fans a little differently, however. Both embroidered radiating lines in the fans, to separate each signature, Waterville in red, and Biddeford alternating blue and red. The women of Waterville divided the fans into ten vanes. One person then penciled in the donors' names and one or more women embroidered them (fig. 5.15). In Biddeford, however, the quilt's organizers divided each fan into six, and donors signed each block in ink.

Blocks in both quilts bear the names of the cities' mayors, as well as merchants and attorneys, and school and church officials. Biddeford's quilt includes signatures of officers of the local WRC and GAR, as well as that of Helen Douglass, wife of Frederick Douglass. One of the blocks in Biddeford's quilt bears what was thought to be the signature of a Cantonese Chinese immigrant with the surname Hop (fig. 5.16).[19] Transliterated, the inscription on the quilt reads Hop Sing Guan, the last word of which translates to place. The first symbol, pronounced Hop, means gathering, and Sing means victory. It is possible that the laundry was run by a man named Sing Hop whose family gave him an auspicious and ambitious name. It is also possible that three words refer to the laundry and that its proprietor's name was something altogether different.[20] Either way, the *Maine Register* for 1900 lists two men, Lung Horp and Sing Horp, who operated laundries on opposite ends of Maine Street. The *Register* entries for Biddeford list three other laundries. One of these was operated by F. L. Cornish, who was likely not Chinese. The American Hand Laundry and Star Laundry do not list the names of their owners.[21] The Waterville *Register* entry lists six laundries, two of which were run by Chinese immigrants. By contrast, the city of Portland listed thirty-two laundries, at least fifteen of

**Fig. 5.16
Detail, Biddeford Fan Fundraising Quilt**
Maine State Museum, 2017.96.1

Detail of the Biddeford fan quilt, showing the inked signatures, including an inscription that is either the signature of a Cantonese man named Hop or Horp, or the name of the laundry business that he operated.

which were owned by Chinese immigrant families.[22] A review of the 1900 *Register* reveals that towns large enough to have two or more laundries generally were home to at least one Chinese-American individual or family, at least judging from the business names. Despite the 1882 Chinese exclusion act, Chinese-American men and in many cases their families could be found in nine Maine counties, from Sanford and Biddeford in the south, to Eden (now Bar Harbor) in the east, and north to Bangor. Despite its British origins, by the time the Biddeford and Waterville GAR/WRC quilts were made, Maine had become much more multi-ethnic than it had been even fifty years before. French Canadians and Acadians, Germans, Italians, Finns, Armenians, and Lebanese all found home in Maine, working in its quarries and woods and in its mills and factories.

☙

Variety was the order of the day in the late 1800s, in the range of colors in a quilt, the number of figures in a redwork or crazy quilt, and in the sheer number of quilts Maine women made between the close of the Civil War and the beginning of the twentieth century.

CHAPTER 5

GALLERY

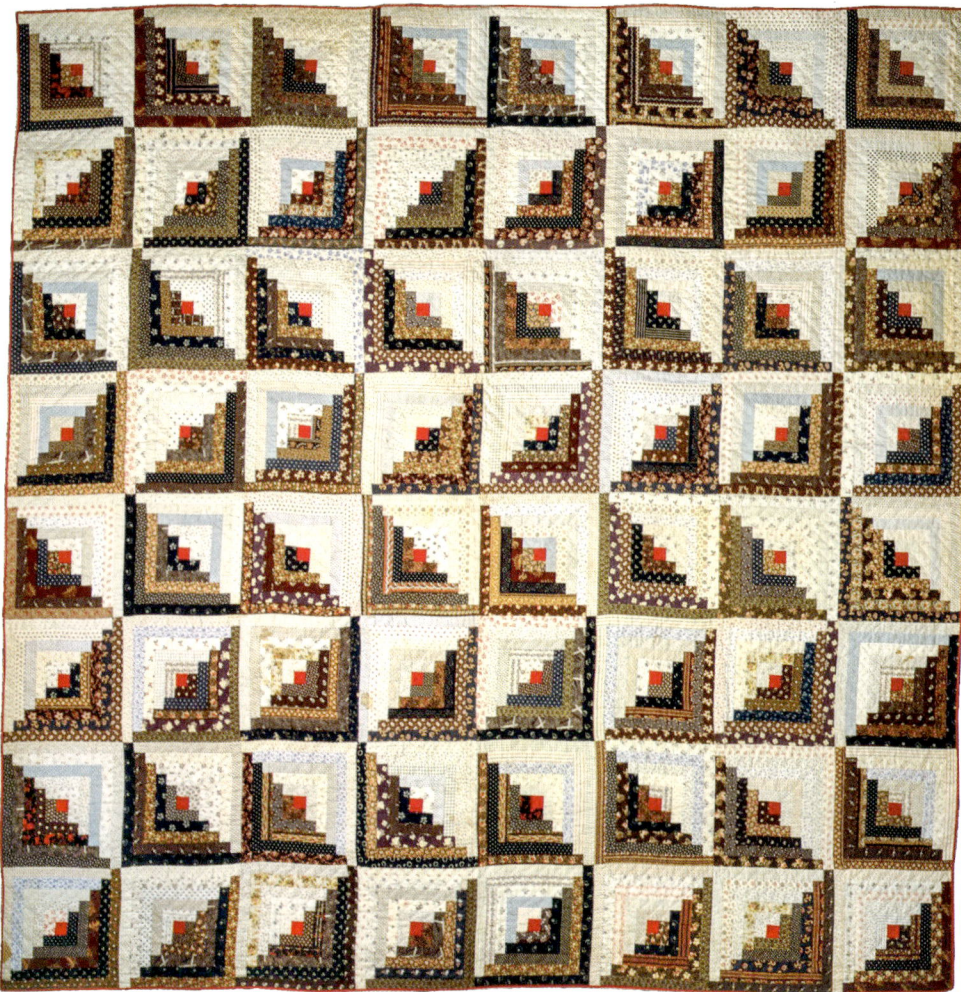

Fig. 5.17
Log Cabin Variation
Made as a wedding gift for Millie Burton Burgess
Probably Carmel, Maine, 1896
103 x 103 inches
Maine State Museum, 92.24.3

This simple but unusual log cabin variation was made as a wedding gift for Millie Burton Burgess and Adolphus Omri Burgess. Millie was thirty-one years old and a schoolteacher in 1896, when she married Adolphus, forty-one, who was a sign painter.[23] She was born in Carmel, Maine, and Adolphus in China, Maine. The couple settled in Holyoke, Massachusetts, where they were married.

118

COTTONS GALORE

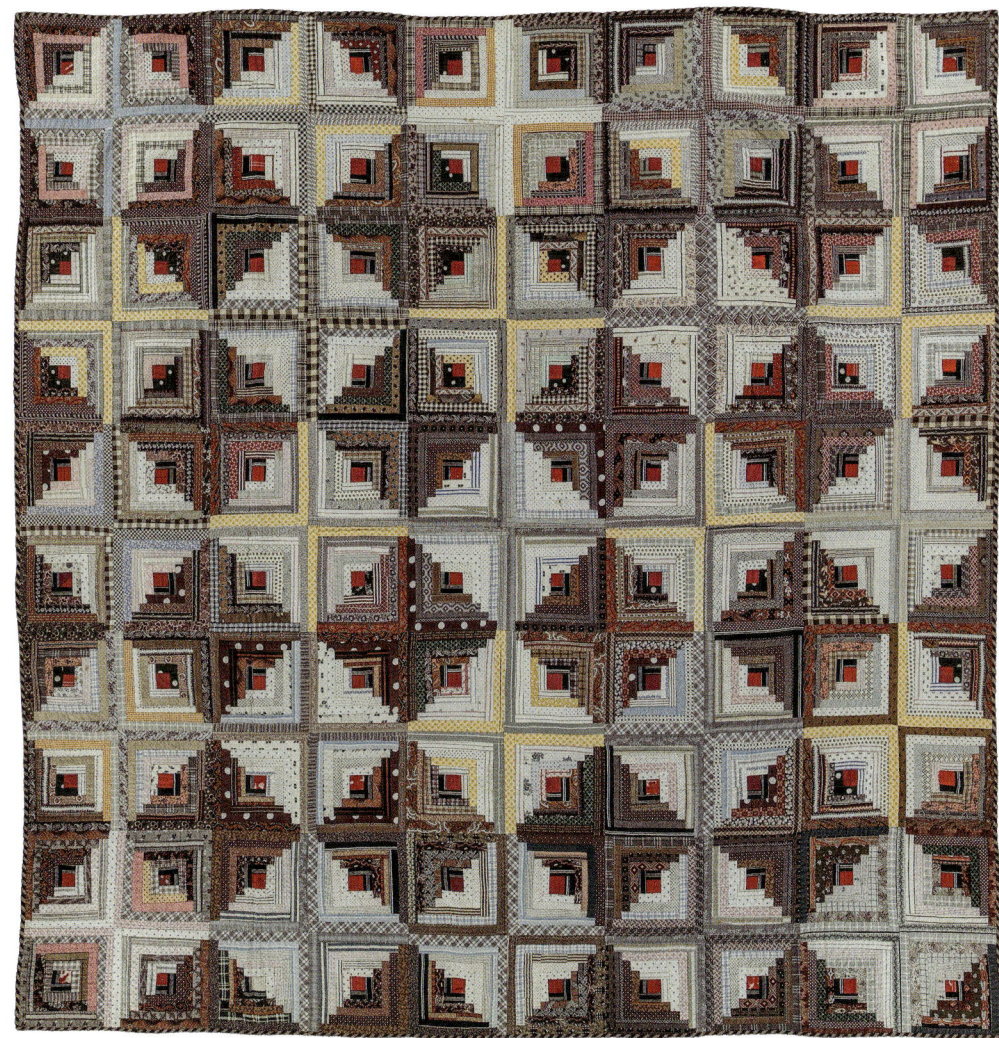

Fig. 5.18
Log Cabin Quilt, Sunshine and Shadow Variation
Made by Eunice Shaw Mayo
Steep Falls, Maine, ca. 1880
78½ x 77¼ inches
Maine State Museum, 2000.105.2

Eunice Mayo's log cabin quilt variation was called Sunshine and Shadow. She apparently enjoyed making such quilts, as the Maine State Museum holds another, similar example she made. The quilt descended in the maker's family before its donation to the museum.

CHAPTER 5

Fig. 5.19
Log Cabin Quilt, Pineapple or Windmill Variation
Attributed to Elizabeth "Eliza" Pineo Farnsworth or her daughter, Charlotte C. Farnsworth Look
Columbia Falls, Maine, 1870s
82 inches x 84 inches
Maine State Museum, 68.98.1

Eliza Pineo of Deblois, Maine, married Joseph Farnsworth of Jonesboro sometime around 1850–1852. The couple moved to Columbia Falls, where their five children were born. Their daughter Charlotte was born in 1853. The quilt descended in the family, but nearly 100 years after its creation, family members could not recall whether Eliza or Charlotte had made it, or if they had worked on the quilt together.

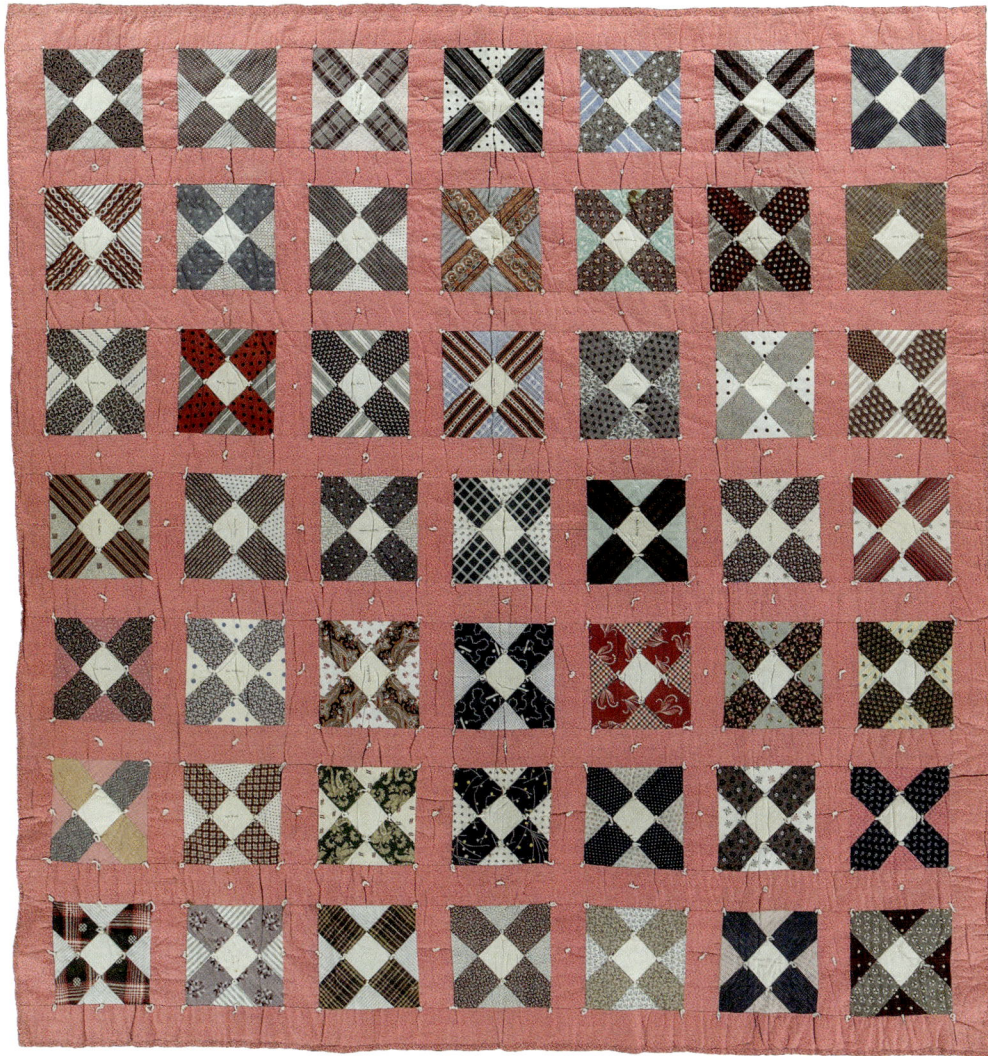

Fig. 5.20
Album Quilt
Made by friends and family of Helen Stockman Merrill
East Auburn, Maine, 1888–1889
84 x 84 inches
Maine State Museum, 2005.91.2

Helen "Nellie" Stockman of East Auburn, Maine, apparently had many friends, a large family, or both. Two nearly identical quilts were made for Stockman before her 1889 marriage to Albert Merrill. The names are inscribed on each block in the same handwriting. At some point the two quilts were separated and traveled down different lines of the family.

CHAPTER 5

Fig. 5.21
Ocean Waves Quilt
Made by or for Helen "Nellie" Stockman Merrill
East Auburn, Maine, ca. 1889
82½ x 76½ inches
Maine State Museum, 2006.40.5

A third quilt that Nellie Stockman Merrill owned includes the same double pink fabric used on the album quilts, as well as many other fabrics. Apart from the fact that it was owned by Nellie Merrill, the history of this quilt is unknown. Merrill may have made it, or a friend or family member who was involved in the creation of Nellie's album quilts might have given it to her.

Fig. 5.22
Detail, Nellie Stockman's Album Quilt
Maine State Museum, 2005.91.2

Detail of one of Nellie Stockman Merrill's quilts, showing handwriting used on both album quilts, and fabrics common to three of her quilts.

Fig. 5.23
Star and Swags Quilt
Attributed to Eveline Greenwood Cushman
Lisbon, Maine, ca. 1872
92¼ x 92¼ inches
Maine State Museum, 81.138.1

Eveline Greenwood Cushman was an accomplished seamstress: getting so many diamond seams to lie flat is a difficult feat. At the last minute, however, she evidently decided that the outside row was too pale and added another. It complicated her appliqué work, which she had mostly finished by that point. Some diamonds cover bits of the appliqué flowers and leaves. The tips of some diamonds have been cut, and others turn slightly to accommodate leaves and flowers.

   Eveline Greenwood was born in Greene, Maine, in 1853. She married Sylvanus Cushman of Lisbon in 1872, and the couple lived and raised their children on their Lisbon farm. By 1880, the census notes that Eveline had a disability, an injured right ankle. It may be that decreased mobility caused by this handicap gave Eveline more time for handwork such as this intricate quilt.

CHAPTER 5

Fig. 5.24
Appliqué and Pieced Quilt
Probably made by Emma Harmons
and other family members
Saco, Maine, 1850s and later
76 x 78 inches
Maine State Museum, 2015.40.2

Emma Harmons of Saco, Maine, was a prodigious quilter. This example may be one that she began and a descendant finished. The piecework was done by hand, but a few appliqué elements were sewn to the foundation by machine. Part of the quilting was worked by hand, and some sewn by machine.

Fig. 5.25
Carolina Lily Quilt
Attributed to Amanda V. Nash Kaler
Waldoboro, Maine, late 1800s
92 x 81 inches
Maine State Museum, 68.174.81

The pattern of this quilt was popular and goes by many names including Carolina Lily, North Carolina Lily, Tiger Lily, Wood Lily, and Mountain Lily.

   Amanda V. Nash was born to a farming family. She had five siblings and was single until the age of 41, when she married Oscar E. Kaler, a ship's joiner. The 1870 census notes that Oscar was a widower with four young children. The children would have been grown by the time he married Amanda. After Oscar died in 1901, Amanda lived alone for some time before moving to a nephew's house in Nobleboro. The quilt she made descended in the Kaler family.

Fig. 5.26
Basket Quilt
Attributed to Mary Bowman Lithgow
Augusta, Maine, 1842–1865
94 x 70 inches
Maine State Museum, 95.118.1

Born in Hallowell, Maine, in 1803, Bowman married Llewellyn Lithgow in 1835. His father and uncles, including Major General William Lithgow, had come to Pownalborough, in what is now Dresden, in 1788, and Llewellyn was born there on Christmas Day, 1796. The couple lived in Dresden, where Llewellyn was a merchant, until he was able to retire at the ripe age of forty, and the couple moved to Augusta in 1839. Mary died in 1868. The Lithgows had no children. A note that was attached to the quilt records that Mary made it in 1842, when she was twelve years old. However, Mary Lithgow was thirty-nine years old and the Lithgows were living in Augusta by then. It is possible that she made it at a family member's home in Hallowell. It is also possible that the quilt was made at a different time.

Fig. 5.27
Robbing Peter to Pay Paul Quilt
Made by a member of the Gagnon or Hinds families
Benton, Maine, 1850–1900
83 x 79 inches
Maine State Museum, 2016.29.2

Several members of the Hinds and Gagnon families of Benton included quilters. The maker of this quilt, which bears the whimsical pattern name Robbing Peter to Pay Paul, used plain white muslin or sheeting and green gingham. The simple checked fabric known as gingham has been woven for nearly 200 years and has never gone out of production. The quilter's choice of fabrics made for a lovely quilt. Unfortunately, the fabrics are difficult to date precisely, and so determine the quilt's maker.

CHAPTER 5

Fig. 5.28
Pieced Cotton Explosion Potholder Quilt
Unknown maker
Maine, ca. 1885
75½ x 75½
Collection of Shelburne Museum, gift of Elizabeth M. Billings and Harriet Miller, 2001-36.
Photography by Andy Duback.

The identity of the woman who made this quilt has been lost. It is a pity, as she was a very talented needleworker. A round pattern like Explosion, or Mariner's Compass, would not seem to lend itself well to the potholder construction method. The maker of this quilt managed it beautifully, however. She bound each round block with red binding, and then crafted curved sashing to fill the spaces between the blocks. About half of the binding segments are bound with light-blue cotton. It may be that the rest were, as well, in a matching blue that has since faded to a pale cream color. The middle points of the compass have faded also. The quilt, which is still dramatic, would have been even brighter in its day.

Fig. 5.29
Ohio Star Potholder Album Quilt
Made by friends and relatives of Octavia Henrietta Bangs
Phillips, Maine, 1870
74 x 83 inches
Maine State Museum, 2014.42.1

Octavia Henrietta Bangs of Phillips was thirty when she made a block of this quilt. She married Elbridge Dill soon after. The quilt was given to Octavia Bangs, perhaps as a wedding gift, and it descended in the family. The makers of the quilt carefully embroidered their names and dates on the quilt. Unfortunately, some of the embroidery floss was not colorfast and bled when the quilt was washed. Some colors of the floss may have had what conservators call inherent vice: that is, they were unstable from the beginning. In a few cases, the dye has destroyed the threads of the floss, and the inscription as well.

CHAPTER 5

Fig. 5.30
Annie's Quilt
Friends and family of Annie Whitcomb Baker; 36 inscribed names
Newcastle or Edgecomb, Maine, 1885
96 x 72 inches
Courtesy of Newcastle Historical Society

"Annie's Quilt," as it is called, was made for Annie Whitcomb Baker of Newcastle, when she married Robert Cochran Clifford of Edgecomb in 1885, when she was thirty-four years old. All of the blocks are appliqué, and most include stylized flowers with their edges framed with decorative trims. A flag is centered in the top row beside two blocks with maritime motifs: a mariner's compass and a block featuring an octant and two fouled anchors. Robert was a farmer, and the couple spent the rest of their lives on a farm, but there are no agricultural motifs on the quilt. Relatives or friends of the couple may have been mariners, an almost certain fact of life in a coastal Maine town. The quilt was hand stitched, and was constructed in a quilt-as-you-go technique, whereby the blocks, batting, and backing were assembled together, in stages.

Fig. 5.31
Detail, Annie's Quilt
Courtesy of Newcastle Historical Society

Detail of the maritime blocks on Annie's quilt, including a mariner's compass, an octant, and fouled anchors.

COTTONS GALORE

Fig. 5.32
Zigzag Postage Stamp Quilt
Mary Augusta Walton Mason
Corinna, Maine, ca. 1890
83 x 78 inches
Maine State Museum, 2009.41.2

Mary Augusta Walton of Alton, Maine, married Leonard Mason in 1883, and the couple settled in Corinna, Maine, where they had a farm. Mason likely made her two postage stamp quilts before her children were born or when they were quite small. Leonard Jr. was born in 1891, and daughter Annie in 1895. Leonard died of an accidental gunshot wound when he was thirteen. The quilts eventually passed to Mason's daughter, Annie Mason Bates (see fig. 7.5).

CHAPTER 5

Fig. 5.33
Overshot Postage Stamp Quilt
Mary Augusta Walton Mason
Corinna, Maine, ca. 1890
90 inches x 70 inches
Maine State Museum, 2009.41.3

Mary Mason's postage stamp quilts are unusual in their design. Most such quilts have no overall pattern and are simply a riot of color (see fig. 5.3). Mason's, however, are carefully laid out, in a pattern of zigzags (fig. 5.32) or concentric rhombuses that recall woven overshot blankets. The fabrics suggest a date of ca. 1890, but it is likely that Mason constructed her quilts before her children were born in 1891 and 1894, as it would have been difficult to lay out such complicated quilts while managing two youngsters.

COTTONS GALORE

Fig. 5.34
The Norwegian Quilt
Possibly made by Harriet Purington
Portland, Maine, 1867
85 ½ inches x 66 ½ inches
Maine State Museum 2020.1.1; photograph courtesy of Camille Breeze, Museum Textile Services

Carl Fredrik Musaus was born in Norway in 1830. He emigrated to the United States, anglicized his name to Charles Frederick Musaus, and became a naturalized citizen and a ship's captain. After his first wife died, he married Marietta Purinton in 1860. Marietta was the daughter of a Portland grocer. She lived with her parents when Charles was away and traveled with him when she could. One of their children was born at sea. In the early and mid-1860s, Charles captained the ship Norwegian. This quilt commemorates that ship and Charles's heritage. It was made around the time that the Norwegian was sold, and Charles took command of a new ship. The quilt bears the names of friends and family members, but may have been made by just one person. An undated letter from Marietta's sister, Harriet, known as Hattie, discusses making a quilt. She may have made the Norwegian quilt. It was constructed using the potholder technique, with each block quilted and bound before the blocks were sewn together. In addition to masonic and religious themes, many of the blocks feature maritime symbols, including the Portland Observatory. This block and others, together with the potholder construction and the red figures on a plain ground, link this quilt to two made in the Portland neighborhood of Munjoy Hill a few years earlier, during the Civil War (see figures 4.10 and 4.11).

6

THAT'S JUST CRAZY

The fashion for crazy quilts grew out of the 1876 Centennial Exposition in Philadelphia. The six-month-long exhibition, which included artwork from other nations, not only inspired a style of quilt, but influenced decorative arts in general.[1] The Aesthetic art movement prized art for beauty's sake and did not limit its definition to canvases. Crazy quilts adopted the art movement's asymmetry; they borrowed imagery from Japanese pottery and prints, from artists like Kate Greenaway, from political banners, book illustrations, and

Fig. 6.1
Crazy Quilt with Brownie
Made by Anne Hadley
Machias, Maine, 1884
81 x 70 inches
Maine State Museum, 88.29.1

Anne Hadley of Machias was a capable embroiderer. Nonetheless, she also made use of commercially available embroidered silks when she made her crazy quilt in 1884.

**Fig. 6.2
Detail, Crazy Quilt with Brownie**
Maine State Museum, 88.29.1

Anne Hadley's quilt included images from popular culture such as this Brownie riding a mouse. In 1884, Palmer Cox's Brownie drawings were becoming popular. His Brownies, Their Book *was published three years later. Hadley's quilt includes pre-embroidered details, as well as her own embroidery. She likely purchased the yellow patch with cattails already embroidered.*

scenes of everyday life.[2] Crazy quilts were so popular that industry responded with traceable embroidery patterns and with ready-made embroidered panels and elements (figs. 6.1 and 6.2).[3] In the 1880s, cotton manufacturers began to print "Crazy Cloth."[4] Called cheater cloth today, this fabric bore printed versions of crazy patches.

Nothing says variety like a crazy quilt. The quilts' makers often took decoration to the extreme, cramming embroidery, painted motifs, three-dimensional flowers, appliqué, millinery flowers, and ribbons into every available nook and cranny. As Beverly Gordon puts it, "The Crazy quilt [has] indeed a bewildering sense of oversaturation. Such a quilt cannot be taken in or processed at a glance; it is first *experienced*, and only gradually are its many components sorted out [author's emphasis]."[5]

Strictly speaking, most crazy quilts are not, in fact, quilts. The decorative surface fabrics are stitched directly onto a foundation fabric (figs. 6.3 and 6.4). Most crazy quilts lack batting and quilting, traits that are also missing from other bedcovers of the late 1800s, such as log cabin and outline quilts. Most crazies were not intended for the bed, but were elements of décor, to be draped over a lap or a piano, or across the back of a couch. The appeal of crazy quilts, unlike pieced cotton quilts, was recognized by quilters and descendants alike. The value crazy quilts held in their makers' families is reflected by a simple fact: in the Maine State Museum collection, it is the only class of quilt for which every maker is known. These prized textiles were often put away in a trunk or newfangled cedar chest and only taken out for special occasions. This was just as well, as silk was the most popular fabric for a crazy quilt. The richness and gloss of the fabric added to the visual texture of the crazy quilt. However, silk is very sensitive to light and does not hold up well. This is especially true of inexpensive silks woven in the late 1800s and early 1900s that were "weighted," that is, treated with metal salts, to appear more valuable.[6] To acquire a large enough variety of fabrics, women traded scraps of silk dress fabric or hat ribbons with friends, or they ordered scraps or kits by mail.[7] Quiltmakers also used velvets and other plush fabrics, sometimes in the same quilt (see figs. 6.7 to 6.16). As the style became more mainstream and less novel, some makers moved the silk crazy quilt out of the parlor and onto the bed, making bedcovers from wool and even humble cotton (fig. 6.5). Maine women often made their decorative crazy quilts from wool scraps, perhaps because wool was such a common fabric in a state with long winters and so many outdoor activities (fig. 6.6).

CHAPTER 6

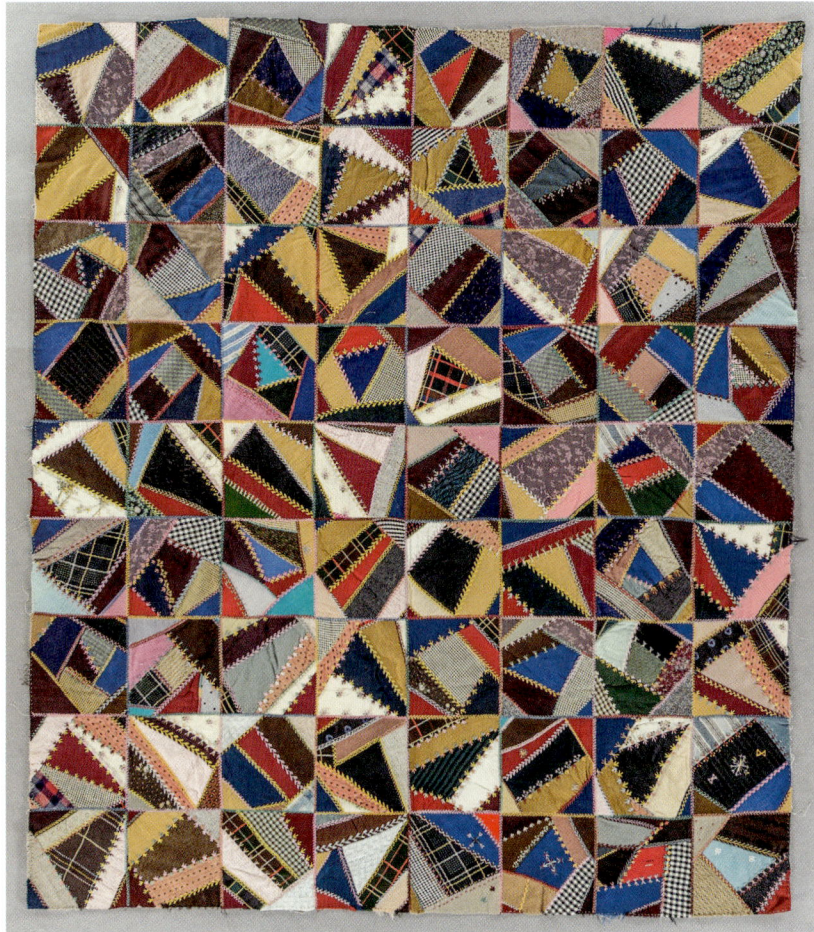

Fig. 6.3
Crazy Quilt Top
Ella M. Wells Parkin
Clinton or Fairfield, Maine,
ca. 1895
76 x 76 inches
Maine State Museum,
2002.66.2

Ella Wells of Fairfield was born in 1875. She was probably in her twenties when she made this crazy quilt top. Ella married John H. Parkin in 1905. Her husband was born in Canada and was a naturalized citizen. The couple settled in Fairfield, where John worked as a carpenter.

Fig. 6.4
Detail, Back of Crazy Quilt Top
Maine State Museum, 2002.66.2

The back of Ella Wells Parkin's quilt shows the embroidered seams where swatches of fabric were sewn to the foundation, and the blocks later stitched together. The black fabric behind two of the blocks would not have shown when the quilt was finished. Most crazy quilts were not quilted but were fastened with ties at block intersections, so that the embroidery on each seam would not be damaged.

Fig. 6.5
Cotton Crazy Quilt
Carrie C. Meservy Ham
Farmingdale, 1910
78½ x 67¾ inches
Maine State Museum, 2019.25.1

Emily Diggs of Farmingdale received this quilt from her Aunt Carrie Ham when she was nine years old. It was carefully stored and never used. The reason may be due to the inscription, which gives the quilt to Emma L. Diggs. Emily was named after several family members named both Emma and Emily. In a letter found with the quilt, she notes that she vastly preferred the latter.

Fig. 6.6
Wool Octagon Crazy Quilt
Made by Mary Jane Haley
Winterport, Maine, 1893
61 x 59 inches
Maine State Museum, 89.30.1

This wool quilt was constructed like a crazy quilt, with pieces sewn to a foundation. However, instead of irregular swatches of silk, Mary Jane Haley chose a pattern of octagons, made up of eight triangles, with squares between them. One of these bears an embroidered inscription: "Mother / Age 60 years / 1893." Some of the triangles are pieces in tidy strips. As in a crazy quilt, embroidery covers every seam. It would have been a warm, heavy lap quilt. The donor remembered seeing it in her grandmother Mary Jane Haley's parlor. It was later used to line another quilt instead of batting, and the family eventually brought it to their camp in Bayside, Maine. When the later quilt was damaged, the family discovered the wool quilt inside it.

CHAPTER 6

By 1884, ladies' publications were predicting the demise of the passé crazy quilt, in favor of new expressions of more traditional patchwork. However, the style continued to be popular, at least in rural areas, for many decades.

COMMUNITY EXPRESSION: A BAILEY ISLAND QUILT MYSTERY

The crazy-quilt trend was at its height in 1890, and women all over the nation were making the exciting new throws for their parlor décor. With around 400 year-round residents, Bailey Island, Maine, is not a big town; nor was it in 1890 when Mary Louise Orr made a crazy quilt (fig. 6.7). It is not known how the crazy-quilt craze reached the community. Some island

Fig. 6.7
Mary Louise Orr's Crazy Quilt
Made by Mary Louise Stover Orr
Bailey Island, Maine, 1890
82 x 62 inches
Maine State Museum, 2000.47.1

Mary Louise Orr of Bailey Island made this quilt for her young daughter, Ethel. It includes silks, velvets, and velveteen fabrics, and three signed ribbons. In addition to embroidery, Orr painted some blocks and adorned others with three-dimensional velvet or silk flowers, as well as flowers made from embroidered chenille.

136

**Fig. 6.8
Detail, Mary Louise Orr's Quilt**
Maine State Museum, 2000.47.1

This painting of a woman in a veil may be a self-portrait of the quilt maker, Mary Louise Stover Orr.

**Fig. 6.9
Detail, Mary Louise Orr's Quilt**
Maine State Museum, 2000.47.1

Anna Morton, wife of Benjamin Harrison's Vice President Levi P. Morton, signed one of the three silk ribbons on the quilt. Collecting signatures was a popular fad in the 1890s.

women likely subscribed to women's magazines or accessed them through friends who did. Although island communities are somewhat removed from the larger society, Bailey Island is close to the mainland. Moreover, most of its inhabitants had access to boats. Portland was not as distant by boat in 1890 as it is by car today, when islanders must cross over the island's famous 1928 cribstone bridge and drive up Orrs Island and the long Harpswell peninsula to reach Brunswick and then head north to coastal towns or south to more populous parts of the state.

Mary Louise Orr used silk, velvet, and velveteen in her quilt. Like thousands of other women, she embellished these lustrous fabrics with embroidery. But she also incorporated metallic trims and made three-dimensional flowers of velvet, satin ribbon, and chenille yarns for some of the blocks. She also painted two portraits on the quilt: a woman in a veil (fig. 6.8) and a young girl, and added images of familiar animals, such as cats, a horse, a dog, and a cow. Mary Louise made the quilt for her daughter, Ethel, who was seven years old in 1890. Ethel may have had some say in the animals that her mother painted, because she was involved in other decisions regarding the quilt: the quilt includes three wide silk ribbons, autographed with the names of famous people (fig. 6.9). At the time, collecting autographs was as big a fad as stitching crazy quilts.

Two of the ribbons' signers were women: American first lady Caroline Harrison, and Anna Morton, wife of Benjamin Harrison's vice president, Levi Morton. The third was poet and abolitionist John Greenleaf Whittier. Ethel sent each of them a ribbon, with a request for an autograph. Evidence for this survives in the form of three letters from Helen Keller, then nine years old, from whom Ethel had also requested an autograph (fig. 6.10). In the first letter, Helen wrote her regrets to Ethel, explaining that she could not sign the ribbon Ethel sent, because she could only write in pencil (this would later change). Ethel and her mother sent gifts to Helen Keller, and she sent a thank-you note. In all, she wrote three letters to Ethel, which were as precious to the Orr family as the crazy quilt itself was. The letters show Helen's use of "square handwriting." She placed a piece of paper over a special grooved board, and with a pencil in her right hand, she formed block-style letters, while guiding the pencil with the forefinger of her left hand.

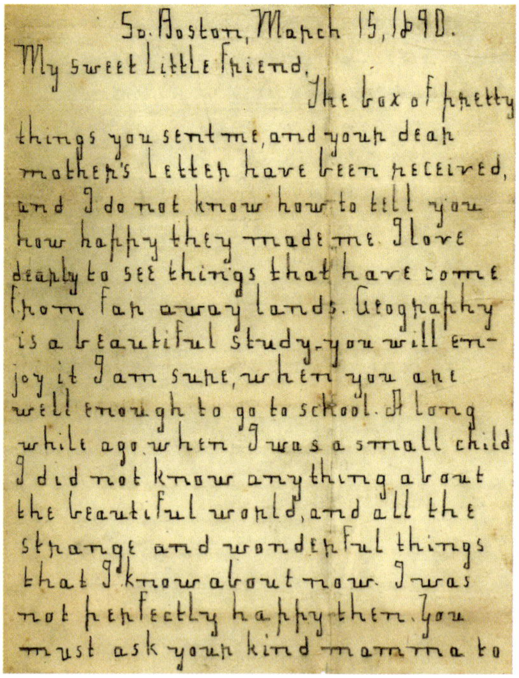

Mary Louise Orr's family cherished the quilt she made for Ethel, and by 2000, when her descendants gave it to the Maine State Museum, they thought it was unlike any other. However, the museum's collection held another crazy quilt, also sewn on Bailey Island (fig. 6.11). That quilt, said to have been made by Mary Louise Orr's third cousin, Addie Mae Johnson, has many similarities to the Orr quilt. It also includes velvets,

Fig. 6.10
Thank-You Note
Helen Keller to Ethel Orr
South Boston, March 15, 1890
10 x 8 inches
Maine State Museum, 2000.99.2

Helen Keller had to turn down the Orrs' request for a signed ribbon. She and Ethel wrote several letters to each other, including this one in which Helen thanked Ethel for gifts she had sent.

Fig. 6.11
Addie Mae Johnson Crazy Quilt
Made by Addie Mae Johnson or Mary Louise Stover Orr
Bailey Island, 1890–1895
64 x 64 inches
Maine State Museum, 84.79.1

This quilt, remarkably similar to the example sewn by Mary Louise Orr, was also made on Bailey Island. The name on the silk ribbon reads "Addie M. Johnson." The two women were related, and it is not known which of them made the quilt.

THAT'S JUST CRAZY

velveteens, and silks. It has three-dimensional flowers made from velvet, silk ribbon, and chenille yarns (fig. 6.12) like those on the Orr quilt (see figs. 6.8 and 6.9); and it has one white silk ribbon, signed Addie M. Johnson (see fig. 6.12).

Johnson's quilt also includes painted highlights, although they are not as abundant or as large as those painted on her Orr cousin's example. However, it is clear the two quilts were based on the same patterns. Some of the sculpted flowers are nearly identical (figs. 6.13 and 6.14), and the painted bees are the same shape, style, and size on the two quilts (figs. 6.15 and 6.16). Addie Mae made or received her quilt before her December 24, 1895, marriage to Charles Annis of Portland.[8]

Fig. 6.12
Detail, Addie Mae Johnson Crazy Quilt
Maine State Museum, 84.79.1

The silk ribbon on Addie Mae Johnson's quilt bears her name. It is not known, however, whether it is her signature or an inscription dedicating the quilt to her.

Fig. 6.13
Detail, Addie Mae Johnson Crazy Quilt
Maine State Museum, 84.79.1

Palette with pink silk roses on Addie Mae's quilt.

Fig. 6.14
Detail, Mary Louise Orr Quilt
Maine State Museum, 2000.47.1

Palette with pink silk roses on Mary Louise's quilt.

Fig. 6.15
Detail, Addie Mae Johnson Crazy Quilt
Maine State Museum, 84.79.1

Block with painted bees on Addie Mae's quilt.

Fig. 6.16
Detail, Mary Louise Orr Quilt
Maine State Museum, 2000.47.

Block with painted bees on Mary Louise's quilt.

The two quilts vary slightly in their overall color scheme and in their fabric choices. The Johnson quilt includes a larger number and variety of printed silks. We may never know if she based her quilt on her cousin's much-admired example, or if Mary Louise Orr made a second quilt for a favorite cousin. As yet, no correspondence or diaries have surfaced about either quilt, and the nature of their relationship remains a mystery.

☙

Women from every corner of the state made crazy quilts, from Caribou and Presque Isle in the far north (see figs. 6.17 to 6.19), to Bailey Island in Casco Bay. They continued to be made into the twentieth century. Aline Neveux of Biddeford completed her wool crazy quilt—which was also a family register—in 1973 (see figs. 6.20 to 6.22). Women continue to make crazy quilts today, as individual artisans or part of the state's several crazy-quilt guilds.

GALLERY

Fig. 6.17
Millinery Crazy Quilt
Made by Sarah Logan Howard
Caribou, Maine, 1939–1940
78.5 x 76 inches
Courtesy of Maine Historical Society, 2015.2

Sarah Logan Howard adorned the sixteen blocks of this crazy quilt with velvety faux flowers and leaves from one of Presque Isle, Maine's, two millinery shops. It is not known whether she worked at the shop or was related by marriage to the milliner. Sarah died in 1943. She was eighty-seven years old.

CHAPTER 6

**Fig. 6.18
Detail, Millinery
Crazy Quilt**
Courtesy of Maine
Historical Society,
2015.2

This composition of this block is more ordered than that of the others. The cotton sateen backing of the quilt is as bold as its design.

**Fig. 6.19
Detail, Millinery
Crazy Quilt**
Courtesy of Maine
Historical Society,
2015.2

Some of the millinery components on the quilt are very large. Perhaps the leaves and flowers Sarah used were those that did not sell well in the shop.

THAT'S JUST CRAZY

Fig. 6.20
Neveux Family Register Crazy Quilt
Made by Aline Neveux
Biddeford, Maine, 1942–1973
80½ x 65½ inches
Maine State Museum, 2009.20.1

Aline Florence Gendron Neveux of Biddeford, Maine, began this quilt during World War II. According to her children, her first block was that commemorating the bombing of Pearl Harbor. All but one of the other blocks in the quilt served as a family register, with a block for her and one for her husband, Eugene, and one for each of their children. Aline added to the blocks as her children grew up. She included the names of their spouses, the dates of their marriages, and the births of each of her grandchildren. She also designed and embroidered motifs for each child and grandchild, such as a tooth for the dentist and a plane for the pilot, and a family of skunks for the youngster who bore that nickname. The quilt bears one other square that represents national events: Aline made a block to honor President John F. Kennedy after his assassination.

CHAPTER 6

Fig. 6.21
Eugene and Aline Neveux with Aline's Quilt
Photo by Richard Danforth for the Biddeford *Journal Tribune*
Biddeford, Maine, 1973
Maine State Museum, 2009.20.2

Aline and Eugene Neveux posed in their living room with Aline's quilt shortly after it was finished.

Fig. 6.22
Detail, Neveux Family Register Crazy Quilt
Maine State Museum, 2009.20.1

Detail of Aline Neveux's quilt showing her block and that of her husband, Eugene. On the sashing of the quilt, Aline stitched "Commencé Janvier 1942" and "Complété Février 1973." She added one date after the completion of the quilt: it bears the date of Eugene's death, February 11, 1974. Aline died in 2001 at age 98. Her children donated the quilt in 2009 on what would have been her 106th birthday.

**Fig. 6.23
Cross Fan Crazy Quilt**
Made by members of the Harrington Methodist Society
Harrington, Maine, 1885
67 x 59 inches
Maine State Museum, 73.3.1

To judge from this quilt, the ladies of the Methodist Society of Harrington, Maine, included talented designers, needleworkers, and artists. They chose a fan pattern, and using crazy quilt techniques, sewed the fans into a brilliant cross. The makers embroidered classic crazy-quilt stitches over the seams of every multi-colored silk vane of the many fans. The negative spaces of the blocks are filled with embroidered motifs, elaborate initials, and small floral paintings. As with most crazy quilts, this was intended to be shown draped over a piano or other piece of furniture. The lace edging and painted silk would not have held up to the hard wear of a bedcover.

**Fig. 6.24
Detail, Harrington Methodist Society Quilt**
Maine State Museum, 73.3.1

The center of the cross includes a delicately painted pink rose and a dedication to Pastor Frank L. Brooks. He was a circuit preacher whose rounds included the Methodist Church in the small town of Harrington. Rev. Brooks must have made a good impression when he began his visits to Harrington in 1885, because the Methodist Society gave him this quilt the same year.

CHAPTER 6

Fig. 6.25
Embroidered Wool Crazy Quilt
Made by Clarissa Packard Folsom
Cambridge, Maine, ca. 1895
64¾ x 47½ inches
Maine State Museum, 2009.82.1

Clarissa Packard Folsom of Cambridge, Maine, made this crazy quilt when she was a widow in her early seventies. Folsom was born in Cambridge, but the family recalls that she lived and may have worked for a time in Livermore Falls, Maine. The quilt passed to her son, and in 1950, it was given to the donor, Folsom's great-granddaughter, as a wedding gift.

THAT'S JUST CRAZY

Fig. 6.26
Detail, Clarissa Folsom's Wool Crazy Quilt
Maine State Museum, 2009.82.1

Clarissa Folsom was skilled with a needle. Each embroidered wool flower on the border of her quilt is about 3/16 of an inch across. The quilt includes several colorways of some dress wools. It is possible that Clarissa worked in the clothing industry before her marriage to Josiah Folsom, or had relatives or friends who did.

CHAPTER 6

Fig. 6.27
Black Crazy Quilt
Made by Vinnie E. Fall Crosby
Albion, Maine, 1888
70 x 53 inches
Maine State Museum, 69.131.1

Vinnie Fall Crosby of Albion took a different approach to a crazy quilt. While each seam is covered by a row of embroidery, all the fabric scraps she used were black wool, rather than the riotous silks that were more often used.

Fig. 6.28
Detail, Vinnie Crosby's Black Crazy Quilt
Maine State Museum, 69.131.1

An embroidered depiction of a Japanese woman was one of the larger motifs in Vinnie Crosby's crazy quilt. Gilbert and Sullivan's Mikado *came out three years before Crosby made her quilt. It was successful enough that it was followed quickly by other plays and musicals such as Jones and Greenbank's* The Geisha, *that sought to capture its popularity. However, Japanese and Chinese motifs were often included in crazy quilts, and it was not necessary to be a music lover to include such exotic designs in one's quilt.*

Fig. 6.29
Crazy Quilt
Bethia Thompson and her neighbors
Round Pond, Maine, 1886
63 x 63 inches
Maine State Museum, 2000.43.1

Bethia Thompson and her friends and neighbors in the fishing village of Round Pond, Maine, made this quilt in 1886. Bethia's quilt traveled with her family, first to a niece, then to a great-nephew in North Carolina. It was sold at that point, and then passed down through another family, first to a sister, and then to a nephew and niece. Luckily, the quilt's history was preserved through all these moves, and it found its way back to Maine.

Fig. 6.30
Detail, Bethia Thompson's Crazy Quilt
Maine State Museum, 2000.43.1

The makers of Bethia Thompson's crazy quilt appliquéd additional insects, flowers, fans, and other motifs over the embroidery of the quilt. They painted some patches, as well, with similar motifs.

CHAPTER 6

Fig. 6.31
Prize-Winning Crazy Quilt
Made by Lucy Marsh
New Gloucester, Maine, 1899
79 x 81 inches
Maine State Museum, 2005.7.890

An envelope that was pinned to this quilt records that it is "Lucy Marsh's Silk Quilt." The quilt won blue ribbons in several fairs, including the New Gloucester & Danville Agriculture Association fair, the Cumberland County Agricultural & Horticulture Society fair; and in 1901, the Maine State Fair.

Fig. 6.32
Detail, Lucy Marsh's Prize-Winning Crazy Quilt
Maine State Museum, 2005.7.890

Detail of Lucy Marsh's quilt and its hand-crocheted lace trim. The pansies at top left are scraps of a printed silk fabric that was also used to back the quilt.

7

THE TWENTIETH CENTURY: COMMUNITY AND CHANGE

The years in Maine between 1865 and 1930 have been called "an age of adjustment."[1] The pace of change Maine experienced in the late 1800s accelerated in the early 1900s. Manufacturing—textiles, shoes, leather goods, wood products, paper—expanded into the edges of Maine's great north woods, as well as along every major waterway. Immigrants poured into Maine to work at mills and factories, replacing those who had left for greener pastures.[2] By 1900, 12 percent of the state's population was French Canadian.[3] Half of Lewiston's population—and 70 percent of its labor force—was French Canadian in 1900, and by 1920 they were a clear majority.[4] By 1912 the railroad had arrived in Aroostook County, and its population had more than tripled, to 74,664.[5] Electricity was making its way north, too. At first the lines powered cities and industry. Electric streetcars moved goods as well as people. By 1915, cities and towns from Kittery to New Sweden and from Turner to Calais enjoyed the convenience of public transportation via streetcar. Maine's booming tourist industry sparked expansion in the power grid as well, as wealthy summer folks demanded the luxury of electricity in their cottages.[6] By 1910, the "two Maines" of today were already defined, as population, services, and lines of transportation concentrated in the south, coastal areas, and major manufacturing centers just inland.

Maine's economy in the 1800s and early 1900s made the most of the state's natural resources: water (for power), trees, fish, granite, and ice. The latter two industries were declining rapidly by 1900, as cement and electric refrigeration took hold. Gradually, extraction depleted resources. Textiles and paper manufacturers moved elsewhere in the late twentieth century. The same was true of agriculture. By the 1990s, many of Maine's dairy farms and nearly all of its chicken farms had closed, and only 3 percent of the state remained in cropland.[7] Throughout the century, tourism and service-based industries expanded as people came north to Vacationland, first by train and then by car. Maine began work on its highways in the 1940s, completing them in the 1970s. Increasing numbers of tourists poured north on the new roads.

In the early part of the century, World War I, the boom of the '20s, the stock market crash of '29, and the Great Depression that followed all affected Mainers. But even before the Great

CHAPTER 7

Depression, the changes to Maine's towns, cities, and rural communities were such that many people looked back to times that they perceived as simpler.[8] This national trend is reflected in Colonial Revival style architecture, furnishings, and quilts (fig. 7.1). Patterns seen as traditional, such as log cabin quilts and crazy quilts, remained popular. Maine women made more prosaic crazy quilts than they had a generation or two before, often using wool or cotton (see figs. 6.5 and 6.6). These quilts were intended for use rather than for display, while serving as touchstones for a past that was perceived as less chaotic than the present.

Fabric colors evolved after World War I. Before the war, dye manufacturing had been centered in Germany. During an initial and abrupt fashion for white during the war when German dyestuffs were not available, American chemists learned quickly, producing colors after the war that were lighter and brighter than those that had been in vogue before the war.[9] New fabrics in lavender, Nile green, pastel blue, pink, yellow, and orange, offered quilters a

Fig. 7.1
Hexagon Quilt
Mary E. Knowlton
Belmont Corner,
Maine, ca. 1930
86 x 76 inches
Maine State Museum,
71.134.2

Mary E. Knowlton lived in the hamlet of Belmont Corner, near Belfast, Maine. This hexagon or "hexie/hexi" pattern is often called Grandmother's Flower Garden. Mary called it "Trip Around the World." She fussy-cut the fabrics so that each hexagonal flower petal looked the same. We do not know whether she made the quilt just before the Great Depression hit. If she made it during the Depression, this somewhat wasteful use of fabrics could represent optimism on Mary's part. It might also imply that she had access through friends or family to fabrics that weren't selling well. The colors in the quilt were for the most part developed after World War I.

Fig. 7.2
Basket of Diamonds Quilt
Nellie E. Batchelder
Sanford, Maine, 1937
91 x 83 inches
Maine State Museum, 95.43.1

Nellie Batchelder embroidered her name and the date on the side of her quilt. She was sixty-seven years old when she completed it. Her husband, William, who had died two years earlier, had been a superintendent at a local woolen mill. Nellie ran their household and raised their son and daughter. After the children had grown, the Batchelders took boarders into their home. Nellie stored her quilt carefully. It does not appear to have been used much, if at all. Nellie died in Sanford in 1953.

cheerful dose of color during difficult times (fig. 7.2). They also looked good under electric lights, which became more common across Maine by mid-century.[10]

And many quilters were struggling. The Depression and the World War II years took their toll on household incomes in Maine, as they did across the country. Farm families could raise food, but cash for animal feed and for fabric was tight. Suppliers of feed, flour, sugar, and other dry staples responded to the Depression by packaging their products in printed cottons. So-called flour sack prints were immensely popular. The fabric in three matching feed sacks was enough to make a dress. Some women and children looked forward to the opportunity for free fabric and made a point of getting to the local feed supplier early on delivery day.[11] Other children fretted, knowing that their classmates would recognize the dress fabric for what it was, and think them poor.[12] Quilters also took advantage of the bright fabric of flour, sugar, and feed sacks, incorporating them into utility quilts and dressier quilts (see figs. 7.2 and 7.3).

CHAPTER 7

Fig. 7.3
Dresden Plate Variation
Jennie L. Gagnon
Benton, Maine,
ca. 1935
73 x 78 inches
Maine State Museum,
2016.29.4

Jennie Gagnon of Benton was a nurse, trained in Massachusetts. She had two teenaged boys at home when she made this quilt, using a pattern published by the McCall company. She went back to work sometime between 1930 and 1940, at the tuberculosis sanitarium in nearby Fairfield, Maine. One imagines that she made the quilt before she returned to a full-time job as a nurse. The overall color scheme of her quilt was similar to that suggested on the front of the pattern envelope, but the colors she chose were softer. She chose to secure the quilt with ties rather than quilting.

Fig. 7.4
McCall Quilt Pattern 74
McCall Pattern Company
New York City, ca. 1935
8 x 6¼ inches
Maine State Museum, 2019.57.1

The McCall Pattern Company included designs for two quilts in pattern 74. The yardage requirements were printed on the back. Inside, construction instructions and paper quilting patterns accompanied the sheets of tissue printed with patterns for each component piece. The company included instructions in French and Spanish, as well as English. Jennie Gagnon would have bought or borrowed a pattern like this when she was getting ready to make her quilt (above).

154

THE TWENTIETH CENTURY

Fig. 7.5
Memory Bouquet Quilt with Additions
Annie L. H. Mason Bates
Dexter, Maine, 1931
95 x 78 inches
Maine State Museum, 2009.41.1

Annie Mason Bates was the daughter of Mary Walton Mason (see figs. 5.32 and 5.33). Annie's quilt is based on the Memory Bouquet patterns designed in 1930 by Eveline Foland, whose work was distributed by the Kansas City Star newspaper. Foland's Memory Bouquet included twenty flowers, each alone in a bowl, ikebana-style. Annie Bates used all but the holly in her quilt. The hand embroidery around each appliqué motif is astonishingly consistent and well executed. When Annie made the quilt, her widowed mother was living with her and her husband. Both women were skilled needleworkers. Many of the floral designs differ from those of Memory Bouquet. It is possible that the two worked together and that one or both designed the extra flower motifs. Annie died in 1981. She and her husband, Carl, had no children, and the quilt passed to a neighbor and friend.

Newspapers joined ladies' magazines like *McCall's* (see fig. 7.4), and became an important resource for quilters, printing quilt patterns in the 1920s and '30s. Papers in the Midwest, Kansas City in particular, published patterns by named designers. Within weeks, or even days, the patterns were printed in newspapers across the country (fig. 7.5). Kits were becoming popular, as well, for those who had the means to purchase them. Thanks to railroads and rural free delivery, women's magazines and private businesses sold patterns and kits by rail and by mail to even the most rural quilters. With crazy quilts, women of the late 1800s rejected the sameness of traditional pieced quilts, but their daughters and granddaughters

embraced the new patterns and consistent aesthetic of kits "as a sign of modernity and progressivism," as Marin F. Hanson observed.[13]

The Depression prompted women to assist their neighbors through quilts, as they had done during the Civil War and World War I. For years, the ladies of Phippsburg, Maine, had organized fundraisers for community needs such as library or firehouse improvements. In the 1930s, they focused on meeting the individual needs of townsfolk who were struggling financially. In 1935 they made an unusual raffle quilt to raise money to buy shoes for children in the town who lacked them (see figs. 7.19 to 7.20). They called it the Song Quilt, because each block depicted a popular song. Rather than raffle the quilt, individuals paid for the right to guess the songs. The quilt's winner was the person who guessed the greatest number of songs.

After the Depression, fewer Maine women quilted until the 1960s and 1970s, when the centennial of the Civil War and the American Bicentennial sparked renewed interest in colonial and nineteenth-century life, and with it, craft. Quilting blossomed again. The renaissance had humble beginnings, full of polyester-blend fabrics and thick poly batting. But suppliers caught on to the demand for more functional fabrics and batting, and by the 1990s quilting was a passionate pastime for women in Maine and across the country. In 1978, a group of like-minded women established the Pine Tree Quilt Guild, dedicated to quilting and quilters in Maine. It was only one resource available to Maine quilters at the time, as magazines, websites, and eventually blogs dedicated to quilting made it possible for women everywhere to quilt in whatever style took their fancy.

OUT OF TURBULENCE, REVIVAL: QUILTS AS VEHICLES OF COMMEMORATION AND PROTEST

Two anniversaries, the 1961–1965 Civil-War Centennial, and the American Bicentennial of 1976, revived interest in history and in quilts in Maine and across the country. As Robert Shaw observed, "After the trauma of the Vietnam War and the scandals of Richard Nixon's presidency, Americans were relieved to be able to celebrate something positive about their country and its heritage."[14] In the late 1800s and early 1900s, the nation's centennial and sesquicentennial sparked and fanned the Colonial Revival. The 1960s and '70s revival was also a romantic look back at the country's founding, but against the backdrops of political turmoil and a multitude of artistic movements. The result was as much Holly Hobby as it was Peter Max: it looked to the past through its own filters, and celebrated with its own joyful, jazzy color palettes.

Against the backdrop of the Bicentennial, textile arts such as quilting, which had seemed passé after World War II, were considered charming once again. Towns across the state revived the idea of an album quilt to commemorate the Bicentennial. Most of these featured landmarks specific to each town, what Robert Shaw called "an album of local history," as well as motifs referencing the founding of the United States, or the Bicentennial itself.[15] Many

THE TWENTIETH CENTURY

Fig. 7.6
Bicentennial Quilt
Green Street Senior Citizens Club
Designed by Mrs. Eleanor R. Baker
Augusta, Maine, 1976
108 x 76 inches
Maine State Museum, 76.72.1

Mrs. Eleanor Baker, a native of New Jersey, had lived in Maine for decades when she designed this Bicentennial quilt for the Green Street Senior Citizens Club. She chose local landmarks important to the group, including several area churches, the State House, the local fire house, the new bridge across the Kennebec River, the block house from Fort Western, the high school, and local businesses including the local power company headquarters and a grocery store. The quilters also included Maine's state flower and bird, the pine tassel and chickadee, as well as national, state, and bicentennial flags and an eagle with a shield. Makers included their names on the quilt, in fabric paint.

Fig. 7.7
"Mister Market" Block Detail, Green Street Seniors Citizens' Bicentennial Quilt
Maine State Museum, 76.72.1

The Mister Market grocery store was one of the more prosaic landmarks the Green Street Seniors included. Details of the storefront, including a blue mailbox, were executed using ballpoint fabric paint such as the Artex or Aunt Martha brands. The floral fabric may represent a flowerbed.

Maine towns were founded not long after the Revolutionary War, and these anniversaries also became fodder for quilts (see figs. 7.16 to 7.17).

Many groups followed their 1840s ancestors' custom whereby individual women contributed blocks with little regard for a common look. The organizers of some commemorative quilts chose common fabrics to be used in each square and tie the quilt together visually. A group of women in Augusta, Maine, included traditional techniques in their quilt, but added a modern touch with fabric paint (figs. 7.6 and 7.7). Fabric paints in ballpoint tubes, such as the Artex and Aunt Martha's brands, became popular around 1970. They could be used on pre-printed or iron-transfer patterns instead of embroidery. However, many women used them freehand, as they might use a colored pencil. Other new surface treatment

157

CHAPTER 7

Fig. 7.8
Girl Scout Quilt
Farmingdale Girl Scout Troop 731
Farmingdale, Maine, 1976
78 x 53 inches
Maine State Museum, 77.3.1

The girls of Troop 731 were from Farmingdale, Maine. The quilt served as a group project, as well as a means for girls to learn to sew and earn a merit badge. Interest in handwork and other traditional crafts grew around the time of the U.S. Bicentennial.

Fig. 7.9
Girl Scout Quilt, Reverse Side
Maine State Museum, 77.3.1

On the reverse side of the quilt, the girls added their names along with patriotic and natural symbols. They used iron-on transfers and fabric crayons.

THE TWENTIETH CENTURY

Fig. 7.10
Bicentennial Quilt
Linda Throckmorton
Cutler, Maine, completed in 1985
60 x 60 inches
Collection of the artist

Linda Throckmorton's quilt includes a map of her town of Cutler, Maine, with its rivers and roads delineated. She linked each landmark to its location in town by embroidering a line to its spot on the map. She included vanished landmarks in her quilt, as well, noting them with a small circle, embroidered by her careful hand.

Fig. 7.11
Detail, Throckmorton Bicentennial Quilt
Collection of the artist

Some of the landmarks Linda Throckmorton included on her quilt feature the types of buildings favored on other bicentennial quilts, such as churches, schools, and for coastal towns, lighthouses. However, Cutler is also home to a Navy VLF facility that communicates with submarines via very low frequency radio. Linda implied the scale of the array by stitching appliqué fog between the embroidered radio antennas. Below this scene, she added a depiction of the Little River Lighthouse.

CHAPTER 7

techniques were used on quilts, as well. Members of Girl Scout troop 731 of Farmingdale, Maine, drew iron-on transfers on the back of the quilt they made in 1976 (figs. 7.8 and 7.9).

Individuals were also inspired to make bicentennial quilts. Linda Throckmorton of Cutler, Maine, embroidered town scenes and maps to commemorate the bicentennial of her hometown (figs. 7.10 and 7.11). Planning and crafting the quilt took several years, and she finished it in 1985. Like many others who made bicentennial and commemorative town quilts, Linda featured Cutler landmarks. Alongside the church, the school, and historic homes, she included the antenna array at the Naval VLF Maine station. This base was built in 1960 to transmit very-low frequency (VLF) radio communication to submarines.

In the turbulent times of the late 1900s, a Bicentennial quilt was a distillation of the spirit of a community. This concept inspired some to use the medium of quilting less as a bedcovering and more as an instrument of protest, as well as one of communication and commemoration. The AIDS Memorial Quilt was never a bed quilt, but a way to memorialize members of a

Fig. 7.12
AIDS Quilt Block
Various makers and locales, 1996
Panel size: 3 x 6 feet; block size 12 x 12 feet (shown)
Courtesy of NAMES Foundation AIDS Memorial Quilt, block 4638

Each panel of the AIDS memorial quilt measures three feet by six feet. Eight panels are combined to form a block. Over two dozen Mainers are commemorated on the quilt, which is too large to be displayed in its entirety. The panels are as varied as the individuals they memorialize. The panel in the upper right was made in memory of Mainer Glenwood Randall.

community by means of an object that conveys comfort: in this case, the comfort conveyed by a quilt was associated with that of the presence of loved ones after their deaths (fig. 7.12). The first incarnation of the quilt, in 1987, comprised over 1900 panels made in honor of people who had died of AIDS. It covered an area larger than a football field and attracted a half-million viewers.[16] The quilt fostered a nationwide community of support at a time when AIDS was little-understood and its victims shunned. Over the years, the quilt has allowed friends and family members a way to memorialize beloved individuals struck down by the disease. It has also served as a means of raising money to better understand and combat AIDS. Today the quilt includes over 48,000 blocks. It remains the largest community art project in the world.[17]

The AIDS memorial quilt may have been partially inspired by a peace protest called "The Ribbon." The rally, which took place in Washington, D.C., and Arlington, Virginia, on August 4, 1985, was organized to protest nuclear proliferation and took place on the fortieth anniversary of the bombing of Hiroshima near the close of World War II. Justine Merritt of Denver came up with the idea to use small quilts, tied together, to protest the nuclear arms race.[18] Fear of nuclear war and its dangers was palpable in the 1980s, and the story was picked up by the media. Reported in magazines as disparate as *McCall's* and *Mother Jones* and by news agencies around the world, the idea of the Ribbon inspired thousands to make quilts for peace. When the components were tied together, the quilt was over fifteen miles long. The concept of using quilts as a protest vehicle was novel. Some protesters considered it as yin to the yang of protest: "Sewing is a traditionally woman's thing. Those aggressive marches are such a masculine thing. I think this is a gentler statement from women."[19] Fifteen thousand people ultimately attended the rally, but the small quilts, each of which was easily carried, also allowed people to take part in the protest remotely. Individuals and groups from all fifty states and Washington, D.C., and from countries around the world took part.[20]

In Maine, individuals and groups from over sixty towns contributed to the Ribbon, representing fourteen of Maine's sixteen counties (figs. 7.13 to 7.15).[21] A representative for the state took Maine's quilts to the Ribbon protest in Washington, D.C., and brought them back again. Reflecting the variety of makers and the unusual circumstances of their creation, the Ribbon quilts range greatly in style, skill, and medium. Many are drawn or painted, especially those made by children. Some show polished artistry and quilting ability. Others appear to be their makers' first attempts at quilting, or even at sewing. Many of Maine's Ribbon quilts are signed. Families, individuals, schools, senior homes, convents, and churches made quilts. Bethel, Maine, was the center of an organized and prolific group: over twenty-five of the 170 surviving examples have inscriptions from that town. Maine's religious organizations were active in the effort. Over thirty-five of the Maine Ribbon quilts have religious themes. Most of those were made by members of churches or church organizations including several convents and Catholic schools, and quilts from Baptist, Methodist, Quaker, and Unitarian Universalist congregations. Other quilts refer to social issues. One quilt bears appliqué motifs of a star and crescent moon, as well as two interlocked female symbols (see fig. 7.14). Its many signatures

CHAPTER 7

Fig. 7.13
"The Ribbon" Quilt Component
Linda Pope
Newcastle Maine, 1985
18 x 36 inches (without ties)
Courtesy of Maine Historical Society, 1990.261.53

Ribbon participants were asked what they would miss in the event of nuclear war. Newcastle resident Linda Pope answered the question with this winter scene of a barn, silo, and snow fence.

Fig. 7.14
"The Ribbon" Quilt Component
Signed with 27 first names
Portland, Maine, 1985
18 x 36 inches (without ties)
Courtesy of Maine Historical Society, 1990.261.119

Twenty-seven people signed this element of the Ribbon quilt, celebrating same-sex relationships. They signed only with their first names or nicknames. This reflects the degree of discomfort many Americans in the 1980s had with homosexuality, and the lack of safety gay people experienced at that time.

Fig. 7.15
"The Ribbon" Quilt Component
Betty Tyler
Brunswick, Maine, Easter, 1985
18 x 36 inches (without ties)
Courtesy of Maine Historical Society, 1990.261.57

Betty Tyler of Brunswick sewed a patchwork garden on her Ribbon block. She filled it with names of friends and called it "Our Garden of Peace and Friendship."

suggest the progress out of the proverbial closet that was being made by gays and lesbians in the 1980s.

REFLECTIONS OF COMMUNITY: THE CASTINE COMMUNITY BICENTENNIAL QUILT

Castine, Maine, has a deep history. In 1996, when artists and historians in the town decided to commemorate the bicentennial of the modern town, they needed a quilt 24 feet wide to accommodate it all (figs. 16–17). It includes seven square blocks depicting scenes from the history of the town. The eight rectangular panels that frame them represent animals and plants in the local environment. Flags of the many political entities that controlled the town fly at the quilt's top, while at the bottom, watercraft of the various eras float in the bay. These range from Etchemin and Wabanaki canoes to the *State of Maine*, the training ship for the Maine Maritime Academy.[22] The arched borders at top and bottom symbolize the greater world and universe of which Castine is a part.

Fig. 7.16
The Castine Community Bicentennial Quilt
Margaret Hodesh, lead designer
Eighty-nine documented makers
Castine, Maine, 1995–1996
82 inches x 24 feet
Courtesy of Castine Historical Society, 1996.75

In the 1600s, the land that is now the town of Castine was the home of an Etchemin leader named Madockawando and his family. The area had been occupied for generations. Baron Jean-Vincent de Saint-Castin, for whom the town is named, commanded the French fort of Pentagoet in the late 1600s, and married Marie Mathilde, Madockawando's daughter.[23] The first panel of Castine's community bicentennial quilt commemorates this period of the town's history, depicting appliquéd figures of a French priest and settlers, Saint-Castin, Mathilde, and members of the local Etchemin community.

CHAPTER 7

Fig. 7.17
Detail, Castine Community Bicentennial Quilt
Courtesy of Castine Historical Society, 1996.75

When completed, the quilt was presented to the Castine Historical Society, where it is on view every summer. It depicts the history of the town of Castine, and its place in the natural environment.

Producing the quilt was a community effort. Guided by local historian Lois Moore Cyr, and with input from many quilters and other interested parties, Margaret Hodesh and Charlene Wiseman designed the quilt. Members of the group worked on components at meetings in local homes and Emerson Hall, the building that serves Castine as its town hall. In all, eighty-nine individuals contributed to the quilt, including sixteen girl scouts, 4-H members, and students from a local school.[24]

Commemoration and protest quilts introduced thousands of Mainers to quilting. They also pushed the definition of a quilt further than ever from its early definitions as bedcoverings

or items of clothing. The 1970s and 1980s saw a resurgence of craft in Maine and across the country. This coincided with a re-evaluation of the definition of fine art. In the last quarter of the 1900s, academically trained artists increasingly saw quilts as a vehicle for artistic expression. Artists began to use quilts as their canvas and fiber art as their medium. In 1971, the Whitney Museum broke new ground with its exhibit "Abstract Design in American Quilts," the first show that treated as fine art what had traditionally been thought of as a somewhat homespun craft, which inspired artists and the public to look at quilts in a new way.[25] Art quilt pioneers and modern-minded traditional quilters alike adapted traditional patterns or stretched traditional formats, as in the wall hangings made for the Blaine House, Maine's governor's residence, in 1996 (see figs. 7.21 to 7.22). Others treated fabric like a traditional fine-art medium, creating non-traditional quilts (fig. 7.18). These trends would continue in the first decades of the 2000s.

Fig. 7.18
Steel Garden
Jo Diggs
Portland, Maine, 1990–1991
70 x 88 inches
Courtesy of the artist

An art-deco grill in the auditorium of the Togus veterans' hospital in Augusta inspired Jo Diggs's quilt "Steel Garden." She created it for a show called "Fabric Gardens," part of an international exhibit of quilts at Expo '90, the International Garden and Greenery Exposition in Osaka, Japan. It was the first quilt competition in Japan that featured work by international quilters.[26] "Steel Gardens" won an honorable mention and award of recognition and toured with the show for three years.

THE TWENTIETH CENTURY

GALLERY

Fig. 7.19
Song Quilt
Made by Emma Perry and other members of the Phippsburg Welfare Club
Phippsburg, Maine, 1935
94 x 76¼ inches
Maine State Museum, 2016.15.1

The thirty blocks of this unusual fundraising quilt each represent a popular song. To win the quilt, donors needed to identify the most songs. During the Depression the Phippsburg Welfare Club raised money for library books, for the fire department, and for shoes for the town's schoolchildren so that they would not need to go to school barefoot or with holes in their shoes. Mrs. James Wyman had the idea for the quilt. The town was home to several men with that name, and her full identity remains unknown. Emma Perry made most of the blocks. Lucia Ferguson, a Phippsburg native living in Boston, won the quilt. She later gave it to a friend, so that it would find a home in Maine.

To build interest in the quilt and give local folk time to think about their answers, the Welfare Club displayed the quilt in a local store, along with a randomly ordered list of the songs on the quilt:

Goodbye Sweet Day (boy & girl on fence)
Silver Threads among the Gold
Old Fashioned Garden
Tiptoeing through the Tulips
The Moon Came Over the Mountain
The Bear Went Over the Mountain
Spinning Wheel in the Parlor
Little Red Schoolhouse
Little Gray Home in the West
Sidewalks of New York
Vacation Days or School Days
My Wild Irish Rose (girl)
Ring the Green Irish Bells
Rose of No Man's Land
Spring Song (blue birds)
Red Wing

Holy City
Three Black Crows
Home Sweet Home
America the Beautiful
Sailing, Sailing
Cowboy Song
Absent (Vacant Chair)
Isle of Capri
Last Rose of Summer
Gypsy Warning
Blue or Pale Moon
Trees
Three Little Pigs
Owl and the Pussycat

Fig. 7.20
Phippsburg Song Quilt: The Sidewalks of New York
Maine State Museum, 2016.15.1

With the song list in hand, one could likely deduce that this block represents "The Sidewalks of New York." Composed in 1894 by Charles Lawlor with lyrics by James Blake, this popular song was recorded by many artists. It was included in a 1935 Shirley Temple movie, Little Miss Marker, *so the song would have been fresh in the minds of those who saw the quilt.*[27]

Fig. 7.21
The Twelve Days of Maine Christmas: A Partridge in a Pine Tree
Clamshell Quilters Ellen Sheehy and Julie Stegna
Damariscotta, Maine, 1995
25 x 24 inches
Maine State Museum, 96.105.1

Based in Damariscotta, the Clamshell Quilters serve as the Lincoln County branch of the Pine Tree Quilt Guild. In 1994 or 1995 the group decided to make a series of banners for Blaine House, the residence of Maine's sitting governors. The blocks would reinterpret the Twelve Days of Christmas with a Maine twist. Thus, this block depicts a Partridge in a Pine Tree. Ellen Sheehy pieced and appliquéd the banner, and Julie Stegna quilted it.

Fig. 7.22
The Twelve Days of Maine Christmas: Four Chickadees
Clamshell Quilters Phyllis Tracy and Diane Newton
Damariscotta, Maine, 1995
25 x 24 inches
Maine State Museum, 96.105.4

Phyllis Tracy stitched the appliqué and Diane Newton quilted the Four Chickadees of the Twelve Days of Maine Christmas, a series of banners for the Blaine House. The other banners in the series include Two Mourning Doves, Three French Hens, Five Tourmaline Rings, Six Canada Geese a-Laying, Seven Mute Swans a-Swimming, Eight Baskets of Berries, Nine Lobsters a-Crawling, Ten Deer a-Leaping, Eleven Beavers a-Building, and Twelve Eagles Soaring.

CHAPTER 7

Fig. 7.23
Fence Posts Lap Quilt
Etta Mary Clark Spearen Page
Guilford, Maine, 1920s
54 x 39¼ inches
Maine State Museum, 2016.5.1

Sometime before 1931, Etta Mary Clark Spearen Page of Guilford, Maine, cut down a quilt she made around 1920 and made it into a lap quilt for her daughter, Virginia Littlefield, who was ill. After Virginia's death in 1931, the family put the quilt away. Some of the silks in it are fragile and shattering. While this is, perhaps, fitting for a quilt made in such a heartbreaking situation, the quilt is too fragile to be exhibited often.

Fig. 7.24
Photograph of Etta Mary Clark Spearen Page with a Quilt
Glass plate negative by an unknown photographer
Guilford, Maine, ca. 1915
5 x 7 inches
Maine State Museum, 82.6.285

In 1908, Etta Mary Clark Spearen made a quilt in the rail fence or fence posts pattern. She used velvets and velveteens, and her rich quilt won first prize in the Piscataquis County fair. Her grandchildren recalled playing with the quilt many years later, until it was tattered from use.[28] The pattern was apparently one that Etta Mary favored, as she made a second rail fence quilt, of silk (see fig. 7.23).

CHAPTER 7

Fig. 7.25
Poultry Ribbon Quilt
Helen Stockman Merrill
East Auburn, Maine, ca. 1910
76 x 70½ inches
Maine State Museum, 2005.91.1

The top of this quilt is made from poultry ribbons. Nellie Merrill, her mother, Ella Noble Niles Stockman, and her paternal grandmother Almira Davis, were all active in the Maine State Poultry Association in the early decades of the 1900s. It is possible that the women and their friends won all the ribbons used to make this quilt. Nellie may have augmented family prizes with surplus ribbons from the Poultry Association.

Fig. 7.26
Detail, Helen Merrill's Poultry Ribbon Quilt
Maine State Museum, 2005.91.1

The poultry ribbons used in the quilt top came from several shows across Maine. Most date between 1904 and 1910.

172

THE TWENTIETH CENTURY

Fig. 7.27
Unfinished Yo-yo Quilt
Marie Rose Eva Lavigne Pelletier
Biddeford, Maine, 1936–1945
90¼ x 54½ inches
Maine State Museum, 93.85.1

In 1936, Marie Rose Pelletier of Biddeford purchased fabric to make a yo-yo quilt. She worked on the quilt off and on for several years. It was still unfinished at her death in 1945. Forty-eight years after her death, her daughter gave the unfinished quilt to the museum, together with its component pieces, thread, and the receipts for the fabric.

Fig. 7.28
Yo-yo Quilt Components and Tools; Fabric Receipts
Marie Rose Eva Lavigne Pelletier
Biddeford, Maine, 1936–1945
Unsewn circles are 4½ inches in diameter
Maine State Museum, 93.85.2-.15

Marie Rose Pelletier did not get to finish her quilt. Because of that, we can see how she made it. After making the individual yo-yo components, she combined them into multicolored blocks with a red edge. She then sewed those into larger strips which she eventually added to the body of the quilt.

173

8

MAINE QUILTS TODAY

Maine quilts produced today are more varied and exciting than ever. Quilters across the state create a wide range of work of astonishing beauty and skill. Some find inspiration in historic quilts: making faithful reproductions of patterns common one hundred years ago,

Fig. 8.1
Love
Mary Heinz Carthage
Belfast, Maine, 2017
96 x 83 inches
Collection of the artist

Love is a common theme in Mary Heinz Carthage's quilts. She makes small art quilts for family members every Valentine's Day. This Valentine is rather larger. She made it in 2017, in time for a red-and-white-quilt theme at the Pine Tree Quilt Guild Maine Quilt Show. Carthage designed the layout of the quilt using a variation of the Cat's Cradle pattern. Julia's Needle Designs produced the Sweetheart Cats patterns she embroidered into the negative spaces in the quilt.

**Fig. 8.2
Back of Mary Carthage's Love Quilt**
Collection of the artist

The reverse side of Mary Carthage's Love quilt features a large expression of the Cat's Cradle block in a frame of red. The simple pattern highlights the red and white quilting. The label in the lower left, carefully sized to fit within lines of quilting, includes two embroidered cats and several inscriptions. In addition to her name and information about the quilt, she expresses love for her "favorite husband," and for the cats that inspired the quilt's design.

**Fig. 8.3
Maine Heritage Quilt**
Wendy Caton Reed
Bath, Maine, 2005
85 x 72 inches
Collection of the artist

Wendy Reed prefers the potholder method of quilt construction (see figs. 3.6 to 3.9). She gives her potholder quilts culinary names. This example uses traditional as well as new appliqué patterns, all of which relate to life in Maine (see also figs. 8.22 to 8.24).

Fig. 8.4
The Quilt: A Life of its Own and Mine
Made by Pat Burns; designed by Diane S. Hire
Stockton Springs, 2013
77 x 60¼ inches
Collection of the artist

When designer Diane Hire decided to publish App Is for Appliqué, *a new series of quilt patterns, she enlisted a dozen quilters from the Stockton Springs area to produce examples of the new designs for the book. Each quilter focused on one of the motifs. Pat Burns's assignment was the tulip, seen at center top of the quilt. Each quilter was free to interpret the designs in her own way. Burns decided to incorporate all twelve elaborate flowers into one quilt. She spent hundreds of hours hand-stitching the motifs and carefully machine quilting. Because of the time it took to make it, she called it simply "The Quilt."*

Fig. 8.5
Frog Pond Farm
Nora Flanagan
Belmont, Maine, 2016
54 x 45 inches
Private collection, photograph courtesy of the artist

Nora Flanagan uses traditional blocks as frames for fanciful landscapes based on farms and the coastline near her Maine home. In this example she has used crazy quilt and log cabin blocks, many of which include central motifs that recall farm life (see also figs. 8.25 and 8.26).

MAINE QUILTS TODAY

Fig. 8.6
Garden Burst
Catherine Worthington
Brunswick, Maine, 2007
21½ x 28 inches
Private collection

Catherine Worthington's quilts begin with fabric she designs herself, creating patterns she paints and embellishes before making them into quilts. Some of the designs, such as this example, are abstract. Others are naturalistic (see figs. 8.27 and 8.28).

making neo-traditional versions, or riffing off one aspect of an antique quilt and creating something completely modern (figs. 8.1 and 8.2). Others combine traditional piecing and appliqué into new quilt expressions (figs. 8.3, 8.4, and 8.5).

A strong community of art quilters resides in Maine. Some, like Catherine Worthington (fig. 8.6) and collaborators Gayle Fraas and Duncan Slade (fig. 8.7), focus on surface treatments.[1] Other artists, including Jude Spacks, create collages in which delicate layers of fabric shade and shape the images depicted (fig. 8.8). Like Worthington, Fraas, and Slade, Spacks incorporates pigment in her work—in this case, paint—although the artists use the medium in different ways.

CHAPTER 8

Fig. 8.7
The Point, Cross River, NW—Jan. 22 and 23
Gayle Fraas and Duncan Slade
Wholecloth quilt, dye painted on cotton, stitched
Boothbay, Maine, 2018
55 x 38 inches
Courtesy of the artists

Gayle Fraas and Duncan Slade "explore the relationship of ornamental surface and portrayal of landscape in quest of a sense beyond place."[2] *They use dyes to create surface design that does not affect the fabric's "hand," that is, its texture and the way that it moves. Some of their quilts are inspired by life events. All celebrate the world around them (see also figs. 8.29 and 8.30).*

Fig. 8.8
Girl Warrior
Jude Spacks
Belfast, Maine, 1996
53 x 55 inches
Courtesy of the artist

Jude Spacks uses a combination of complex textile collage and paint to produce her quilts. A single eye can include over two dozen carefully placed fragments of printed fabric. A quilt can take years to complete. (See also figs. 8.31 to 8.33).

Until recently, traditional quilters and fiber-artist quilters had little interaction or overlap in terms of artistic support. The Pine Tree Quilt Guild (PTQG) attracted mostly traditionalists and neo-traditionalists, while arts and fine-crafts guilds embraced art-quilt makers. That dichotomy is changing. The quilt guild mounts a state-wide show every summer. In 2018 they showcased the work of Susan Carlson of Harpswell, whose work features freehand raw-edge fabric collage (fig. 8.9), and in 2017 the best of show award went to contemporary quilter Sarah Ann Smith of Hope, Maine (fig. 8.10).[3]

CHAPTER 8

Fig. 8.9
Crocodylus Smylus
Susan Carlson
Harpswell, Maine,
2015
6 x 22 feet
Courtesy of the artist

For Susan Carlson, the tactile aspect of a quilt is the most intriguing, as can be seen by her rich collage quilts. This twenty-two-foot-wide example was the centerpiece at the Pine Tree Quilt Guild's 2018 Maine Quilt Show (see also figs. 8.34 and 8.35).

Membership in the Pine Tree Quilt Guild has grown steadily since its founding in 1978. Today it boasts over sixty-five local chapters across the state, and the group supports quilters with classes, meetings, teaching kits, its annual show, and scholarships for individual quilters learning new techniques. The local chapters range from community-centered sewing circles to more broadly based groups of artisans who specialize in a particular type of quilt, such as crazy quilts. One chapter, Art Quilts Maine, offers its membership the community of a traditional quilt chapter while focusing on nontraditional design.

One class of contemporary quilting that is frequently overlooked is that made by Wabanaki artisans. In the nineteenth century, Wabanaki clothing was decorated with both beads and intricate lacings of ribbon appliqué (see figs. 2.19 to 2.25). While other Native communities also worked with silk appliqué, the delicacy and artistry of Wabanaki silk ribbon appliqué was unsurpassed. At once traditional and innovative, the art form is beginning a slow resurgence among Wabanaki artists and artisans. Jennifer Neptune, Penobscot artist, curator, herbalist, and teacher, is at the vanguard of this renaissance (fig. 8.11).

Several Maine organizations support art quilters and highlight their work. The state's craft guilds, such as the Maine Craft Association, the Maine Crafts Guild, and Designing Women, all count quilters among their membership and in their fine-craft shows. Maine Fiberarts in Brunswick champions contemporary artists in a wide range of media, including sculptural knitting, hooked rugs and wall hangings, weaving, felt sculpture, and basketry, as well as quilting. Founded in 2000, it offers a place for artists to show their work, to learn, teach, and mentor. The internationally known Haystack Mountain School of Crafts on Deer Isle is both

Fig. 8.10
She Persisted in Her Quest to Reach the Shore and Sing the Anthem of the Sea
Sarah Ann Smith
Hope, Maine, 2017
59 x 80 inches
Courtesy of the artist

Sarah Ann Smith's collage quilt, She Persisted in Her Quest to Reach the Shore and Sing the Anthem of the Sea, *won best of show at the Maine Quilt Show in 2017 and has been on exhibit at shows around the country ever since. In her quilts, the surface texture created by the quilting is as important to the composition as the many layers of fabric in play (see also figs. 8.36 to 8.38).*

MAINE QUILTS TODAY

Fig. 8.11
Charles Shay, Wearing an Appliqué and Beadwork Collar
Jennifer Neptune
Indian Island, Maine, 2009
22¼ x 19½ inches
Private collection; photograph courtesy of the artist

Penobscot elder Charles Shay wearing Jennifer Neptune's ribbon-appliqué and beadwork collar at a 2009 presentation about its construction. The collar is based on an example in the Smithsonian's National Museum of the American Indian. The original was once worn by Shay's ancestors (see fig. 2.24; see also 8.39 to 8.41).

a retreat where artists can recharge and a venue where masters can teach. A new artist residency program in Monson, Maine, offers comparable opportunities for quilt artists to learn and teach. Whether they make art quilts or neo-traditional quilts, many quilters teach. Some offer workshops on technique at quilt shows across the country, as well as for local guilds and art schools, maintaining websites that showcase their work and advertise their workshops.

Maine's art quilt community is growing, but by far the largest number of Maine quilters practice the art in a more traditional way, making and reinterpreting time-honored patterns. Ironically, while some art quilters have embraced hand-quilting, many traditional quilters no longer quilt by hand. Instead, they send their quilts to be long-arm quilted. A long-arm quilting machine employs rollers to keep the quilt taut and features a sewing mechanism at the end of an adjustable arm that can operate freely in any direction. True to their name, these machines have the capacity to sew the length of an entire quilt. Patterns are computerized and can be as simple or as complex as time and budget allow. Early examples of long-arm quilting were not popular at quilt shows, but in the last twenty years the complexity and capacity of the machines and the artistry of the designs have grown along with the talent of the long-arm operators, and machine-sewn quilts have become the norm. Most traditional quilters send out at least some of their quilts to long-arm artists.

Like most art quilters, traditional quilters often have several projects going at once. Some they complete at home, but other quilts are community affairs, such as challenge quilts, in which everyone in the quilt group makes a sample based on a theme or incorporating an unusual piece of fabric. As in previous centuries, when women made patriotic quilts during the Civil War (see fig. 4.4), or came together to make memorial quilts for friends or family members who had died of AIDS (see fig. 7.12), making a quilt can help an artisan cope with the pain of grief and fear. After the attacks of September 11, 2001, Evelyn Sabean of Farmington was moved to make a quilt to commemorate those whose lives were lost (fig. 8.12). She wanted to "visually express a positive message in the face of tragedy."[4] She focused on the firefighters who died trying to save others, and depicted an angel comforting a fallen firefighter.

Fig. 8.12
The Strength Behind Our Heroes
Evelyn Sabean
Farmington, Maine, 2001–2002
49 x 46 inches
Maine State Museum,
2017.51.1

Evelyn Sabean included numbers on the firefighter's hat—091101 and 345—that commemorate the date of the September 11, 2001, attack and the number of firefighters killed that day, or who died as a result of their work on 9/11. The number rose from 343 to 345 while Evelyn was sewing the quilt, and she had to change the number on the hat accordingly. The purple and yellow border fabric includes the first stanza of the song "God Bless America."

Debbie Gagne was an RN working at the Veterans Administration Hospital at Togus in Augusta in 2000. She and her colleagues were seeing more veterans at the newly established women's health clinic there. Gagne approached her superiors with an idea to help the women express their pride in their service by means of a group "memory quilt." Marion "Vella" Smith of Chelsea worked with the veterans and sewed their blocks into a quilt, and Gagne documented each block (fig. 8.13). Veterans of several conflicts contributed to the quilt, honoring women who fought in every American war since World War I. Some participants noted that working on the quilt helped them overcome their sense of being an outsider as a female veteran. Whether working alone or in a group, many traditional quilters find solace in quilting. A great number use their art as outreach as well, making charity quilts, or as some prefer to call them, community quilts.

Fig. 8.13
Memory Quilt
Marion "Vella" Smith and female veterans
Chelsea, Maine, 2000
82 x 54½ inches
Maine State Museum, 2019.39.1

The veterans from the women's health clinic at Togus hospital used a range of atypical materials in their quilt blocks, including fabric paint, glitter glue, photo transfers, and fabric flowers, as well as more traditional methods such as appliqué and embroidery. The blocks were personal expressions of pride in service and of healing.

QUILTS FOR A CAUSE

"I feel like I have purpose."

Jackie Manton, quilter, March 11, 2019

Quilt groups in the 1800s tended to be ladies' benevolent societies whose members quilted. In the late 1900s and early 2000s, they instead became quilting groups that also did benevolence work, as women learned the joy of creating quilts but also that of learning together, sharing, and creating community. The widow of a veteran who was stationed at the former Brunswick Naval Air station, Jackie Manton took up quilting as a way to cope after the early death of her husband. "It saved me," she has said.[5] She made quilts for her kids and grandkids but "a person needs only so many quilts." So now she makes charity quilts exclusively. Manton is the organizer for two groups' charity quilts: quilting them, collecting and documenting donated quilts, packing and sending them to the various groups, and keeping track of the thousands of quilts the women in the groups have made over the years. Manton's service to veterans and local families in crisis offers a glimpse of the now-invisible work carried out by generations of sewing circles who made bed quilts for wounded Civil War soldiers, or to raffle off so that the children of those made poor by the Depression would have shoes to wear to school. Following in the footsteps of the women who made those quilts, today's quilters find community in using their needlework to help others.[6]

Like women across the country, individual quilters, quilt chapters, and sewing groups all over the state make quilts for many causes. These can be raffle quilts to benefit local or state quilt groups or for a local church. Chapters and individuals make quilts for local families who have lost their homes to fire or suffered other losses. But most charity quilts are sent outside their home towns. The output is impressive. Beth Dawson of Dresden, Maine, estimates that she makes ten to twelve quilts a year, some for her extended family, but most for charities. Working for two quilt groups, Jackie Manton gathers, documents, and sends hundreds of quilts a year to nearly a dozen charities.

Charity, or community, quilts fall into four categories: quilts for veterans, for people in crisis, for children in crisis, and for animals. Cancer centers across the state receive quilts for patients. For veterans, the national group Quilts of Valor is mentioned most often as a recipient of Maine charity quilts (figs. 8.14 and 8.15). Other quilts for veterans are sent to local nursing homes, the Maine veterans' hospital at Togus, and to hospice centers.[7] Jackie Manton

Fig. 8.14
Constitution Quilt of Valor
Jackie Manton
Topsham, Maine, 2019
72 x 59½ inches
Private collection

The Quilts of Valor organization prefers the colors red, white, and blue for its quilts. Jackie Manton added an image of the U.S. Constitution, and a bald eagle. The eagle, the national bird of the U.S., has long been worked into quilts as a patriotic symbol.

has a hard time making veterans' hospice quilts, because the painful situation is close to home for her. She finds solace in the thought that her quilts give healing to veterans at the end of life, as well as comfort to their families.

Like many quilt groups across the state, those that Jackie Manton and Beth Dawson work with make quilts for various children's charities: the Ronald McDonald House in Portland, the Maine Children's Cancer Program, and Wrap-a-Smile (fig. 8.16).[8] The latter is a partner of Rotaplast International, a medical-outreach group associated with Rotary International that surgically eliminates cleft palate and other deformities, as well as burn scars. Quilt groups also respond to requests from the neonatal intensive care unit (NICU) at Maine Medical Center in Portland for "scent blankets" and light-blocking quilts. The latter cover an incubator, giving the infant inside a respite from the activity of the NICU. Scent blankets are twelve-inch-square quilts, small enough to fit into an infant's incubator (see fig. 8.16). The baby's mother ensures that her scent is on the quilt by, for example, putting the quilt in her bed overnight. The nurses then place the tiny quilt beside the baby. When infants leave the NICU for home, the subtle, familiar scent on the quilt calms children and makes their transition easier. Some quilters make twenty-five-inch square quilts to give to the parents of children who die in hospitals.

Fig. 8.15
Quilt of Valor Presentation
Jackie Manton
Brunswick, Maine,
September, 2019
Private collection;
photograph courtesy of Jackie Manton

Through Quilts of Valor, veteran C. Pete Eastman received Jackie Manton's Constitution quilt. The pair posed outside of the Brunswick, Maine, Elks' Lodge after the presentation ceremony.

Each group that receives quilts has specific needs and guidelines that quilters must follow. For Wrap-a-Smile, the quilt must be small enough to wrap around a child before, during, and after surgery. The color white is considered inauspicious by many cultures, so quilters avoid that color when making Wrap-a-Smile quilts. For hospice patients, a bed quilt might be too heavy, so quilters provide lap quilts with very light batting. In addition to size requirements, some groups find their recipients have color preferences. The most popular color combination for Quilts of Valor, for example, is red, white, and blue. Many quilters enjoy incorporating bright, cheerful fabrics in their quilts for children and veterans. As Jackie Manton puts it, "I want it to look happy when it goes out."

At first consideration, animals might not appear to be likely recipients of charity quilts. However, a need exists. After natural disasters, animal shelters can be overwhelmed, and

Fig. 8.16
Three Charity Quilts for Children
Members of the Kaleidoscope Quilters group
Mid-coast Maine, 2019
Left to right, clockwise: 55 x 45½; 12 x 12; 34 x 29½ inches
Private collections

The members of the Kaleidoscope Quilters group make hundreds of quilts a year for charity. The largest of these three will go to Wrap-a-Smile; the smallest is a scent quilt for a premature infant. The third was made for a child with cancer. The quilts' makers do not know the recipients. They make the quilts to specifications from the different institutions that give them to young patients.

smaller animals are often kept in stacked wire kennels. For large dogs in standard kennels, blankets serve as a warm, soft place of comfort. For cats and small dogs in stacked cages, however, blankets are too large. Agencies provide quilt groups with the dimensions needed, and quilters supply them in return with sturdy, warm, and simply made utility quilts for lost pets in very stressful situations.

As quilt groups meet the needs of one charity, they make quilts for different beneficiaries, and then circle back to the earlier group as needs arise. Individual members also make quilts for causes they are interested in, such as Project Linus, a nonprofit organization that provides homemade blankets to children in need, or a local homeless shelter for veterans. Some groups provide colorful pillowcases for foster children. They put a small stuffed animal inside, as well as small things the child will need. Often, the pillowcase and its contents are the only things the children have to call their own.

"People say 'It's just a quilt.' But that's not true," Manton says. "It's more than just a quilt. It's comfort. It's warmth. It's a superhero cape if you're a child. It's a tent you can hide under when things are too much. It keeps me giving. I could stay at home and do so much more,

CHAPTER 8

but I pick up my stuff and go [to quilt-group sewing sessions]. Why do I do that? I'm more inward than social. [But] this is a story about women. Women help themselves while staying connected. You don't know the impact of what you give away, but you do know the feeling you get when you give something that can change someone's life.

"I know the best women in the world."

REFLECTIONS OF COMMUNITY: A QUILT FOR A CAUSE IN LEWISTON-AUBURN

In the first two decades of the 2000s, Maine has become more racially and ethnically diverse, thanks in part to an influx of immigrants of color. In much the same way that Irish

**Fig. 8.17
Green Dot Quilt**
Green Dot L.A.
Lewiston and Auburn, Maine, 2018
48 x 42 inches
Collection of Green Dot L.A.

Green Dot L.A., a Lewiston-Auburn, Maine, social action group made this quilt as a subtle way for local businesses and organizations to take a stand against bullying and racial harassment.

**Fig. 8.18
Detail, Green Dot Quilt**
Collection of Green Dot L.A.

The border of the quilt includes language empowering the viewer to act with kindness to create a safe community.

and French immigrants in the 1800s faced angry discrimination, Maine's new residents have occasionally faced harassment and violence. The cities of Lewiston and Auburn have a large Franco community, a legacy of the cotton mills and shoe factories of the late 1800s and early to mid-1900s. But this heritage has not made the twin cities free from such events. To counter the impulse for harassment and prevent it from becoming more widespread, a local group, Green Dot L.A., has partnered with Green Dot, a nationwide anti-violence and anti-bullying organization, to help local residents safely respond to and defuse harassment against immigrants, as well as against other groups and individuals.[9] Working together, they have designed a program specific to the needs of the Lewiston-Auburn community and trained forty-six local leaders to implement it. These individuals represent eighteen businesses and organizations that include police departments, public schools, the YMCA, churches, and Bates College. They, in turn, spread the word by means of presentations and workshops, as well as by example.

Green Dot members and supporters made a quilt as another way of reaching out. The quilt includes the motto: "No one can do everything but everyone can do something. Kindness counts. Let's make Lewiston-Auburn safe for everyone" (figs. 8.17 and 8.18). Local businesses, schools, and other organizations sign up to host the Green Dot quilt. By hanging it in public places, local organizations show their support for the Green Dot project and take a silent stand against violence in the community.

DAILY LIFE IN A MAINE COMMUNITY: THE "CIRCLE A DAY" QUILT OF JUDY ROCHE

After illness left her with hand tremors, long-time quilter Judy Roche recuperated using the physical therapy she knew best: hand sewing. Beginning in mid-December 2016, Roche sewed a circle of fabric onto a five-inch square background. The grounds she used were white or off-white prints, and the circles were bright colors (fig. 8.19). Roche chose fabrics that fit her day: when she faced an ant infestation in the house, she chose a print that featured ants on a picnic tablecloth; on a day when her husband Pat mowed the lawn her circle was grass-green; a book Roche was reading titled *Murder on a Starry Night* sparked the use of a navy-blue print with yellow stars. Other days she used fabrics that she and Corienne Kramer produced for

CHAPTER 8

**Fig. 8.19
Circle-a-Day Quilt**
Judy Roche
Belfast, Maine,
2016–2019
82 x 71 inches
Collection of the
artist

This bright quilt holds a secret: every day, when Judy Roche finished making a block, she wrote the date on the back of it, along with a comment about the day's activities. The quilt is in effect a diary quilt, an account of a year in the life of a Maine woman in the early twenty-first century.

Chanteclaire Fabrics, the designer of which had asked Roche to reproduce antique prints from her quilt and fabric collections. After sewing each small block, Roche carefully cut away almost all of the fabric behind each circle, leaving just enough for a quarter-inch seam. She then sewed the blocks into strips before stitching the strips together to form the quilt top.

In 2016, several bloggers were making similar quilts. However, Roche's version is different from those she was inspired by: on the reverse of each block she penned an inscription. On the circular, ¼-inch seam allowance of each circle, she wrote the date and something about her day (figs. 8.20 and 8.21). The back of a block featuring ears of corn includes the entry: "Oct 7.

**Fig. 8.20
Detail, Judy Roche's Circle-a-Day Quilt**
Collection of the artist

Judy Roche chose the central fabric of each quilt block to reflect the day. Some related to something she did during the day. A few fabrics reference the day's weather. Others reflect holidays, visits from friends, or even her mood on a given day.

**Fig. 8.21
Detail, Judy Roche's Circle-a-Day Quilt**
Collection of the artist

The back of each block of Judy Roche's quilt includes the date and a brief description of the day's activities. This image shows the reverse side of the blocks in figure 8.20.

CHAPTER 8

Farmers market. Drove to Unity. Amish meats + cast iron frying pan. Saw Amish cutting down corn stalks." Roche sewed her blocks in order by date. She had just enough room left on the quilt top to include blocks that spelled out her name and the year that she finished the quilt top, 2017. The result is a quilt diary, a view of a year in the life of Roche and her community, albeit one that is hidden from view inside a quilt. Roche has finished the quilt like a pillowcase so that the inscriptions can be accessed when the need arises.

☙

Twenty-first-century quilters in Maine are creating works that quilters before them could not have dreamed of. At the same time, their work is shaped in similar ways to that of quilters of fifty or one hundred or even 250 years ago. Tradition and innovation are reflected in Maine quilts from every era. Some quilters have been moved by the simple desire to be covered at night by something beautiful. Others have had a strong drive for self-expression. Most quilters have discovered inspiration, feedback, consolation, and support in a network of like-minded artisans and artists. As they have done for 250 years in Maine, quilts continue to offer comfort and community.

GALLERY

The makers of historic quilts cannot reveal the inspirations or ideas they had as they were designing or sewing their work. Contemporary quilters can. Seven individual artists and one collaborative duo share their thoughts about their work, below.

Wendy Caton Reed

I made my first quilt at the age of nine under the tender tutelage of my Edgecomb, Maine, neighbor, Arzetta Poole. I'll never forget the first time I entered her tiny sewing room and spied the towering pile of brightly colored feedsack prints on the table beside her treadle machine. I was immediately hooked! Mrs. Poole taught me more than simply how to hold a needle and thread. She showed me how to enjoy the process of quiltmaking, and to realize that the journey was every bit as important as the destination. I am forever grateful for her gentle guidance. There is a bit of Mrs. Poole in every quilt I make.

Sharing my craft with organizations and individuals in need is important to me. I prefer to call them "community" quilts, as I don't like the stigma attached to the word "charity." My local group, Kaleidoscope Quilters, donates hundreds of quilts each year and I am thankful to be a part of it.

My quilts reflect my personality and my love for traditional designs. They don't need to make a statement, but there is always a reason for their creation. I want to make a connection with the recipient or the viewer of my quilts. With proper care, they will be here long after I have gone, thus creating a sort of immortality. I hope that people will handle my quilts one hundred years from now and feel a sense of what I was trying to convey. After all, a quilt without a story is simply a pretty blanket.

CHAPTER 8

Fig. 8.22
Pan Blackened Quilt
Wendy Reed
Bath, Maine, 2015
47 x 36 inches
Maine State Museum,
2020.22.1

Wendy Reed frequently makes quilts using the potholder method. She often gives these works culinary names. In this case the title refers to the antique and reproduction "neon" fabrics that feature bold colors on a black background. Reed mixes traditional appliqué patterns with original designs in this quilt, resulting in a thoroughly modern interpretation of antique motifs.

Fig. 8.23
Reverse, Wendy Reed's Pan Blackened Quilt
Maine State Museum, 2020.22.1

The lively reverse side of Pan Blackened demonstrates one of the benefits of working in the potholder technique. The bar near the top of the quilt is its sleeve, used to hold a bar or dowel to hang the quilt on the wall.

Fig. 8.24
Half-Baked Jane
Wendy Reed; based on an 1863 design by Jane Stickle
Bath, Maine, 2015
70 x 70 inches
Collection of the artist

In 1863, Jane Blakely Stickle of Shaftsbury, Vermont, made a quilt that is known today as the "Dear Jane" quilt. Wendy Reed stitched her own version of the quilt, making each of the 169 blocks using the potholder method. The original had a border of alternating wedges, as did Reed's. However, she disliked the effect, and removed them. She added this undulating border instead, and dubbed the quilt "Half-Baked Jane." Like the body of the quilt, Reed's original border was made of potholder blocks. She reused them, making a small quilt she called "Leftovers."

Nora Flanagan

I love my farmers' market friends. My community includes potters, painters, knitters, weavers, felters, and other quilters. My fellow vendors know the cycle of "idea-create-take-to-market."

I was born in Bangor, grew up in Portland, and went to college in Boston. I have lived out west and down south. Ultimately, Maine wins every time.

Painting and sewing have been my focus since my youth. Fortunately, my mother grandmother, and sisters (and later, some brothers) were all big sewers. Our dining room table always had patterns and projects on it. The first quilt I made (at age 19) started out as patchwork and evolved into an album-style quilt featuring mementos of my summer. Farms, harbors, and Maine scenes are still a favorite theme for my quilts.

In addition, my quilt guild community is always helpful, educational, and friendly. With them, I can always talk quilts, fabric, and techniques.

Fig. 8.25
Moonlight Sonata
Nora Flanagan
Belmont, Maine, 2019
50 x 42 inches
Collection of Judy Roche, photograph courtesy of the artist

Nora Flanagan made this fanciful coastal scene for a fellow quilter who loves fabrics. She named the sailboat Someday.

Fig. 8.26
Black Horse Farm
Nora Flanagan
Belmont, Maine, 2018
50 x 40 inches
Private collection, photograph courtesy of the artist

The coast of Maine is never far away from Nora Flanagan's heart. It can be seen in the background, below this hilltop farm.

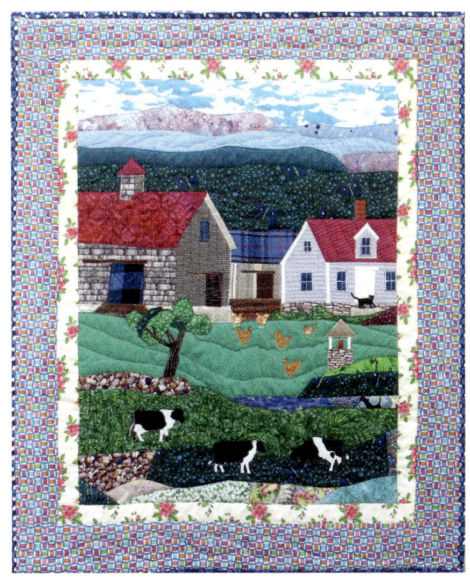

Catherine Worthington

Catherine Worthington is a studio textile artist living in Brunswick, Maine, with a BFA in textile design from the University of Massachusetts in Dartmouth. She recently retired from over twenty years as an artist-mentor at Spindleworks in Brunswick, an arts program for adults with disabilities. Catherine's studio practice consists of painting cloth and composing art quilts as well as designing and creating original textiles.

She notes: "A lot of my textile art reflects the beauty of nature's landscapes from gardens to the sea and the creatures that live there. Inspired by the natural world, I am compelled to create and capture its color, texture and charm."

Using textile paints on cloth, she creates colorful textured and patterned fabrics to use as her palette when composing wall pieces. Her process of cutting, piecing, and stitching adds depth and dimension. As she explores the medium of textile painting she explores the balance between abstraction and representation. "My art quilts are interpretations of real places and I hope to capture the attention of the viewer by creating a feeling or familiar place to connect with."

Catherine teaches surface design classes and workshops in the mid-coast Maine community and beyond. Her art quilts are part of many private collections and she has exhibited her work for eighteen years throughout Maine, New England, and Florida. Her work has found permanent residence in three hospitals in Maine as well as a local church. She is a member of Designing Women, Harlow Gallery, Maine Crafts Association, Maine Crafts Guild, and Maine Fiberarts.

Fig. 8.27
Rocks and Reflections
Catherine Worthington
Brunswick, Maine, 2016
41 x 34 inches
Courtesy of the artist

Many of Catherine Worthington's wall quilts offer visions of familiar places seen through a lens of her own creation in which different seasons or times of day occupy the same scene.

CHAPTER 8

Fig. 8.28
Shore Birds
Catherine Worthington
Brunswick, Maine, 2018
15½ x 28 inches
Courtesy of the artist

Catherine Worthington interprets the world around her, using painted fabrics of her own design to bring to life Maine landscapes and wildlife.

Gayle Fraas and Duncan Slade

Gayle Fraas and Duncan Slade have been in a continuous visual dialogue for forty-five years. Most of their works are printed and painted with synthetic dyes on cotton, subverting the tools and materials of the industrial mid-century for rural studio practice. Designed and executed by either one or in collaboration, all are signed Fraas·Slade.

Fraas·Slade was selected for "The New American Quilt" at the Museum of Contemporary Crafts in 1976. This seminal exhibit surveyed quilts by a disparate group of artists from across the country for whom personal expression took precedence over technical acuity, and alternative materials and processes combined with traditional. Fraas·Slade was again selected for "The Art Quilt" that opened in Los Angeles in 1986, the exhibit that first used the term "art quilt" and demonstrated the global veracity of an art form with folk art roots.

When digital tools arrived with the millennium, the artist team's 2007 "Watermarks" exhibit included works that were printed and stitched elsewhere via digital files, assessing how making things would be transformed in the twenty-first century. Most recent work, however, continues by hand.

The work of Fraas·Slade is included in the collections of: Philadelphia Museum of Art, Baltimore Museum of Art, Peabody Essex Museum, Museum of Art and Design, and the International Quilt Study Center and Museum at the University of Nebraska. Corporate collections include: Fidelity Investments, Nuveen Inc., Hilton Corporation, and Elmira College. Public collections in Maine include: Portland Public Library, Lincoln Health St. Andrews, Department of Marine Resources, Boothbay Harbor, and the University of Maine/Orono.

CHAPTER 8

Fig. 8.29
Ram Island, Sheepscot River
Gayle Fraas and Duncan Slade
Boothbay, Maine, 2011
24 x 24 inches
Courtesy of the artists

Fraas·Slade's wholecloth quilt is dye-painted on cotton. The quilt offers multiple ways to view the same island.

Fig. 8.30
Ram Island, Boothbay
Gayle Fraas and Duncan Slade
Boothbay, Maine, 2004
36 x 36 inches
Courtesy of the artists

In the dye-painted wholecloth quilt Ram Island, Boothbay, *Fraas·Slade offer the illusion of a pieced quilt through their quilting patterns. It is part of a series exploring signal flags.*

Jude Spacks

I started making pictures with cloth after my eighth-grade home economics teacher let me take home the box of fabric scraps at the end of class. I cut up and re-used the awful skirt with wobbly hems I'd made, too.

I came to the art quilt movement of the '80s from the art side. In college, I'd studied oil painting, concentrating on portraiture. Then I started composing portraits using fabrics. In recent years I've experimented with combining textiles and paint. The representational fabric collage process I developed involves looking closely at a photo of the subject. I begin in the center, with the eyes—each of which may contain 50+ tiny pieces of cloth—and work outwards from there, gluing shape to adjacent shape in an intricate jigsaw of colors, textures and patterns; the backing goes on last.

This takes a while—sometimes many years—as an abundance of diverse materials collaborate to create a new form. Fabrics come through my hands carrying the vitality of the ecology where they originate and the cultural inheritance of all who farmed, spun, wove, dyed, designed, marketed, and transported them. Every scrap contributes to the essence shining through an emerging artwork.

We live so intimately with textiles—wearing them, seeing and touching them constantly—they tend to evoke a rich layering of personal association. We're connected to cloth. This warmth of connection helps bring a portrayal to life as the viewer makes eye contact with its parts and wholeness.

Fig. 8.31
Presence
Jude Spacks
Belfast, Maine, 1997
67 x 38 inches
Courtesy of the artist

Not all of Jude Spacks's portraits portray humans. She approaches every type of portrait from the same perspective, beginning each work with the subject's eyes.

CHAPTER 8

Fig. 8.32
Portrait of Fannie Lou Hamer
Jude Spacks
Belfast, Maine, 2017
42 x 34 inches
Courtesy of the artist

This sensitive portrait of voting and civil rights activist Fannie Lou Hamer (1917–1977) speaks to Jude Spacks's artistic abilities and her strong drive for social justice. It combines a painted portrait with the expressive cloth eyes that are the artist's forte.

Fig. 8.33
Detail, Portrait of Fannie Lou Hamer
Courtesy of the artist

Detail of Jude Spacks's mixed-media portrait of Fannie Lou Hamer, showing the fabrics in the eyes.

Susan Carlson

Quilts are tactile, even those that hang on the wall as artwork, as I have discovered numerous times, after gently discouraging people from touching them. It's the tactile nature of a quilt that rouses memories in people of warmth, of comfort, of family. For three decades I've been creating fabric collage quilts. Over the years, my favorite subjects have been my family (I include pets as family). I keep these quilts close to me, hanging in my home and studio. It is a comfort for me to see them, to be surrounded by them, reminded of the memories that inspired them.

Quilting has traditionally been a community event. I find my quilting community on the road when I travel to teach fabric collage, with students and other teachers. I also find community in the brave new world of the internet, writing a weekly blog on fabric collage that is read by thousands, and creating online groups where those practicing fabric collage can share work and support one another, regardless of ever meeting each other, or where they happen to live in the world.

My large quilts of animals are my signature pieces. "Specimens" is the title of the grouping of my favorite quilts featuring endangered, extinct, and unique animals. When one never sees a rhinoceros or a saltwater crocodile in real life, these animals and their plight can become abstract, easily overlooked, forgotten. I hope my quilts make people see these wondrous creatures with fresh eyes, making them real again, something worth saving.

Fig. 8.34
Dixie Dingo Dreaming (Pippin)
Susan Carlson
Harpswell, Maine, 2011
48 x 48 inches
Courtesy of the artist

Susan Carlson's pets are members of her family. Here she imagines her southern rescue dog Pippin as a Dixie dingo.

Fig. 8.35
Polkadodo
Susan Carlson
Harpswell, Maine, 2006
40 x 43 inches
Courtesy of the artist

All the fabrics Susan Carlson chose for her dodo quilt had polka dots. The fabrics inspired the name of the piece, Polkadodo. *The work is part of her* Specimens *series.*

Sarah Ann Smith

When Sarah Smith's family returned to the U.S. when she was six, she had lived on four continents. Shortly after that, a neighbor girl made her an apron for her doll. Sarah promptly started sewing clothes for her troll dolls, and she hasn't stopped sewing or traveling since. In 1988, Sarah began quilting, which morphed into the perfect marriage of two of her favorite things: sewing and art. Sarah was not one of those "natural born" artists; it wasn't until she was in her 40s that she was able to teach herself and take online art courses.

Sarah says her birthplace was a geographical accident: she should have been born in Maine. After living all over the world and moving way too many times, she finally found home when she arrived with her family in 2004. Maine's everyday beauty in all seasons inspires her work, as do her family and critters.

Sarah's award-winning work has been juried into shows around the world, including the inaugural Rising Stars exhibit at International Quilt Festival 2017, and is in public and private collections. She authored *ThreadWork Unraveled* and *The Art of Sarah Ann Smith . . . so far*; has had her work published regularly and internationally in magazines, online, and in books; teaches nationwide; has a video workshop *Art Quilt Design, from Photo to Threadwork*; and has appeared on *Quilting Arts TV* and on *The Quilt Show*.

Sarah is also Hope town selectman, member and committee volunteer for the Studio Art Quilt Associates, quilt teacher, pattern designer, and mom living in Hope, Maine, with her husband, a pug, two cats and assorted dust bunnies.

Fig. 8.36
Milkweed No. 1
Sarah Ann Smith
Hope, Maine, 2015
30 x 41 inches
Collection of Frank Klein; photograph courtesy of the artist

Sarah Ann Smith's larger-than-life milkweed pods capture the essence of an early autumn day.

CHAPTER 8

Fig. 8.37
Descended from the Stars
Sarah Ann Smith
Hope, Maine, 2015
40 x 40 inches
Courtesy of the artist

The quotation around Sarah Ann Smith's labyrinth in Descended from the Stars *reads: "We have descended from the stars. We have risen through the forms of thousands of animals. We have passed through the lives of our ancestors, our grandparents, and our parents. And now we have been born into the moment of our supreme existence. We have a life. What will we do with it? Mirza Khan."*

Fig. 8.38
Pink Oyster Mushrooms
Sarah Ann Smith
Hope, Maine, 2018
50 x 30 inches
Private collection; photograph courtesy of the artist

The quilting of Sarah Ann Smith's Pink Oyster Mushrooms gives them both depth and elegance that is echoed by their gold rims.

Jennifer Neptune

Jennifer Neptune is a master basketmaker, beadworker, and Maine guide from the Penobscot Nation. Based on Indian Island, Neptune specializes in miniature baskets, beadwork reproductions, silk ribbon appliqué, and porcupine quill jewelry. She is an accomplished artist and has won several awards for her basketry and beadwork at national Native American art markets, including first and second place ribbons at the Heard Museum Indian Market.

She is the manager of the Penobscot Nation Museum and director of the Maine Indian Basketmakers Alliance, where she has worked for more than twenty years helping other artists sell and market their work.

Jennifer has a degree in anthropology with a minor in Native American Studies and a museum studies minor/certificate program from the University of Maine. She interned at the Farnsworth Museum of Art in Rockland, Maine. Jennifer curated a Wabanaki Basketry exhibit at the Hood Museum of Art at Dartmouth University and exhibits at the Colby Museum of Art and the Portland Museum of Art. Jennifer serves as a trustee of the Abbe Museum and the Hudson Museum, and as an advisor for the Maine State Museum.

CHAPTER 8

Fig. 8.39
Chief's Collar
Jennifer Neptune
Indian Island, Maine, 2009
22¼ x 19.5 inches
Private Collection; photograph courtesy of Jennifer Neptune

Reproduction of a traditional Penobscot Chief's collar. The original collar, collected from Indian Island, Maine in the early 1900s, is in the collection of the National Museum of the American Indian (see fig. 2.24).

Fig. 8.40
Rabbit Bag
Jennifer Neptune
Indian Island, Maine, 2012
24 x 11 inches
Private collection; courtesy of the artist

Double-sided bag with wool and glass bead appliqué. The figure of a rabbit smoking a pipe is a Wabanaki motif often seen engraved into birchbark designs.

Fig. 8.41
Work in Progress
Jennifer Neptune
Indian Island, Maine
Courtesy of the artist

Detail of silk ribbon appliqué and beadwork along the edge of a traditional Penobscot woman's peaked cap.

NOTES

INTRODUCTION

1 John Finley, *Kentucky Quilts, 1800–1900* (Louisville: The Kentucky Quilt Project, Inc., 1982), 15–16.

2 The quilt documentation projects have also inspired a documentation project for embroidered samplers. See http://samplerconsortium.org/about.html.

3 See Ruth E. Finley, *Old Patchwork Quilts and the Women Who Made Them* (Philadelphia and London: Lippincott, 1929); Carrie A. Hall and Rose G. Kretsinger, *The Romance of the Patchwork Quilt in America* (New York: Bonanza Books, 1935); and Patsy and Myron Orlofsky, *Quilts in America* (New York: Abbeville Press, 1974). All promoted the idea that American quilting was born out of a necessary frugality in the early days of colonization.

4 Mrs. Pullan, *The Lady's Manual of Fancy-Work* (New York: Dick & Fitzgerald, 1858), 95.

5 Eliza Leslie, *The House Book: or, A Manual of Domestic Economy* (Philadelphia: Carey & Hart, 1843), 311.

6 Dawn C. Adiletta, "A Matter of Taste: The Aesthetic Movement and Connecticut Crazy Quilts," in Lynne Z. Bassett, ed., *What's New England About New England Quilts? Proceedings of a Symposium at Old Sturbridge Village, June 13, 1998* (Sturbridge, MA: Old Sturbridge Village, 1999), 92–103.

7 Regina Lee Blaszczyk, *The Color Revolution* (Cambridge, MA: MIT Press, 2012), 198–200.

8 Linda Eaton, *Quilts in a Material World: Selections from the Winterthur Collection* (New York: Harry N. Abrams, in association with The Henry Francis du Pont Winterthur Museum, Inc., 2007), 164–87.

9 *A Girl's Life Eighty Years Ago, Selections from the Letters of Eliza Southgate Bowne* (New York: Charles Scribner's Sons, 1887), 56–57.

CHAPTER 1

1 Jane C. Nylander, *Our Own Snug Fireside: Images of the New England Home, 1760–1860* (New York: Alfred A. Knopf, 1993), xi. See also Roderick Kiracofe, *The American Quilt: A History of Cloth and Comfort, 1750–1950* (New York: Clarkson Potter, 1993), 46, 61.

2 Stephen J. Hornsby and Richard W. Judd, eds., *Historical Atlas of Maine* (Orono, ME: University of Maine Press, 2015), plate 8; Edwin A. Churchill, "English Beachheads in Seventeenth-Century Maine," in *Maine: The Pine Tree State from Prehistory to the Present,"* ed. Richard W. Judd, Edwin A. Churchill, and Joel W. Eastman (Orono, ME: University of Maine Press, 1995), 51–60.

3 See Hornsby and Judd, plate 10.

4 Hornsby and Judd, plates 12–13.

5 Jeffrey Phipps Brain, *Fort St. George: Archaeological Investigation of the 1607–1608 Popham Colony, Occasional Publications in Maine Archaeology Number 12* (Augusta, ME: The Maine State Museum, Maine Historic Preservation Commission, and Maine Archaeological Society, 2007), 131–37. Archaeological investigations at Fort Richmond (1740–1755) in Richmond, Maine, recovered shards of several Chinese export porcelain vessels. J. N. Leith Smith, John P. Mosher, William Burgess, and Kåre Mathiasson, "Archaeological Phase II Intensive Survey of Fort Richmond for the Route 197 Bridge Replacement and Road Realignment, MDOT PIN12674.00 Between Richmond, and Dresden, Maine," unpublished manuscript on file at the Maine Historic Preservation Commission, Augusta, Maine, 2011, 24, 26–27, 31–32, 50–53.

6 Joel Lefever, "Family Connections," in *Blog of the Old York Historical Society* (York, ME, December 10, 2015), https://oldyorkmuseums.wordpress.com/2015/12/10/family-connections/

7 See Janice E. Frisch in *American Quilts in the Industrial Age, 1760–1870,* ed. Patricia Cox Crews and Carolyn Ducey (Lincoln: University of Nebraska Press, 2018), 196–98, 201–3, 221–22, 286.

NOTES

8   The name Vaughan has been spelled various ways in the historical record. Vaughan, with an A, was favored by the family, so is used here.

9   Catalog record for 1975.0048, Winterthur Museum; Deborah E. Kraak, "Early American Silk Patchwork Quilts," in *Textiles in Early New England: Design, Production, and Consumption, The Dublin Seminar for New England Folklife Annual Proceedings, 1997* (Boston: Boston University, 1999), 25–26; Linda Eaton, *Quilts in a Material World: Selections from the Winterthur Collection* (New York: Harry N. Abrams and The Henry Francis du Pont Winterthur Museum, 2007), 65, 134–35.

10   Linda Eaton, *Quilts in a Material World*, 65, 134–35.

11   Lynne Z. Bassett, "Inspired Fantasy: Design Sources for New England's Whole-Cloth Wool Quilts," *The Magazine Antiques*, vol. 178, no. 3 (September 2005), 125.

12   Bassett, *Massachusetts Quilts*, 170; see also Laurel Thatcher Ulrich, *A Midwife's Tale: The Life of Martha Ballard, Based on Her Diary, 1785–1812* (New York: Vintage Books, 1990), 143, 146.

13   Bassett. "Inspired Fantasy," 124, 127.

14   Bassett, "Inspired Fantasy, 123.

15   Lynne Zacek Bassett, ed., *Massachusetts Quilts: Our Common Wealth* (Hanover, NH: University Press of New England, 2009), 4; Lynne Z. Bassett and Jack Larkin, *Northern Comfort: New England's Early Quilts, 1780–1850* (Nashville, TN: Rutledge Hill Press, with Old Sturbridge Village, 1998), 15.

16   Tandy Hersh, "Eighteenth-Century Quilted Silk Petticoats Worn in America," *Uncoverings*, vol. 5 (1984): 84–85.

17   Bassett, *Massachusetts Quilts:* 4.

18   See, for example, the expression of motifs in the quilts illustrated in Lynne Z. Bassett, "'Spun me some worsted to quilt with': New England's Early Wool Quilts," in *What's New England about New England Quilts? Proceedings of a Symposium at Old Sturbridge Village, June 13, 1998*, ed. Lynne Z. Bassett (Sturbridge, MA: Old Sturbridge Village, 1999), 2–14.

19   Bassett and Larkin: *Northern Comfort*, 15.

20   Ulrich, *A Midwife's Tale*, 135, 136, 143, 144, 146; Robert R. McCausland and Cynthia MacAlman McCausland, *The Diary of Martha Ballard, 1785–1812* (Camden, ME: Picton Press, 1992), 175–77, 205–7, 345.

21   Two such threads are clearly visible, but a third may be present: the first thread of the warp is often hidden by the weft threads as they turned. See Susan Greene, *Wearable Prints, 1760–1860, History, Materials, and Mechanics* (Kent, OH: Kent State University Press, 2014), 38.

22   Greene, *Wearable Prints*, 39.

23   Lynne Z. Bassett, personal communication, March 19, 2018.

24   Janneken Smucker, "Early Nineteenth-Century Embroidered Bedcovers," *Winterthur Portfolio* 42:4 (2009): 224–42; see also Lynne Z. Bassett in *American Quilts in the Industrial Age, 1760–1870*, ed. Patricia Cox Crews and Carolyn Ducey (Lincoln: University of Nebraska Press, 2018), 42–44.

25   SI 88838 catalog records.

26   SI 190856 catalog records.

27   Abby Y. Palmer of Whitefield, Maine, signed and dated her pieced, embroidered wool quilt in 1841. It is now in the collection of the Museum of Fine Arts, Boston, accession number 42.515.

28   Laurel Thatcher Ulrich, *The Age of Homespun, Objects and Stories in the Creation of an American Myth* (New York: Alfred A. Knopf, 2001), 415.

29   Smucker, "Early Nineteenth-Century Embroidered Bedcovers," 231.

30   Jennifer Swope, personal communication, October 2, 2019.

31   Jennifer Swope, personal communication, October 2, 2019.

32   Lynne Z. Bassett, auction lot description; James D. Julia auction January 31, 2008, lot 796.

33   Bassett, James D. Julia auction.

34   Bassett, James D. Julia auction.

35   Linda Eaton, *Printed Textiles: British and American Cottons and Linens, 1700–1859*, rev. ed. (New York: Monacelli Press, 2014), 51.

36   Eaton, *Quilts in a Material World,* 67.

NOTES

CHAPTER 2

1 Alexander Hamilton, reprinted in: *Alexander Hamilton's Famous Report on Manufactures: Made to Congress December 5, 1791, in his Capacity as Secretary of the Treasury* (Boston, MA: The House Market Club and Porter Publishing, 1892), 6; Joyce Butler, "Rising Like a Phoenix: Commerce in Southern Maine, 1775–1830," in *Agreeable Situations: Society, Commerce, and Art in Southern Maine, 1780–1830*, ed. Laura Fecych Sprague (Boston, MA: Northeastern University Press and the Brick Store Museum, 1987), 15–35.

2 Stephen J. Hornsby and Richard W. Judd, eds., *Historical Atlas of Maine* (Orono, ME: University of Maine Press, 2015), plate 25. See also plates 23–27 and 31.

3 Laurel Thatcher Ulrich provides a summary of weaving in Topsham, Maine, based on the 1810 census. Weavers were found in families in town and on farms, and from a variety of backgrounds. "Eighty-eight percent of the town's households claimed to have made cloth, and 56 percent owned looms." Laurel Thatcher Ulrich, *The Age of Homespun: Objects and Stories in the Creation of an American Myth* (New York: Alfred A. Knopf, 2001), 309, 467.

4 Paul E. Rivard, *A New Order of Things: How the Textile Industry Transformed New England* (Hanover, NH: University Press of New England, 2002), 5.

5 Laurel Thatcher Ulrich, " 'From the Fair to the Brave': Spheres of Womanhood in Federal Maine," in *Agreeable Situations: Society, Commerce, and Art in Southern Maine, 1780–1830*, ed. Laura Fecych Sprague, 218.

6 Butler, "Rising Like a Phoenix," 31.

7 Paul E. Rivard, *Made in Maine: From Home and Workshop to Mill and Factory* (Charleston, SC: History Press, 2007), 117.

8 Rivard, *Made in Maine*, 116.

9 Rivard, *Made in Maine*, 117; Rivard, *New Order*, 69.

10 Susan E. Greene, *Wearable Prints, 1760–1860: History, Materials, and Mechanics* (Kent, OH: Kent State University Press, 2014), 415–16. The technology was imported from Ireland. See Florence Montgomery, *Textiles in America* (New York: W. W. Norton & Company and the Winterthur Museum, 1985), 205, and Greene, *Wearable Prints*, 416.

11 Greene, *Wearable Prints*, 422.

12 Linda Eaton, *Printed Textiles: British and American Cottons and Linens, 1700–1850* (New York: The Monacelli Press, 2014), 269–76.

13 For a summary of the hardships and opportunities the war brought, see Butler, "Rising Like a Phoenix," 27–31.

14 Complex rules regarding coastal trade and customs registry played another major role. See Hornsby and Judd, *Historical Atlas of Maine*, plate 20.

15 Ulrich, *Age of Homespun*, 413.

16 Eaton, *Printed Textiles*, 52.

17 Sumpter Priddy III, *American Fancy: Exuberance in the Arts, 1790–1840* (Milwaukee, WI: Chipstone Foundation, 2004).

18 Jane Radcliffe notes that various published accounts report Poor's birth year as 1807. His gravestone, however, notes that he "DIED Sept. 10, 1845, AEt. 42." (Personal communication, August 14, 2019.)

19 Rufus Porter, *A Select Collection of Approved, Genuine, Secret, and Modern Receipts, for the Preparation and Execution of Various Valuable and Curious Arts, as Practised by the Best Artists of the Present Age* (Concord, MA: c. 1820), 37.

20 Lynne Zacek Bassett, "Stenciled Bedcovers," *The Magazine Antiques*, vol. x (February 2003), 73.

21 The author stopped counting after identifying fifty-nine examples by 2003; many more examples have come to light since then.

22 Bassett, "Stenciled Bedcovers," 72.

23 The Whittier stenciled spread was sold by the Gould Auction Company on February 21, 2004.

24 https://www.ancestry.com/family-tree/person/tree/77533246/person/42366491467/facts.

25   "A paper label sewn to the bedcover upon receipt is inscribed in nineteenth-century script, 'Hand painted by / Miss Emily Morton in / 1826 aged sixteen years. / Mrs J. C. Barrett.' Another later paper label written in green ink reads 'Painted by hand—by / Miss. Emily Morton, aged / 16 years—Done in 1826 / Miss. Morton lived in / Thorndyke, Maine—.'" http://emuseum.history.org/view/objects/asitem/search@/0?t:state:flow=f8d03867-f8d5-4845-b0a9-483f611eacce. Genealogical research on Ancestry.com uncovered an Emily Morton of the correct birth year in the correct county. She married Sargent Coffin (1806–1845) in 1833 and produced three children before Sargent's death. In 1848, she married Robert H. Hunt (1825–1900); she had two children with her second husband.

26   Kyle Dane, Dane Genealogy Book, Geni.com, available at https://www.geni.com/photo/view/6000000041362666835?album_type=photos_of_me&end=&photo_id=6000000012852726207&project_id=&start=&tagged_profiles=

27   Sarah Anna Emery, *Reminiscences of a Nonagenarian* (Newburyport, MA: William H. Huse & Co., 1879), 245.

28   The Worcester Historical Museum in Worcester, Massachusetts, has a quilted pelisse with matching quilted bonnet and bag with a local provenance, accession number 1976.787.

29   Alice Morse Earle, *Two Centuries of Costume in America, 1620–1820* (Williamstown, MA: Corner House Publishers, 1974; originally published in 1903), 253.

30   Harriet Beecher Stowe, *Poganuc People: Their Loves and Lives* (1878), 182: ". . . and the ferns came up with their woolly hoods on, like prudent old house mothers…."

31   Laureen A. LaBar, "Identity, Communication, and the Role of Diplomacy in Wabanaki Dress," in *Dressing New England: Clothing, Fashion, and Identity: The 2010 Dublin Seminar for New England Folklife Annual Proceedings* (Deerfield, MA: Trustees of Historic Deerfield, 2014): 10-27.

32   LaBar "Wabanaki Dress," 19.

33   Henry Adams, *The Life of Albert Gallatin* (Port Townsend, WA: Loomanics Unlimited, 1993), 12.

34   Bruce J. Bourque and Laureen A. LaBar, *Uncommon Threads: Wabanaki Textiles, Clothing, and Costume* (Seattle, WA: The Maine State Museum and Washington University Press, 2009), 99, 105.

35   Bourque and LaBar, *Uncommon Threads*, 105-7.

36   The name Socabasin is spelled various ways by different families. Nina Fletcher Little, who once owned the painting, spelled it Soccabeson, and the Abby Aldrich Rockefeller Museum has titled the painting using that spelling. Passamaquoddy Tribal Historian Donald Soctomah provided information on Denny (or Denni) Socabasin and her family.

37   Bourque and LaBar, *Uncommon Threads*, 23-33.

38   Gilbert T. Vincent, *Masterpieces of American Indian Art from the Eugene and Clare Thaw Collection* (New York: Harry N. Abrams, Inc., and the New York State Historical Association, 1995), 25.

39   Jennifer Neptune, personal communication, 2009.

40   LaBar, "Wabanaki Dress," 19-21.

CHAPTER 3

1   Lynne Zacek Bassett, ed., *Massachusetts Quilts: Our Common Wealth* (Hanover, NH: University Press of New England, 2009), 269.

2   See, for example, Carolyn Ducey, *Chintz Appliqué: from Imitation to Icon* (Lincoln, NE: International Quilt Study Center and the University of Nebraska, 2008), 10-11, plates 3-4.

3   Stephen J. Hornsby and Richard W. Judd, eds., *Historical Atlas of Maine* (Orono: University of Maine Press, 2015), plate 37.

4   Lauren Whitley, "The Textile Industry," in *Massachusetts Quilts: Our Common Wealth,* ed. Lynne Zacek Bassett (Hanover, NH: University Press of New England, 2009), 147.

5   A mill in Waldoboro employed just three people in 1850, and one in Alfred, only six. Hornsby and Judd, *Historical Atlas*, plate 48; Paul E. Rivard, *A New Order of Things: How the Textile Industry Transformed New England* (Hanover, NH: University Press of New England, 2002), 80-83.

6   Samuel L. Harris, *The Maine Register and National Calendar, for the year 1843* (Augusta, ME: Daniel C. Stanwood, 1843), 135.

NOTES

7   Hornsby and Judd, *Historical Atlas*, plate 48.

8   Rivard, *New Order*, 72, 74.

9   Thomas Wilson O'Brien, Invoice Book, 1842–1857, Portland, Maine, folio 139, Joseph Downs Collection of Manuscripts and Printed Ephemera, Winterthur Library.

10 George Adams, *The Maine Register for the Year 1855: Embracing State and County Officers, and an Abstract of the Laws and Resolves; Together with a Complete Business Directory of the State, and a Variety of Useful Information* (Portland, Hallowell, Augusta, and Bangor, ME: Blake and Carter; George R. Davis; Masters, Smith & Co., Edward Fengo; and David Bugbee & Co., 1855), 290–410.

11 Hornsby and Judd, *Historical Atlas*, plate 47.

12 Rivard, *New Order*, 34.

13 Whitly, "Textile Industry," 147; Hornsby and Judd, *Historical Atlas*, plate 42.

14 Paul E. Rivard, *Made in Maine: From Home and Workshop to Mill and Factory* (Charleston, SC: History Press, 2007), 120–21.

15 Bassett, *Massachusetts Quilts*, 291.

16 Parts of this essay were previously published. Pamela Weeks, "One Foot Square, Quilted and Bound," in *Uncoverings* 2010, ed. Laurel Horton (Lincoln, NE: American Quilt Study Group, 2010).

17 Janet Rae and Margaret Tucker, "Quilts with Special Associations," in Rae, Tucker, et al., *Quilt Treasures of Great Britain: The Heritage Search of The Quilters Guild* (Nashville, TN: Rutledge Hill Press, 1995), 181. The authors make the distinction among inscribed, autograph, and signature quilts. Loretta B. Chase, as co-curator of "Women's Writes," an exhibit at the New England Quilt Museum, Lowell, MA, May-June 2010, suggests the more inclusive term "inscribed" in place of "signature."

18 Xenia Cord, "Signature Quilts, Part 1," on the website *Celia Eddy's Quilt Story*. http://www.quilt.co.uk/quilting-articles.asp?idNo=19. The author discusses the differences between the public and private spheres of inscribed presentation quilts.

19 Dorothy Cozart, "A Century of Fundraising Quilts, 1860-1960," in *Quiltmaking in America: Beyond the Myths*, ed. Laurel Horton (San Francisco: American Quilt Study Group, 1994), 156-63.

20 Persis Sibley Andrews, Diary (transcription), Hamlin Memorial Library, Paris Hill, ME.

21 Parts of this essay were previously published. Pamela Weeks, "One Foot Square, Quilted and Bound," in *Uncoverings* 2010, ed. Laurel Horton (Lincoln, NE: American Quilt Study Group, 2010).

22 Hamlin's wife, Sarah Jane Emery, died in 1855, after twenty-two years of marriage. He married Sarah's half-sister, Ellen Vesta Emery, the following year. Both sisters made blocks for the quilt.

23 For more information on potholder quilts, see Pamela Weeks, *Potholder Quilts* (Atglen, PA: Schiffer Publishing Co., in preparation; due 2020).

24 *Godey's Ladies Book*, January 1835, 41.

25 Sarah Annie Frost, *The Ladies' Guide to Needle Work: being a complete guide to all types of Ladies Fancy Work* (1877; Mendocino, CA: R. L. Shep, 1986), 128.

26 Stephanie Hatch, interview with author, Boxford, MA, September 12, 2006.

27 Robert Bishop, William Secord, and Judith Reiter Weissman, *The Knopf Collectors' Guides to American Antiques: Quilts, Coverlets, Rugs and Samplers* (New York: Alfred A. Knopf, 1982), 21.

28 Many thanks to Pam Weeks for all her help and encouragement with this research.

29 In 1881, Annie Sturdivant Lowe, wife of Captain Marcellus Lowe and daughter of Captain Ephraim Sturdivant, took command of the ship when her husband died suddenly toward the end of a five-year voyage. Her son, Sumner, was born at sea the previous year. Phyllis Sturdivant Sweetser, ed., *Cumberland, Maine in Four Centuries* (Cumberland, ME: Town of Cumberland, Maine, 1976), 74.

30 Floyd W. Norton, *Norton's Hand-Hewn History of Maine and Its Representative Town of Cumberland* (Cumberland. ME: Cumberland Books, 2017), 12, 17. Thank you, Thomas C. Bennet, for bringing this to LAL's attention.

31 Phyllis Sturdivant Sweetser, 53–59.

32 Phyllis Sturdivant Sweetser, 53–59. Hornsby and Judd, *Historical Atlas*, plate 32.

33 Mrs. F. R. (Mary E.) Sweetser, *History of the Town of Cumberland Maine* (Yarmouth, ME: A. F. Tilton, 1921), 20–22, 33.

34 Mrs. F. R. (Mary E.) Sweetser, 25.

35 Mrs. F. R. (Mary E.) Sweetser, 20–22.

36 The location of the Craig quilt is currently unknown. The LSC quilt sold at auction in 2010, before this research began, and is in private hands. The authors were, however, able to examine the quilt and photographed most of the quilt before it sold. The Comet quilt is currently unavailable for examination, and its documentation remains incomplete.

37 Hebrews 6:19.

38 John 15:5.

39 Thomas C. Bennett, ed., *Vital Records of Cumberland, Maine 1701-1892* (Yarmouth, ME: Islandport Press, 2009), 248.

40 Thomas C. Bennett, ed., expanded list of "Cumberland Center Deaths," unpublished ms.

41 Blocks with men's names have been assigned to their wives on the basis of the couples' social ties, if not the ties to the blocks' makers. In no case did this assignment change the number of quilts linked to the wives' names.

42 Genealogical information for this essay was found from Maine marriage records and the find-a-grave index on ancestry.com.

43 Census data from ancestry.com.

44 State News, *Bangor Daily Whig*, 25 March 1882, 1

45 Wayne Wheeler, "The Portland Breakwater Light Station," reprinted from the U.S. Lighthouse Society's *The Keeper's Log*, Spring 2004, 2 and 4; 1860 Federal Census Mortality Schedule from Ancestry.com.

46 Wayne Wheeler, "The Portland Breakwater Light Station," reprinted from the U.S. Lighthouse Society's *The Keeper's Log*, Spring 2004, 2 and 4.

47 Harry Gratwick, *The Forts of Maine: Silent Sentinels of the Pine Tree State* (Charleston, SC: The History Press, 2013), 42–45.

48 Harry Gratwick, *The Forts of Maine*, 42–45.

49 Mason Philip Smith, *Confederates Downeast* (Portland, ME: Provincial Press, 1985), 103–4.

50 Bassett, *Massachusetts Quilts*, 270.

51 Lori G. Ginzburg, *Women and the Art of Benevolence* (New Haven, CT: Yale University Press, 1990), 1.

52 Rev. C. Gayton Pickman, in *An Address before the East Cambridge Christian Temperance Society* (Boston, MA: C. C. Little and J. Brown, 1845), 30, cited in Lori G. Ginzburg, *Women and the Art of Benevolence*, i.

53 Ginzburg, *Women and the Art of Benevolence*, 98–100.

54 The 1851 prohibitory liquor law became known as "the Maine law." It was unpopular as written and was repealed in 1856. However, many local communities retained liquor laws until prohibition was written into the State constitution in 1885. The state was effectively dry until 1933, and restrictive laws on the sale of alcohol continued into the late twentieth century.

CHAPTER 4

1 Henry Worcester, "Maine State Agency in Washington," in *Report of the Adjutant General of the State of Maine for the Years 1864 and 1865*, James W. Hanson, ed., vol. 1 (Augusta, ME: Stevens and Sayward, 1866), 105.

2 Sarah "Say" White letter, Skowhegan, September 17, 1863, MSM acc.# 2002.37.167.

3 Laureen A. LaBar, *Maine Voices from the Civil War* (Augusta, ME: Maine State Museum, 2013), 12.

4 Lynda L. Sudlow, *A Vast Army of Women: Maine's Uncounted Forces in the American Civil War* (Gettysburg, PA: Thomas Publications, 2000), 235–36.

5 Printed in the *Union and Journal*, March 27, 1863, cf. Sudlow, *A Vast Army of Women*, 12.

6 Various authors. "Minutes of the Ladies Beneficent Association of North New Sharon, Me." Unpublished manuscript, private collection.

NOTES

7   "Minutes of the Ladies Beneficent Association of North New Sharon, Me."

8   Special thanks to Linda Bean who provided funds so that the Maine State Museum could acquire this exceptional quilt.

9   William Willis, *The History of Portland* (Somersworth, NH: New Hampshire Publishing Company, facsimile of the second edition, 1972), 239–42.

10   Martin Dibner, ed., *Portland: Greater Portland Landmarks*, second edition (Augusta, ME: Greater Portland Landmarks; J. S. McCarthy Printers, Maine, 1986), 9.

11   Compiled by the Workers of the Writer's Program of the Works Projects Administration in the State of Maine, *Portland City Guide* (Portland, ME: The Forest City Printing Company, 1940), 274.

12   Willis, *The History of Portland*, 730.

13   The Brick Store Museum, Kennebunk, ME, accession file #2543.

14   The Mystic Seaport Museum, Mystic, CT, accession file #1968.24.

15   Research on the families was done on Ancestry.com.

16   Jack Coggins, *Arms and Equipment of the Civil War* (Garden City, NY: Doubleday & Company, Inc., 1962), 132.

17   Anita B. Loscalzo, "Massachusetts and the Sewing Machine," in Lynne Zacek Bassett, ed., *Massachusetts Quilts: Our Common Wealth* (Hanover, NH: University Press of New England, 2009), 164–65.

18   Loscalzo, "Sewing Machine," 164.

19   In 1917 Augusta Quimby Frederick reminisced about the quilt's construction at a meeting of the Woman's Alliance in Belfast. Quoted in Megan Pinette, "Hurrah for the Boys of the Pine Tree State," in Pamela Weeks and Don Beld, *Civil War Quilts* (Atglen, PA: Schiffer Publishing, Ltd., 2011), 40.

20   Megan Pinette, personal communication, June 2011.

CHAPTER 5

1   George Adams, *The Maine Register for the Year 1855: Embracing State and County Officers, and an Abstract of the Laws and Resolves; Together with a Complete Business Directory of the State, and a Variety of Useful Information* (Portland, Hallowell, Augusta, and Bangor, ME: Blake and Carter; George R. Davis; Masters, Smith & Co., Edward Fengo; and David Bugbee & Co., 1855), 290–410.

2   Richard W. Judd, in Stephen J. Hornsby and Richard W. Judd, eds., *Historical Atlas of Maine* (Orono, ME: University of Maine Press, 2015), part III introduction, before plate 38.

3   Libby Bischoff, "At Work in Maine: Selected Photographs of Labor," in *Maine Photography: A History* (Lanham, MD: Maine Historical Society and Down East Books, 2016). Lewis Hine photographed children who worked in Maine factories in 1909. Some probably began work at six to eight years of age.

4   Jane C. Nylander, *Our Own Snug Fireside: Images of the New England Home, 1760–1860* (New York: Alfred A. Knopf, 1993), ix.

5   Nylander, *Our Own Snug Fireside*, x.

6   Hornsby and Judd, *Historical Atlas of Maine*, plate 24.

7   Hornsby and Judd, *Historical Atlas of Maine*, plate 24.

8   *Maine: The Pine Tree State from Prehistory to the Present*, Richard W. Judd, Edwin A. Churchill, and Joel W. Eastman, eds. (Orono, ME: University of Maine Press, 1995), 338.

9   Hornsby and Judd, *Historical Atlas of Maine*, plate 47.

10   Judd, Churchill, and Eastman, *Maine: The Pine Tree State*, 334.

11   Simon Garfield, *Mauve* (New York: W. W. Norton and Co., 2000), 24, 35–36.

12   Susan Greene, *Wearable Prints, 1760–1860, History, Materials, and Mechanics* (Kent, OH: Kent State University Press, 2014), 527.

13   William Collins Hatch, *A History of the Town of Industry: Franklin County, Maine* (Farmington, ME: Press of Knowlton, McLeary & Co, 1893), 786.

14   Louisa May Alcott, *Little Women* (New York: Grosset and Dunlap, 1915), 9–10.

15   John Bunyan, *The Pilgrim's Progress from This World to That Which Is to Come* (New York: United States Book Company, [undated]), 208.

16   http://www.newenglandlighthouses.net/tenants-harbor-light-history.html.

17 Dorothy Cozart, "A Century of Fundraising Quilts: 1860-1960," in *Uncoverings, 1984,* ed. Sally Garoutte (Mill Valley, CA: The American Quilt Study Group, 1985), 44.

18 Maine Maritime catalog records. See also a related image: https://www.mainememory.net/artifact/27950?popup=1

19 Thanks to Dr. James White, of the University of North Carolina, Chapel Hill, for the transliteration.

20 Further thanks to T. J. and Roza Kwok-Ling Mueller who translated the name.

21 Grenville M. Donham, *Maine Register, State Year-Book and Legislative Manual* (Portland, ME: Grenville M. Donham, 1890), 882. The Biddeford Maine directory found on Ancestry.com lists the surname as Hop, not Horp.

22 Donham, *Maine Register,* 541 and 393-94.

23 Massachusetts marriage records and genealogical information from Ancestry.com.

CHAPTER 6

1 Virginia Gunn, "Crazy Quilts and Outline Quilts: Popular Responses to the Decorative Art/Art Needlework Movement, 1876-1893," in *Uncoverings, 1984,* Sally Garoutte, ed. (Mill Valley, CA: The American Quilt Study Group, 1985), 131.

2 See, for example, Penny McMorris, *Crazy Quilts* (New York: E. P. Dutton, Inc., 1984), 13, 18-21.

3 For an example of applied embroidery, see Beverly Gordon, "Regularly Irregular," in *American Quilts in the Modern Age, 1870-1940,* ed. Marin F. Hanson and Patricia Cox Crews (Lincoln, NE: University of Nebraska Press, 2009), 130.

4 See McMorris, *Crazy Quilts,* 24, for an image of such fabric, as well as an 1886 advertisement for "Crazy Cloth."

5 Gordon, "Regularly Irregular," 132.

6 Jacqueline Field, Marjorie Senechal, and Madelyn Shaw, *American Silk, 1820-1930: Entrepreneurs and Artifacts* (Lubbock, TX: Texas Tech University Press, 2007), 105-7; Howard L. Needles, *Handbook of Textile Fibers, Dyes, and Finishes* (New York: Garland STPM Press, 1981), 49.

7 McMorris, *Crazy Quilts,* 16-17.

8 Addie Mae Johnson was probably born on Orr's Island, in 1870 or 1872. The family recalls that she was living on Bailey Island in 1888, and that she and Charles Annis were married that year. However, state records show that they were married in 1895.

CHAPTER 7

1 Nathan R. Lipfert, Richard W. Judd, and Richard R. Wescott, "New Industries in an Age of Adjustment," in *Maine: The Pine Tree State from Prehistory to the Present*, ed. Richard W. Judd, Edwin A. Churchill, and Joel W. Eastman (Orono, ME: University of Maine Press, 1995), 420.

2 Hornsby, Stephen J., and Richard W. Judd, eds., *Historical Atlas of Maine* (Orono, ME: University of Maine Press, 2015), plates 41, 56.

3 Judd, Churchill, and Eastman, *Maine: The Pine Tree State*, 453.

4 Hornsby and Judd, *Historical Atlas of Maine*, plate 42; Judd, Churchill, and Eastman, *Maine: The Pine Tree State*, 459.

5 Hornsby and Judd, *Historical Atlas of Maine*, plates 41, 43.

6 Hornsby and Judd, *Historical Atlas of Maine*, plate 44.

7 Richard H. Condon and William David Berry, "The Tides of Change: 1967-1988," in Judd, Churchill, and Eastman, *Maine: The Pine Tree State*, 557.

8 Marin F. Hanson, "American Quilts in the Modern Age, 1870-1940," in *American Quilts in the Modern Age, 1870-1940,* ed. Marin F. Hanson and Patricia Cox Crews (Lincoln: University of Nebraska Press, 2009), 1-2.

9 Hanson, "American Quilts in the Modern Age," 13.

NOTES

10   Patricia Cox Crews and Carolyn Ducey, eds., *American Quilts in the Industrial Age, 1760–1870* (Lincoln, NE: The International Quilt Study Center and Museum Collections and University of Nebraska Press, 2018), 84–85.

11   Always keeping in mind that horse feed was no good as a source of fabric, because the molasses in the feed stained the cloth brown. Dorna Tracy, personal communication, 2003.

12   "But we were all poor," noted Ella Lanphier Burgoine, discussing how her sister had hated their flour sack clothing; personal communication, August 10, 2018.

13   Hanson, "American Quilts in the Modern Age," 16.

14   Robert Shaw, *American Quilts: The Democratic Art, 1780–2007* (New York: Sterling Publishing Co., 2009), 281.

15   Shaw, *American Quilts: The Democratic Art*, 281.

16   Information about the AIDS quilt was obtained via their website: https://www.aidsquilt.org/about/the-aids-memorial-quilt

17   AIDS quilt website.

18   Marianne Philbin, ed., *The Ribbon: A Celebration of Life* (Asheville, NC: Lark Books, 1985), 10–13.

19   Bernice Barton of Evanston, Illinois, quoted in an August 4, United Press International news article: "15-mile 'peace' ribbon wrapped around Washington landmarks," https://www.upi.com/Archives/1985/08/04/15-mile-peace-ribbon-wrapped-around-Washington-landmarks/5758491976000/

20   Don Wilcox, "The People," in Philbin, *The Ribbon: A Celebration of Life*, 17, 24–25.

21   Maine Historical Society accession records for 1990.261. Many of the Maine examples were not signed; Piscataquis and Washington counties may have been represented in those quilts.

22   The Etchemin later became the modern Penobscot, Passamaquoddy, and Maliseet tribes. In 1701, the three groups and the MicMac tribe formed the Wabanaki Confederacy. Bruce J. Bourque, "Ethnicity of the Maritime Peninsula, 1600–1759," *Ethnohistory* 36, no. 3 (1980): 257–84; Bruce J. Bourque and Laureen A. LaBar, *Uncommon Threads: Wabanaki Textiles, Clothing, and Costume* (Seattle, WA: Maine State Museum and University of Washington Press, 2009): 11–18.

23   Marie Mathilde, or Molly Mathilda, was the baptismal name of Madockawando's daughter. Her original name was Pidianiske Bunny McBride. *Women of the Dawn* (Lincoln, NE: University of Nebraska Press, 1999), 7.

24   The full history of the quilt and images of each square are available on the website of the Castine Historical Society: https://www.castinehistoricalsociety.org/castine-community-bicentennial-quilt/ and http://www.castinehistoricalsociety.org/wp-content/uploads/2017/05/quilt-article001.pdf. Thanks to Paige Lilly for tracking down the details.

25   Ironically for a show on abstract art, the curators omitted mention of the names of the quilts' creators, as well as the context for their creation.

26   Asahi Shimbun, in Jean Andrews, *Fabric Gardens: An International Exhibition of Quilts at Expo '90* (Athens, OH: Dairy Barn Arts Center, 1990), i.

27   https://www.imdb.com/title/tt0025410/soundtrack.

28   MSM catalog records.

CHAPTER 8

1   Gayle Fraas and Duncan Slade are featured in Christine Macchi and Carol Jones, *Fiber Art Masters: A Visual Tour of Maine Artists' Work and Studios* (Topsham, ME: Maine Fiberarts: 2016), 14–15.

2   Gayle Fraas and Duncan Slade, personal communication, June 29, 2019.

3   Susan Carlson is featured in Christine Macchi and Carol Jones, *Fiber Art Masters*, 6–7.

4   Maine State Museum 2017.51.1 Catalog records.

5   All quotes by Jackie Manton were given in the course of an interview in her home on March 11, 2019.

6   My sincere thanks to Jackie Manton, Beth Dawson, Mary Reynolds, Mary Carthage, and Sue Rivers. They and others shared with me information about the many charities that receive quilts.

7   Through the group's gifts of quilts, Quilts of Valor seeks to provide comfort and healing to armed service members and veterans.

NOTES

8   The Ronald McDonald House is a charity with a mission to "keep families with sick children together and near the care and resources they need." They operate in two Maine cities, Bangor and Portland, and have homes, rooms, and mobile stations nationwide.

9   The group does not focus only on violence against immigrants. Their website states that "Green Dot Lewiston Auburn is an initiative by a group of local volunteers who are committed to making our Twin Cities community a better and safer place by teaching strategies for better and safer responses to hurtful and hateful words and behaviors. In this way, we aim to reduce the occurrence and impact of harassment, assault, domestic and partner violence, and other forms of power-based interpersonal threats and violence." http://greendotla.org/who.

BIBLIOGRAPHY

Adams, George. *The Maine Register for the Year 1855: Embracing State and County Officers, and an Abstract of the Laws and Resolves; Together with a Complete Business Directory of the State, and a Variety of Useful Information.* Portland, Hallowell, Augusta, and Bangor: Blake and Carter; George R. Davis; Masters, Smith & Co., Edward Fengo; and David Bugbee & Co., 1855.

Adams, Henry. *The Life of Albert Gallatin.* Port Townsend, WA: Loomanics Unlimited, 1993.

Adiletta, Dawn C. "A Matter of Taste: The Aesthetic Movement and Connecticut Crazy Quilts." In *What's New England About New England Quilts? Proceedings of a Symposium at Old Sturbridge Village, June 13, 1998.* Edited by Lynne Z. Bassett. Sturbridge, MA: Old Sturbridge Village, 1999, 92–103.

Alcott, Louisa May. *Little Women.* New York: Grosset and Dunlap, 1915.

Andrews, Jean. *Fabric Gardens: An International Exhibition of Quilts at Expo '90.* Athens, OH: Dairy Barn Arts Center, 1990.

Andrews, Persis Sibley. Diary (transcription). Hamlin Memorial Library, Paris Hill, ME.

Bassett, Lynne Zacek, ed. *Massachusetts Quilts: Our Common Wealth.* Hanover, NH: University Press of New England, 2009.

Bassett, Lynne Z. "Inspired Fantasy: Design Sources for New England's Whole-Cloth Wool Quilts." *The Magazine Antiques,* vol. 167, no. 3 (September 2005): 120–27.

———. " 'Spun me some worsted to quilt with': New England's Early Wool Quilts." In *What's New England about New England Quilts? Proceedings of a Symposium at Old Sturbridge Village, June 13, 1998.* Edited by Lynne Z. Bassett. Sturbridge, MA: Old Sturbridge Village, 1999: 2–14.

———. "Stenciled Bedcovers." *The Magazine Antiques,* vol. 163 (February 2003).

Bassett, Lynne Z., and Jack Larkin. *Northern Comfort: New England's Early Quilts, 1780–1850.* Nashville, TN: Rutledge Hill Press, with Old Sturbridge Village, 1998.

Benes, Peter, ed. *Dressing New England: Clothing, Fashion, and Identity: The Dublin Seminar for New England Folklife Annual Proceedings, 2010.* Deerfield, MA: Trustees of Historic Deerfield, 2014.

Bennett, Thomas C., ed. *Vital Records of Cumberland, Maine 1701–1892.* Yarmouth, Maine: Islandport Press, 2009.

———. "Expanded List of 'Cumberland Center Deaths.'" Unpublished manuscript, 2009.

Bischoff, Libby. "At Work in Maine: Selected Photographs of Labor." In *Maine Photography: A History.* Lanham, MD: Maine Historical Society and Down East Books, 2016.

BIBLIOGRAPHY

Bishop, Robert, William Secord, and Judith Reiter Weissman. *The Knopf Collectors' Guides to American Antiques: Quilts, Coverlets, Rugs and Samplers.* New York: Alfred A. Knopf, 1982.

Blaszczyk, Regina Lee. *The Color Revolution.* Cambridge, MA: MIT Press, 2012.

Bourque, Bruce J. "Ethnicity of the Maritime Peninsula, 1600–1759," *Ethnohistory* 36, no. 3 (1980): 257–84.

Bourque, Bruce J., and Laureen A. LaBar. *Uncommon Threads: Wabanaki Textiles, Clothing, and Costume.* Seattle, WA: The Maine State Museum and Washington University Press, 2009.

Brain, Jeffrey Phipps. *Fort St. George: Archaeological Investigation of the 1607–1608 Popham Colony, Occasional Publications in Maine Archaeology Number 12.* Augusta, ME: The Maine State Museum, Maine Historic Preservation Commission, and Maine Archaeological Society, 2007.

Brown, Eliza Southgate. *A Girl's Life Eighty Years Ago: Selections from the Letters of Eliza Southgate Bowne.* New York: Charles Scribner's Sons, 1887.

Bunyan, John. *The Pilgrim's Progress from this World to that which is to Come.* New York: United States Book Company [undated].

Butler, Joyce. "Rising Like a Phoenix: Commerce in Southern Maine, 1775–1830." In *Agreeable Situations: Society, Commerce, and Art in Southern Maine, 1780–1830.* Edited by Laura Fecych Sprague, 15–25. Boston, MA: Northeastern University Press and the Brick Store Museum, 1987.

Coggins, Jack. *Arms and Equipment of the Civil War.* Garden City, NY: Doubleday & Company, Inc., 1962.

Condon, Richard H., and William David Berry. "The Tides of Change: 1967–1988." In *Maine: The Pine Tree State from Prehistory to the Present.* Edited by Richard W. Judd, Edwin A. Churchill, and Joel W. Eastman, 554–85. Orono, ME: University of Maine Press, 1995.

Cord, Xenia. "Signature Quilts, Part 1," on the website *Celia Eddy's Quilt Story.* http://www.quilt.co.uk/quilting-articles.asp?idNo=19

Cozart, Dorothy. "A Century of Fundraising Quilts: 1860–1960." In *Uncoverings, 1984.* Edited by Sally Garoutte, 41–53. Mill Valley, CA: The American Quilt Study Group, 1985.

———. "A Century of Fundraising Quilts, 1860–1960." In *Quiltmaking in America: Beyond the Myths.* Edited by Laurel Horton. San Francisco: American Quilt Study Group, 1994.

Crews, Patricia Cox, and Carolyn Ducey, eds. *American Quilts in the Industrial Age, 1760–1870.* Lincoln, NE: University of Nebraska Press, 2018.

Dibner, Martin, ed. *Portland: Greater Portland Landmarks*, second edition. Augusta, ME: Portland Greater Landmarks; J. S. McCarthy Printers, 1986.

Donham, Grenville M. *Maine Register, State Year-Book and Legislative Manual.* Portland, ME: Grenville M. Donham, 1890.

Ducey, Carolyn. *Chintz Appliqué: From Imitation to Icon.* Lincoln, NE: International Quilt Study Center and the University of Nebraska, 2008.

Earle, Alice Morse. *Two Centuries of Costume in America, 1620-1820.* Williamstown, MA: Corner House Publishers, 1974; originally published in 1903.

Eaton, Linda. *Printed Textiles: British and American Cottons and Linens, 1700-1850.* New York: The Monacelli Press, 2014.

———. *Quilts in a Material World: Selections from the Winterthur Collection.* New York: Harry N. Abrams and The Henry Francis du Pont Winterthur Museum, Inc., 2007.

Field, Jacqueline, Marjorie Senechal, and Madelyn Shaw. *American Silk, 1820-1930: Entrepreneurs and Artifacts.* Lubbock, TX: Texas Tech University Press, 2007.

Finley, John. *Kentucky Quilts, 1800-1900.* Louisville: The Kentucky Quilt Project, Inc., 1982.

Finley, Ruth E. *Old Patchwork Quilts and the Women Who Made Them.* Philadelphia and London: Lippincott, 1929.

Frost, S. Annie. *The Ladies' Guide to Needle Work: Being a complete guide to all types of Ladies' Fancy Work.* (1877). Mendocino, CA: R. L. Shep, 1986.

Garfield, Simon. *Mauve* New York: W. W. Norton and Co., 2000,

Ginzburg, Lori G. *Women and the Art of Benevolence.* New Haven, CT: Yale University Press, 1990.

Gordon, Beverly. "Regularly Irregular." In *American Quilts in the Modern Age, 1870-1940.* Edited by Marin F. Hanson and Patricia Cox Crews, 126-76. Lincoln: University of Nebraska Press, 2009.

Greene, Susan. *Wearable Prints, 1760-1860, History, Materials, and Mechanics.* Kent, OH: The Kent State University Press, 2014.

Gunn, Virginia. "Crazy Quilts and Outline Quilts: Popular Responses to the Decorative Art/Art Needlework Movement, 1876-1893." In *Uncoverings,* vol. 5 (1984). Edited by Sally Garoutte, 131-52. Mill Valley, CA: the American Quilt Study Group, 1985,

Hall, Carrie A., and Rose G. Kretsinger, *The Romance of the Patchwork Quilt in America.* New York: Bonanza Books, 1935.

Hamilton, Andrew. *Alexander Hamilton's Famous Report on Manufactures: Made to Congress December 5, 1791, in His Capacity as Secretary of the Treasury.* Boston, MA: The House Market Club and Porter Publishing, 1892.

Hanson, Marin F., and Patricia Cox Crews, eds. *Quilts in the Modern Age, 1870-1940.* Lincoln, NE: University of Nebraska Press, 2009.

Harris, Samuel L. *The Maine Register and National Calendar, for the year 1843.* Augusta, ME: Daniel C. Stanwood, 1843.

BIBLIOGRAPHY

Hatch, William Collins. *A History of the Town of Industry: Franklin County, Maine*. Farmington, ME: Press of Knowlton, McLeary & Co, 1893.

Hersh, Tandy. "18th-Century Quilted Silk Petticoats Worn in America." In *Uncoverings*, vol. 5 (1984): 83–98.

Hornsby, Stephen J., and Richard W. Judd, eds. *Historical Atlas of Maine*. Orono, ME: University of Maine Press, 2015.

Judd, Richard W., Edwin A. Churchill, and Joel W. Eastman, eds. *Maine: The Pine Tree State from Prehistory to the Present*. Orono, ME: University of Maine Press, 1995.

Kiracofe, Roderick. *The American Quilt: A History of Cloth and Comfort, 1750–1950*. New York: Clarkson Potter, 1993.

Kraak, Deborah E. "Early American Silk Patchwork Quilts." In *Textiles in Early New England: Design, Production, and Consumption, The Dublin Seminar for New England Folklife Annual Proceedings, 1997*. Boston: Boston University, 1999.

LaBar, Laureen A. *Maine Voices from the Civil War*. Augusta, ME: Maine State Museum, 2013.

———. "Identity, Communication, and the Role of Diplomacy in Wabanaki Dress." In *Dressing New England: Clothing, Fashion, and Identity: The Dublin Seminar for New England Folklife Annual Proceedings, 2010*, 10–27. Deerfield, MA: Trustees of Historic Deerfield, 2014.

Lefever, Joel. "Family Connections." In *Blog of the Old York Historical Society*. York, ME, December 10, 2015. https://oldyorkmuseums.wordpress.com/2015/12/10/family-connections/

Leslie, Eliza. *The House Book: or, A Manual of Domestic Economy*. Philadelphia, PA: Carey & Hart, 1843.

Lipfert, Nathan R., Richard W. Judd, and Richard R. Wescott, "New Industries in an Age of Adjustment." In *Maine: The Pine Tree State from Prehistory to the Present*, edited by Richard W. Judd, Edwin A. Churchill, and Joel W. Eastman, 420–47. Orono, ME: University of Maine Press, 1995.

Loscalzo, Anita B. "Massachusetts and the Sewing Machine." In *Massachusetts Quilts: Our Common Wealth*. Edited by Lynne Zacek Bassett. Hanover, NH: University Press of New England, 2009.

Macchi, Christine, and Carol Jones. *Fiber Art Masters: A Visual Tour of Maine Artists' Work and Studios*. Topsham, ME: Maine Fiberarts: 2016.

McBride, Bunny. *Women of the Dawn*. Lincoln, NE: University of Nebraska Press, 1999.

McCausland, Robert R., and Cynthia MacAlman McCausland. *The Diary of Martha Ballard, 1785–1812*. Camden, ME: Picton Press, 1992.

McMorris, Penny. *Crazy Quilts*. New York: E. P. Dutton, Inc, 1984.

Montgomery, Florence M. *Printed Textiles*. New York: Viking Press, 1970.

Montgomery, Florence M. *Textiles in America*. New York: W. W. Norton & Company and the Winterthur Museum, 1985.

Murray, Craig C. *Benjamin Vaughan (1751–1835): The Life of an Anglo-American Intellectual*. New York: Arno Press, 1982, 409.

Needles, Howard L. *Handbook of Textile Fibers, Dyes, and Finishes*. New York: Garland STPM Press, 1981.

Norton, Floyd W. *Norton's Hand-Hewn History of Maine and Its Representative Town of Cumberland*. Cumberland, ME: Cumberland Books, 2017.

Nylander, Jane C. *Our Own Snug Fireside: Images of the New England Home, 1760–1860*. New York: Alfred A. Knopf, 1993.

Orlofsky, Patsy, and Myron Orlofsky. *Quilts in America*. New York: Abbeville Press, 1974.

Philbin, Marianne, ed. *The Ribbon: A Celebration of Life*. Asheville, NC: Lark Books, 1985.

Pickman, Rev. C. Gayton. In *An Address before the East Cambridge Christian Temperance Society*. Boston, MA: C. C. Little and J. Brown, 1845.

Pinette, Megan. "Hurrah for the Boys of the Pine Tree State." In Pam Weeks and Don Beld, *Civil War Quilts*. Atglen, PA: Schiffer Publishing, Ltd., 2011.

Porter, Rufus. *A Select Collection of Approved, Genuine, Secret, and Modern Receipts, for the Preparation and Execution of Various Valuable and Curious Arts, as Practised by the Best Artists of the Present Age*. Concord, MA: c. 1820.

Priddy, Sumpter III. *American Fancy: Exuberance in the Arts, 1790–1840*. Milwaukee, WI: Chipstone Foundation, 2004.

Pullan, Mrs. *The Lady's Manual of Fancy-Work*. New York: Dick & Fitzgerald, 1858.

Rae, Janet, and Margaret Tucker. "Quilts with Special Associations." In *Quilt Treasures of Great Britain: The Heritage Search of the Quilters Guild*. Janet Rae, Margaret Tucker, et al. Nashville, TN: Rutledge Hill Press, 1995.

Rivard, Paul E. *A New Order of Things: How the Textile Industry Transformed New England*. Hanover, NH: University Press of New England, 2002.

———. *Made in Maine: From Home and Workshop to Mill and Factory*. Charleston, SC: History Press, 2007.

Shaw, Robert. *American Quilts: The Democratic Art, 1780–2007*. New York: Sterling Publishing Co., 2009.

Smith, Mason Philip. *Confederates Downeast*. Portland, ME: Provincial Press, 1985.

Smucker, Janneken. "Early Nineteenth-Century Embroidered Bedcovers." *Winterthur Portfolio* 42:4 (2009): 224–42.

Sprague, Laura Fecych, ed. *Agreeable Situations: Society, Commerce, and Art in Southern Maine, 1780–1830*. Boston, MA: Northeastern University Press and the Brick Store Museum, 1987.

Sudlow, Lynda L. *A Vast Army of Women: Maine's Uncounted Forces in the American Civil War*. Gettysburg, PA: Thomas Publications, 2000.

Sweetser, Mrs. F. R. (Mary E.). *History of the Town of Cumberland Maine.* Yarmouth, ME: A. F. Tilton, 1921.

Sweetser, Phyllis Sturdivant, ed. *Cumberland, Maine in Four Centuries.* Cumberland, ME: Town of Cumberland, Maine, 1976.

Ulrich, Laurel Thatcher. *The Age of Homespun: Objects and Stories in the Creation of an American Myth.* New York: Alfred A. Knopf, 2001.

———. *A Midwife's Tale: The Life of Martha Ballard, Based on Her Diary, 1785–1812.* New York: Vintage Books, 1990.

———. "'From the Fair to the Brave': Spheres of Womanhood in Federal Maine." In *Agreeable Situations: Society, Commerce, and Art in Southern Maine, 1780–1830,* edited by Laura Fecych Sprague, 215–25. Boston, MA: Northeastern University Press and the Brick Store Museum, 1987.

Various. "Minutes of the Ladies Beneficent Association of North New Sharon, Me." Unpublished manuscript. Private collection.

Vincent, Gilbert T. *Masterpieces of American Indian Art from the Eugene and Clare Thaw Collection.* New York: Harry N. Abrams, Inc., and the New York State Historical Association, 1995.

Weeks, Pam, and Dan Beld. *Civil War Quilts.* Atglen, PA: Schiffer Publishing, Ltd., 2011.

Wheeler, Wayne. "Little-Known Lighthouses: The Portland Breakwater Light Station," reprinted from the U.S. Lighthouse Society's *The Keeper's Log,* Spring 2004, 12–17.

Whitley, Lauren. "The Textile Industry." In *Massachusetts Quilts: Our Common Wealth.* Edited by Lynne Zacek Bassett, 145–48. Hanover, NH: University Press of New England, 2009.

Wilcox, Don. "The People." In *The Ribbon: A Celebration of Life.* Edited by Marianne Philbin. Asheville, NC: Lark Books, 1985, 17–25.

Willis, William. *The History of Portland.* Somersworth, NH: New Hampshire Publishing Company, facsimile of the second edition, 1972.

Worcester, Henry. "Maine State Agency in Washington." In *Report of the Adjutant General of the State of Maine for the Years 1864 and 1865,* vol. 1. Edited by James W. Hanson. Augusta, ME: Stevens and Sayward, 1866.

Writers' Program, Works Projects Administration in the State of Maine. *Portland City Guide.* Portland, ME: The Forest City Printing Company, 1940.

INDEX

Page numbers in *italics* indicate illustrations

Abstract Design in American Quilts (exhibit), 165
Addie Mae Johnson Crazy Quilt, 139, 140
agricultural motifs, 128
AIDS and AIDS memorial quilt, *160–161*, 183
AIDS Quilt Block, 160
Album Quilt, 57, 122
album quilts: appliquéd blocks, 57, 95; construction methods, 57–58, 60–61; friendship quilts, 57, 60, 61; inscribed quilts, 60–62; pieced blocks, 57; potholder quilts, 62–66
Alcott, Louisa May, 110
Alexander, ME, 110
Allen, Polly, 4–5, *33*
American Bicentennial, 1976, 156, *158*
American folk art, xi
American Hand Laundry, 116
American Indian. *See* Native Americans; specific tribes
American Legion, 115
American Revolution, 1, 23, 32, 36–38
Andrews, Persis Sibley, 62
Annie's Quilt, 128
Annis, Charles, 139
appliqué: *Antlers Quilt, 112*; and *Pieced Quilt, 124*; potholder quilts, 62, *63*, *64*, 64–66, 75, 99; printed patterns, 57; silk ribbon, 46, 47–48, 49, *50–51*, 180, 213
Appliqué and Pieced Quilt, 124
Appliqué Antlers Quilt, 112
Appliqué Quilt 111: digital restoration, 112
Arlington, VA, 161
art quilts, 10, 177–178, *179*, 180, 182
Art Quilts Maine, 180
Auburn, ME, 59

backs and backing, 6, 8, 10, 204
Bailey Island, ME, 136–140
Ballard, Martha, 13
Baltimore, MD, 57
Bangor, ME, 46, 117
Bar Harbor, ME, 117
Bark Messenger Quilt, 60, *68*, 75, *76*, 77; detail, *75–77*
baroque designs, 7, 8
Basket of Diamonds Quilt, 153
basket of flowers motif, 22
Basket Quilt, 125
Bassett, Lynne, 7, 22, 39–40, 42–43, 60, 85, xi
Batchelder, Susan, 64
Bath, ME, 42
batting, 7, 32, 65, 133, 156, 186

bed: hangings, 1, *2*, 19, *19*, 51; quilts, 13, 15, 160, 185, 186; rugs, 18–19
bed covers: embroidered, xi, 1, 18, *18*, 19, 22, pieced, 18–19, 23; stenciled, 39–41, *41*
bedcovers. *See* bed covers
Belfast Flag Quilt, 103
Bethel, ME, 161
Bicentennial Quilt by Castine Community, *163–164*
Bicentennial Quilt by Green Street Seniors, *157*
Bicentennial Quilt by Linda Throckmorton, *159*
Bicentennial Quilts, xii 156, *157*, 160, *163–164*
Biddeford, ME, 36, 59, 116
Birds Flying in the Air, Redwork Quilt, 108
Bishop, Robert, 66
Black Crazy Quilt, 148
Black Horse Farm, 197
Blanchard, Jane, 72
Blanchard, Saba Gray, 78
Blanchard family, 77–78, 79
block printing, *33–34*
blocks: in album quilts, 57–58, 60, 61–63, 65–66, 72; in embroidered quilts, 4–5, 19, 22, 100; machine-quilted, 101–102; in medallion quilts, 2–3, *3 4*, *5*, 20; in pieced quilts, 2, *3*, *20*, 100; potholder quilts, 62–63, 65–66, *100*, 100–101
blogs, 156
bonnets and hoods, 12, 44, *44–45*
Breakwater Lighthouse Quilt, 82, 83–84
Brick Store Museum (BSM), 14, *15*, 100
Bridgton, ME, 39
British: fashion tastes, 12–13; needlework traditions, 1–3, 5, 8, 23; textile imports/exports, 14, 32, 36–37
Brunswick, ME, *33*, 137, 180, 198
Brunswick Naval Air Station, ME, 184
Bulman, Mary Swett, 1
Bunyan, John, 110

calendering, 6, 8, 10
calico, xii, xiii 65
Cape Elizabeth, ME, 79–84
Cape Elizabeth Album Quilt, 80–81
caps, 47, *47*, 48, *48*
Captain Wilson Quilt, 70, 76
carding mills, 32
Carlson, Susan, 179, 207, *208*, 209
Carolina Lily Quilt, 124
Carver, Rachel Calderwood, 28
Castine, ME, 163–164
Castine Community Bicentennial Quilt, 163–164

INDEX

Centennial Exposition, Philadelphia, PA, 132
Chadwick, Perlina, 10–11
challenge quilts, 183
Chanteclaire Fabrics, 190
Chapman, Rachel, 24–26
charity quilts. *See* fundraiser quilts
Charles Shay, Wearing an Applique and Beadwork Collar, 180
Charm Quilt, 107
charm quilts, 106, xiv
Chief's Collar, 214
Child, Lydia Maria, 39
Chinese immigrants, 116–117
chintz, xii, 39, 57
Circle-A-Day quilt, 187–188, 190
Circle-a-Day Quilt, 189–190, *190*, *191*
Civil War, xii, xiv, 58, 62, 65, 91–92, 96, 99–102
Civil War Centennial, 154
Civil War veterans, 114–116
clothing and identity/status, 46, 48, 51
Colesworthy Album Quilt, 58
Colonial Revival Style, 152, 156, xii, xiv
colors, 5, 9, 19, 21–22, 34, 36, 40, 43, 61, 75, 116–117, 152, 188; mauve, 106; Prussian blue, 39
Comet Quilt, 73, 76, 79
commemorative quilts, 156, 157, 160–161, 163, 183
community, reflections on: Cape Elizabeth, ME, 80–85; fundraising quilts in the late 1800s: 113–117; North Haven, ME: 18–23; Quilt for a Cause in Lewiston-Auburn, ME: 188–189
community and group quilting, 58, 61–62, 65–66, 79, 84, 92, 162, 181–182
community expression: Bailey Island Quilt Mystery, 134–138
Compass Rose Quilt, 73
Confederacy, 96
Connecticut, xiii
Constitution Quilt of Valor, 185
contemporary quilts, 174, 179–180, 182–184, *199–212*
copperheads, Civil War 91
Copperplate Printed Wholecloth Quilt, 34, 52
copperplate printing, 34–35, *36*, *37*, 37
Cotter, Anne Drain, 110, *112*
Cotton Crazy Quilt, 135
cotton fabrics: availability of, 36–38, 58–59, 106, 151; British exports and imports, 14, 32, 33, 36–37; mill production of, 58–60, 91, 105–106
cotton gin, 91
coverlets. *See* bed covers
Cozart, Dorothy, 113, 114
C4 quilts: common attributes of, 67, 72, 76, 77, 78; core quilts, 67, 72, 77 *See also* Ladies' Sewing Circle
cradleboards, 48

Craig Quilt, 74, 75, 78
Crazy Cloth/cheater cloth, 133
crazy quilts, 132–133, *134*, *135*, 137, *138–140*, *142–150*, 152, 155
Crazy Quilt Top, 134
Crazy Quilt with Brownie, 132–133
crewel embroidery, 18–19
Crocodylus Smylus, 180–181
Cross Fan Crazy Quilt, 145
Cumberland, ME: Cumberland Center Congregational Church (C4), 67, *67*, 72, 78–79; Ladies Sewing Circle (LSC) of the Center Cumberland Congregational Church, 67, 72, 75–76, 78–79; maritime trades in, 66–67, 75
Cumberland Center Congregational Church(C4), 67–67, 72, 78–79
Cumberland Historical Society, 71
cut corner quilts, 9, 15–16, *16*, *21*, *41*
Cutler, ME, 160
Cyr, Lois Moore, 164

Damariscotta Mills, ME, 32
Davis, Louise Griffin, 62
Davis-Dow Quilt, 93, *94*, xiv
Dawson, Beth, 185–186
Delectable Mountains Quilt, 109, 110, 113
Descended from the Stars, 212
Deserted Village (fabric pattern), 35
Designing Women, 180
design motifs: agricultural, 76; basket of flowers, 22; eagle, 22, 76; feather, 8, 9, 10, 15; fish, 22, 81; floral, 4, 7, 8, 10, 14–15, 22, 41; fouled anchor, *75*, 76; religious, 76, 110, 161; tree of life, 4, 7, 8, 9, 10, 24, 26, 57
design motifs, traditional: embroidered, 18–19; local influence on, 21, 22–23; in printed fabrics, 34–35, 40, 41
Diagonal Stripe with Uneven Nine Patch, 55
Dixie Dingo Dreaming (Pippin), *206*
Douglass, Frederick, 116
Douglass, Helen, 116
Dow, Neal, 85
Dresden, ME, 185
Dresden Plate Variation, 154
Dyer, Lucy, 20–22
dyes and dyeing, 22, 32, 33–34, 39–40, 59, 106, 152

eagle motif, 22, 76
Earle, Alice Morse, 44
Eden (Bar Harbor), ME, 117
Embargo of 1807, 22
Embroidered Bedcover, 18
Embroidered Quilt, 19
Embroidered Wool Crazy Quilt, 146
Embroidered Wool Strip Quilt, 23

233

INDEX

embroidery: on bed covers, 1, *18–19*, 22, xi; on crazy quilts, *137*; on quilts, 1, 3–4, 18–19, *19*, 23, *29*, 110, 137; on redwork quilts, 110; on wool crazy quilt, *144*; on wool strip quilt, *23*
Emery, Ellen Vest, 62
Emery, Sarah Anna, 43–44
Emery, Sarah Jane, 62
Etta Mary Clark Spearen with a Quilt, 171
Eugene and Aline Neveux with Aline's Quilt, 144

fabrics: availability of, 10, 22, 32, 36–38, 59, 106, 110, 151; paints, 157; reused scraps/pieces, 6, 10, 14, 20, 23, 133
Fall River, MA, 59
Falmouth, ME, 10, 60
Falmouth Album Quilt, 88
family histories and quilts, 64, 79–84, 133, 135, 137
Fan Fundraising Quilt, 114, *115*
Fanning, Robbie, 65
Fanning, Tony, 65
Farmington, ME, 183
feather motif, 8, 9, 10, 15
Fence Posts Lap Quilt, 170
fiber art, 165, 179
fish motif, 22, 81
Flanagan, Nora, 196, *197*
floral motif, 4, 7, 8, 10, 14–15, 22, 41
flour sack prints, 153
Flying Geese Quilt, 54
Flying Geese Strip Quilt with Harrison Print, 56
Fort Gorges, ME, 84
fouled anchor motif, *75*, 76
Fraas, Gayle, 177
frames for quilting, 7, 10
Frances Berry Orbeton, 96, *97*
Francis Stanislaus in his Regalia, 50
Freeport, ME, 1, 18, *18*
Free Will Baptist Church Society, 92
French Canadians, 106, 116, 117, 151
Friendship Quilt, 63
friendship quilts, xi, 57, 60, 61, *63*, 66, 110,
Frog Pond Farm, 176
Frost, S. Annie, 65
fulling mills, 32, 59
fundraiser quilts, xii, 60–65, 99–101, 110, 113–116, 156, 184–187
Furber, Jenny, 96

Gagne, Debbie, 184
Garden Burst, 177
gays and lesbians (LBGTQ), 163
Germany, 106, 152
Gilded Age, xi
Girl Scout Troop 731, 160
Girl's Own Book (Child), 39
Girl Warrior, 179

glass beadwork, 213, 46, 47, 51, *182*, 215
glazing, 6, 10
Godey's Ladies Book, 64
Gordon, Beverly, 133
Grana, Debra, 64, 80
Grand Army of the Republic (GAR), 114, 116, 117
Great Depression, 151–152
Green Dot Organization, 188–189
Green Street Senior Citizens Bicentennial Quilt, 157
grids and gridlines, 6, 8

Half-Baked Jane, 195
Hallowell, ME, 3, 10, 13, 45
Hamilton, Alexander, 32
Hamlin, Hannibal, 62
handlooms (cotton), 33
Harmons, Emma, 17, 124
Harpswell, ME, 137, 179
Harrington, Mrs., *8–9*
Harrison, Caroline, 137
Hatch, Stephanie, 63, 64, 66
Haystack Mountain School of Crafts, 180
Hexagon Quilt, 152
Hodesh, Margaret, 163, 164
homespun, 6, 165, x
Hope, ME, 179
Hop Sing Guan, 116
household production: of items during the Civil War, 91–92; of textiles, 6–7, 8, 10, 14, 20, 21–23, 32–33
household production of textiles, 7, 8, 10, 14, 21–23, 32
Hubbard, Sarah Hodge Barrett, 45
Humphrey, Lucy Weston, 78
Hussey/Tarbox Wholecloth Quilt, 7

immigrants and immigration, 105–106, 116–117, 149, 186–187
Indian Island, ME, 47, 50, 51
industrialization, xii, 58–60, 99–101, 105–106
Industrial Revolution, 32–33, 35–36, 37, 38, xii
inscribed quilts, 60–62
intaglio printing, 34
interior decoration of homes, 39, 40, 132
Isle au Haut, ME, 27, *27*

Jane Blanchard Quilt, 71
Jenny Furber's Album Quilt, 96
Johnson, Addie Mae, 138, *138–140*
Judd, Richard, 105

Keller, Helen, 137–138

LaBar, Laureen, x, 14, 26, 79
Ladies' Aid Societies, 91–92
Ladies' Beneficent Association, ME, 92, 96
Ladies' Benevolence Society, MA, 84

234

INDEX

Ladies' Guide to Needlework, (Frost), 65
Ladies' Sewing Circle (LSC), 67, 72, 75–76, 78, 79
Ladies' Sewing Circle Quilts, 68, 69, 70, 71, 72, 73, 74, 76
lap quilts, 186
Laurel Leaves Quilt, 90
Leavitt, Sarah, 63
Lewis, Mary Octavia, *95*
Lewiston, ME, 151
Lewiston-Auburn, ME, 188–189
Libby family, *19, 20, 53,* 59
Libby Family Cotton Quilt, 53
Libby-Freeman Album Quilt, 59
Lincoln, Abraham, 62
Little Women (Alcott), 110
log cabin pattern, xiii, 106, 133, 152
Log Cabin Quilt, Barn Raising Variation, 106
Log Cabin Quilt, Pineapple or Windmill Variation, 120
Log Cabin Quilt, Sunshine and Shadow Variation, 119
Log Cabin Variation, 118
long arm quilting, 182–183
Love, 174
Lowell, MA, 59
Lyre Quilt, 72, 75

Maine: and the American Revolution, 1, 23, 32, 36–37; and the Civil War, 58, 62, 65, 91, 96, 99–102, 154; history, 1–2, 10; industrialization, xii, 32–33, 36, 37–38, 58–60, 99–102, 149–150, multiethnicity, 117; Native Americans in, 1, 46–51, 161; statehood (1820), 1; textile mills in, 32–33, 58–60, 91, 105–106
Maine Childrens' Cancer Program, 186
Maine Cotton and Woolen Manufacturing Company, 33
Maine Craft Association, 180
Maine Crafts Guild, 180
Maine Fiberarts, Brunswick, ME, 180
Maine Heritage Quilt, 175
Maine Historical Society (MHS), 14, 15, *43*
Maine Medical Center, 186
Maine Quilt Heritage, 15, 64
Maine Register, 59, 105, 116, 117
Maine statehood, 1820, 1
Maine State Museum, 39, 114, 131, xii
Maine textile mills, 32–33, 58–60, 91, 105–106
Maliseets, 46, 47
Mann, Bruce, ix
Manton, Jackie, 184–185
maritime trades, 60, 66, 105 *See also* nautical themes
Mary Bulman Bedcoverings, 2
Mary Carthage's Love Quilt, back, 175
Mary Louise Orr's Quilt, 134, 135, 137
Masonic symbols, 84, 101

Massachusetts: expansion of mills, 58–60, 105–106; quilt styles and fashions, 18
Massachusetts Quilts: Our Common Wealth, xiii
Matinicus Island, ME, 110
mauve, 106
McCall's (magazine), *154,* 155, 161
Medallion Detail, Polly Allen's Quilt Top, 5
medallion quilts, 1–2, *3, 4–5, 9, 11,* 20, *33, 37,* 92
Medallion Quilt with Engraved Copperplate Printing, 37
Memory Bouquet Quilt with Additions, 155
Memory Quilt, 184
memory quilts, 184
Merrill, Davis, 79
Merrill, Helen "Nellie" Stockman, *122*
Merrill, Louville, 76
Merrill, Mary Ellen Wyman, 76, 79
Merrill family, 72, 76, 79
Merrill Quilt, 69
Merritt, Justine, 161
Micmac Peaked Cap, 48
Micmacs, 46–47, *48*
mid-Atlantic region: album quilt origins, 57; quilt types and designs, 2, 12
Milkweed No.1, 209
mill girls, 59
mills: girls working in, 59; and industrialization, 32–33, 36, 37–38, 58–60, 99–101, 105–106
mills, types of: carding: 32; cotton and production, 58–60, 91, 105–106; fulling, 32, 33; textile and growth of, 58–60, 159–160; woolen, 58–59, 106
"Mister Market" block detail, *157*
Molly Molasses, 47, *47*
monochromatic/multiple colors, *34, 36*
Monson, ME, 182
Moody, Lemuel, Capt., 99
Moonlight Sonata, 197
Morton, Anna, 137
Morton, Emily, 41
Mother Jones (magazine), 161
Mount Vernon, ME, 40–41
Munjoy Hill, Portland, ME, xiv, 99, *100,* 101
Munjoy Hill Civil War Quilts, 100
Mystic, CT, 101
Mystic Seaport Museum, 100, 101

Native Americans: clothing, 46–51; settlements, 1, 46
nautical themes, 75–76. *See also* maritime trades
Neptune, Francis Joseph, 48
Neptune, Jennifer, 49–50, 182, 213
Neveux, Aline, 140, *143*
Neveux Family Register Crazy Quilt, 143
New England region: mills and industrialization, 32–33, 58–60, 99–101, 105–106; quilt types and designs, 2, 6, 8, 12, 40, 62–66
New Hampshire, 8, 18

INDEX

North Haven (North Vinalhaven), ME, 20–22, 28, *28*
North New Sharon, ME, 92
Nylander, Jane, 1

Oak Leaf and Reel Potholder Quilt, 64
Ocean Waves Quilt, 122
Octavia Lewis Civil War Quilt, 95
Ohio Star Potholder Album Quilt, 127
Orbeton, Frances Berry, 96, *97*
Orbeton-Tillson Quilt, 98
Orr, Ethel, 138–139
Orr, Mary Louise, 136–138, 140
Orrs Island, ME, 137
Osgood, Mary, 67
Overshot Postage Stamp Quilt, 130

palampore, 57
Palermo, ME, 29, *29*
Pan Blackened Quilt, 194
paper piecing and templates, 3, 113
Paris Hill Album Quilt, detail, 63
Paris Hill Baptist Church, 62
Passamaquoddies, 46, 47, 48
Passamaquoddy Cradleboard Wrappers, 48
patchwork, xii, 3, 65–66, 92, 110, 136, 196
patriotic symbols and quilts, xiii, 76, 92, 183
Paul, Catherine Rice, 19–20
peaked caps, 47–48
Peaks Island, ME, 114
pelisses, 42–44, *42–44*
Pembroke, ME, 115
Penobscot Chief's Collar, 50
Penobscot Peaked Cap, 47
Penobscots, 46–47, 50
Perkin, William, 106
Perlina Chadwick's Wool Medallion Quilt, back, 11
petticoats, *12–14*, 15, 23
Philadelphia, PA, 132
Phippsburg, ME, 156
Pickman, C. Gayton, Rev., 85
pieced and embroidered: wool quilts, 19–20
Pieced and Embroidered Quilt, 29
Pieced and Embroidered Wool Quilts, 20, 21, 29, 30, 31
Pieced Cotton Explosion Potholder Quilt, 126
pieced cotton medallion, 3, 4
Pieced Cotton Medallion Top, 5, 33
Pieced Cotton Quilt, 35, 36
pieced quilts: album, 57; medallion, 1–3, 4, 11
Pieced Star Quilt, 38
Pieced Wool Medallion Quilt, front, 11
Pieced Wool Quilts, 19, 27, 28
pigments, 34, 39–40, 177
Pilgrim's Progress (Bunyan), 110

Pine Tree Quilt Guild (PTQG), 156, 179–180
Pink Oyster Mushrooms, 212
Plymouth, MA, 21
Poganuc People (Stowe), 44
Point Cross River, January 22 and 23, 178
Poland Corner Methodist Church, 79
Poland Corner Methodist Church Quilt, 78
Polkadodo, 209
Poor, Jonathan D., 39
Porter, Rufus, 39
Portland, ME, 10, 59, 92, 100, 101, 116, 137. *See also* Munjoy Hill, Portland, ME
Portland Breakwater Lighthouse Quilt, 83–84
Portland Company, The, 99–101
Portland Flag Quilt, 104
Portland Observatory, ME, 99
Portrait of Fannie Lou Hamer, 206
postage stamp quilts, xii, *107*, 110, *129,*
Postage Stamp Triangle Quilt, 107
Potholder Album Quilt, 86
potholder quilts, 62–66, 75, *86*, 99, *126*, *127*
Poultry Ribbon Quilt, 172
Presence, 205
presentation quilts, 61–62, 65
Pring, Martin, 21
printed patterns, xiv, 57, 65, 133, *154*, 155–156
Prize-Winning Quilt, 150
Project Linus, 187
protest quilts, xii, 156, 160–161, 164
Prussian blue, 39
Pumpkin Hood, 44, 45

Quakers, 44
Quilt: A Life of its Own and Mine, 176
Quilt Alliance, xi
quilt-as-you-go quilts. *See* potholder quilts
quilt documentation, xi, xiii
Quilted Bonnet, 45
Quilted Bonnet lining 45
Quilted Bonnet Cover, 44
quilted clothing, 12–14, 42–45
Quilted Hood, 45
quilting: frames for, 7, 65; organizations for (Maine), 180; xiv, revival of, 154, 158–159, 172, 177–182; as a social activity, xi–xii, 7, 13, 92
Quilting Design for the Hussey/Tarbox Wholecloth Quilt, 7
Quilting Design of Rachel Chapman's Quilt, 26
Quilting Detail, Brick Store Petticoat, 15
quilting frames, 7, 65
Quilt of Valor Presentation, photograph, *186*
quilts: for animal shelters, 187–188; for a cause, 184–186; for sale, 113; and sewing machines, 101–102, 105
Quilt of Valor Presentation, photograph, *186*

INDEX

quilts: for animal shelters, 187–188; for a cause, 184–186; for sale, 113; and sewing machines, 101–102, 105

quilts, details of: Addie Mae Johnson's Crazy Quilt, 137, 139; Album Quilt by/for Nellie Stockman Merrill, 122; Applique Quilt by Anne Cotter, 111; Bark Messenger, 75, 77; Birds Flying in the Air, Redwork Quilt by Etta Hall, 108; Black Crazy Quilt by Vinnie Crosby, 146; Cape Elizabeth Album Quilt, 81; Captain Wilson Quilt, 76; Castine Community Bicentennial Quilt, 164; Circle-a-Day Quilt by Judy Roche, 189, 191; Crazy Quilt by Bethia Thompson, 149; Crazy Quilt with Brownie, 133; Cross Fan Crazy Quilt by Harrington Methodist Society, 145; Davis-Dow Quilt, 94; Embroidered Wool Crazy Quilt by Clarissa Folsom, 145; Fan Fundraising Quilt (Waterville), 115; Flying Geese and Harrison Print, 56; Green Dot Quilt, 189; Ladies Sewing Circle Quilts, 76, 77; Libby Family Quilt, 53; Mary Louise Orr Quilt, 137, 139, 140; Millinery Crazy Quilt, 142; "Mister Market" block detail, 157; Neveux Family Register Crazy Quilt, 144; Oak Leaf and Reel Potholder Quilt, 64; Orbeton-Tillson Quilt, 98; Pan Blackened Quilt by Wendy Reed, 194; Pieced and Embroidered Wool Quilt by Lucy Dyer, 22; Pieced and Embroidered Wool Quilt / Paul Family, 20; Pieced Cotton Medallion Top, 33; Pieced Wool Medallion Quilt by Perlina Chadwick, 11; Portland Flag Quilt, 104; Portrait of Fannie Lou Hamer, 204; Poultry Ribbon Quilt by Helen Merrill, 172; Prize-Winning Crazy Quilt by Lucy Marsh, 150; Serene Wight Baskets and Poinsettias Quilt, 89; Silk Medallion Quilt by Martha Agry Vaughan, 4; Throckmorton Bicentennial Quilt, 159; Wool Medallion Quilt, 11

quilts for a cause, 182–186
quilts for animal shelters, 185–186
Quilts for Sale in Alameda Hall, Bath, 113
quilts See specific names and types
Quilt with Replaced Corners, 17

Rabbit Bag, 215
Ram Island, Boothbay, 203
Ram Island, Sheepscot River, 202
redwork embroidery, 110
Reed, Wendy Caton, 193, 194, 195
regalia, 47, 48–50
religious motifs and themes, 76, 110, 161
Rhode Island, xiii, 12
The "Ribbon," 160, 161, 162
Ribbon Appliqué and Beadwork Panels, 51
Rivard, Paul, 32, 59
Robbing Peter to Pay Paul Quilt, 125
Roche, Judy, 189–192
Rocks and Reflections, 199

Romantic Movement, ix, x, 42
Ronald McDonald House, 186
Rotoplast International, 186
Rufus Porter Museum, 39

Sabean, Evelyn, 181
Saco, ME, 17, 59, 92, 106
Salem, MA, 43–44
Sanford, ME, 117
Scarborough, ME, xiii, 19
scent blankets, 186
Sebasticook, ME, 11
Sedgwick, ME, 5
selvage threads, 9, 14
September, 11, 2001, 183
Serene Wight Baskets and Poinsettias Quilt, 89
sewing machines, 101–102, 105
Shay, Charles, 49, 182
Shelburne Museum, 18
She Persisted in Her Quest to Reach the Shore and Sing the Anthem of the Sea, 180–181
She Street, 66–67
ships: Bark Messenger, 60, 68, 72, 75–76, 77, 79; Caleb Cushing, 84; Dakota, 66; Grapeshot, 66; Potoosic, 101; State of Maine, 163
Shore Birds, 200
signature quilts. See inscribed quilts
silk fabric: in clothing, 12, 14, 23, 42–43, 44–45, 50–51, 178; in quilts, 3, 12, 23, 63, 132–133, 137, 139, 140
silk fabric, x, xi, xii, 32; pelisse, 42, 43; weighted, 133
silk ribbon appliqué, 47–48, 49, 50, 51, 180, 213
Sing Hop, 116
Skowhegan, ME, 91
Slade, Duncan, 177, 201
slavery, 91
Smith, Marion "Vella," 184
Smith, Sarah Ann, 179, 210
Smucker, Jannekin, 19, 22
Soccabeson, Denny, 48, 49
Soldiers' Aid Society, 92
Solon, ME, 19–20
Song Quilt, 154, 165
Song Quilt: The Sidewalks of New York, 154, 156, 165, 166
Soule, Martha Babson Lane, 1, 18–19
Southgate, Eliza, xiii
Spacks, Jude, 177, 204
Springvale, ME, 33
Stanislaus, Francis, 49, 50–51
Star and Swags Quilt, 123
Star Quilt, 55
State of Maine (ship), 163
Steel Garden, 166
Stenciled Bedcover, 40, 41
stencils/stenciling, 39–41, 61, 61

INDEX

Stowe, Harriet Beecher, 44
Strength Behind Our Heroes, 183
Sweetser, Lucy, 79
Sweetser, Mary Jane Pittee, 78

Taunton, MA, 59
Tenant's Harbor Light, 110
textiles: growth of mills, 58–60, 159–160; household production of, 6–7, 8, 10, 14, 20, 21–23, 32–33; imported, 14, 32, 33, 36–37
textiles, printed: block printing, 33–34; cheater cloth, 131; copperplate printing, 34–35; cylinder printing, 35–36; new colors in, 106, 110; stenciling, 39–41
Thank You Note, 137
"The Ribbon," 159, *160*, 161
The Ribbon Quilt Component, 160
Thomes, Abbie, 67
Thomes-Osgood Album Quilt, 76, 78–79, 87
Thorndike, ME, 41
Three Charity Quilts for Children, 187
Throckmorton, Linda, 159
Throckmorton Bicentennial Quilt, 159
Tillson, Davis, Brig. Gen., 96, *97*
Togus, ME, 184
Tolman, Ellen, 110
Trapunto Quilt, 16
tree of life motif, 4, 7, 8, 9, 10, 24, 26, 57
Troy, ME, 37
T-shaped quilts. *See* cut corner quilts
Turner, Delphos, 29
Twelve Days of Maine Christmas: A Partridge in a Pine Tree, 167; *Four Chickadees*, 167

Union (U.S.), 91, 114–115, xiv
U.S. Sanitary Commission, 92

Vaughan, Martha Agry, 3–4
velvet, xi, 133, 137–138
Vermont, xiii, 18, 19
Veterans Administration Hospital, ME, 184
Vienna, ME, 40
Villars, Alexander Henry Charles, 49

Wabanakis, xii, xiv, 46–47, 163, 180
wadding, 42, 44, 65
Wallace, Burton Tolman, 110
Wallace, Thaddeus, 110
War of 1812, 22, 36, 48, *49*
Washington, D.C., 161
Watercolor Portrait of Denny Soccabeson, 49
Waterville, ME, 8, *9*, 116
Waterville Register, 116
Weeks, Pamela, 60, 62, 63
weighted silk, 133
Wentworth, Eunice, 18
West Lebanon, ME, 18
Weston, Mary Ann, 78
White, Sarah "Say," 91
Whitney Museum, 165
Whittier, John Greenleaf, 137
Whittier, Nanna Bradley, ix, 40
Wholecloth Quilt, 8
wholecloth quilts, 1, 6–9, 10, 14, 15
Wilson Museum, *35*, 36
Winter, Sarah Bowman, 42–44
Wiscasset, ME, 66
Wiseman, Charlotte, 164
women: Civil War activities of, 91– 92, 96, 99, 154; mill workers, 59–60; of She Street, 66–67; social action, 84–85; support for GAR, 114–117; veterans/health care of, 184
Women's Relief Corps (WRC), 115–116, 117
woolen mills, 58–59, 106
Wool Medallion Quilt, 9
Wool Octagon Crazy Quilt, 135
Wool Wholecloth Quilt, 6, 24
wool wholecloth quilts, *6–9, 24*
Work in Progress, 215
World War I, 151–152, 156
World War II, xii, 153, 156, 161
Worthington, Catherine, 177, 198
Wrap-A-Smile, 186

Yo-Yo Quilt, unfinished, *173*

Zegart, Shelley, xi

ACKNOWLEDGMENTS

Maine Quilts: 250 Years of Comfort and Community is the culmination of ten-plus years of off-and-on research, squeezed in where time allowed, followed by several years of steady effort. Over the course of this time I visited over thirty museums in five states and was welcomed into dozens of private homes across Maine. The help and cooperation of these many curators, quilters, and quilt collectors made this project successful. People told stories, went down rabbit holes of genealogical dead ends, found obscure references, and plied me with iced tea and home-baked bread. I live in fear that I will forget to mention someone who assisted me in this long process and beg their understanding. Thank you, friends and colleagues, for your help, your information, and your encouragement. Any errors that found their way into the book are, of course, my own responsibility.

This book was the companion to an exhibition at the Maine State Museum that was originally timed for the state's bicentennial in 2020. Funding for the project was given by the Coby Foundation under the guidance of Ward Mintz. Coby's support for *Maine Quilts* made the exhibition possible, and I am forever grateful. The Society of Winterthur Fellows also supported *Maine Quilts*, allowing me to examine rare Maine quilts in the Winterthur collection. The Elsie and William Viles Foundation contributions were a loving addition to the quilt that Elsie bought for the museum thirty-eight years ago. The Friends of the Maine State Museum raised funds for quilt conservation. The Pine Tree Quilters Guild's pledged support of the exhibition and book means more to me than they know. And always, I am grateful for the generous financial support of the people of Maine and the executive and legislative branches of state government. Their support of the Maine State Museum is a gift to us all.

One of the richest personal rewards of the *Maine Quilts* project has been the friendships that have flourished during its long creation. Lynne Zacek Bassett and Pam Weeks contributed essays to the book. They also coached me through its creation, serving advice, tea, and cocktails as required. Viva curatroika! Cyndi Black and Wendy Reed shared their knowledge, their enthusiasm, and records of the Maine Quilt Heritage documentation project, an invaluable resource representing hundreds of hours spent collecting the stories of Maine's history and quilts. Deb Grana not only lent a quilt, she also researched it and a related quilt and wrote an essay with me about it. She has shared her collection generously. Without the Maine Quilt History Study Group, founded by Judy Roche, teacher, quilter, designer, and mentor, I would be utterly lost. Sue Rivers, Mary Reynolds, Mary Carthage, Pat Burns, Glenna Quigley, Rainey Doyle, Wendy Reed, Cyndi Black, Diane Dixon, Janice Capano, and Lisa Hayden have been great company in the study group as we have learned together. I am in awe of their knowledge and their quilting talents. I am also in awe of Cyndi's ability to talk me into making a study quilt for the Pine Tree Quilters Guild show when I had never made a quilt before. Now I am hooked. Conservators Camille Breeze and Gwen Spicer

ACKNOWLEDGMENTS

conserved several quilts in the collection. The book and exhibition will be all the more beautiful thanks to their work.

Quilters shared stories. Beth Dawson, Jackie Manton, Dona Smith, Mary Carthage, and Mary Reynolds told me of their experiences making charity/community quilts. Katherine "Kay" Fowler, Deb Grana, Dick Knight, Jane Owens, Sandy Stubbs, Connie Sweetser, Sylvia Wallace, and Gail Worthen lent antique quilts for the book and exhibit. Contemporary quilt artists Pat Burns, Mary Carthage, Susan Carlson, Susan Cooper, Jo Diggs, Nora Flanagan, partners Gayle Fraas and Duncan Slade, Jennifer Neptune, Jane Owens, Wendy Reed, Sue Rivers, Judy Roche, Sarah Ann Smith, Jude Spacks, Linda Throckmorton, and Cathy Worthington all lent quilts or contributed photographs of their work.

Brian and Elaine Sipe, Joni Banks and Steven Cox, James Francis, Stephanie Hatch, George LaBar, Kitty Murray, Donald Soctomah, Charlie Burden, Beth Donaldson, Dana Doerfler, Mary Ann Douglas, Gayle Fraas and Duncan Slade, Jennifer Neptune, and Jane Radcliffe all contributed to my research directly and indirectly. And there is more still to do (I still need to get back to the County, Brian). Kim Baird, Nessa Reifsynder, Sue Reich, Deborah Kraak, Kathy Metelica Cray, Susan Price Miller, thank you for your help, friendship, egg sandwiches, and enthusiasm. T. J. and Roza Kwok-Ling Mueller, thank you for identifying the Chinese individual who signed the Biddeford quilt. To Callie Lavoie and the many wonderful quilters at Pine Tree Quilters Guild, my thanks for your continued support of the Maine State Museum.

Without the volunteers who worked on this project, there simply would not be an exhibit or book. I cannot express how thankful I am for their hard work, their incredible contributions, and their patience. To Dianne Dowd, Dave Fuller, Deb Grana, Leah Haraden, my husband Scott Murray, Gary Fuller, Mary Reynolds, Sue Rivers, and Fran Townsend, I can only say a most inadequate "Thank you *so* much!"

Folks at museums and historical societies across the state and beyond were warm and welcoming, despite their busy schedules. I cherish the give-and-take of information and ideas I experienced with them. Thanks very much to: Marianne Martin at the Abby Aldrich Rockefeller Folk Art Museum and the Colonial Williamsburg Foundation; Lee and Sandra Cummings at the Aroostook Historical and Art Museum of Houlton; Matt Bishop at the Bangor History Center; Deborah Dyer at the Bar Harbor Historical Society; Megan Pinette at the Belfast Historical Society; Leanne Hayden and Kathryn Hussey at the Brick Store Museum; Paige Lilly at the Castine Historical Society; Carolyn Small and Linda Fulda at the Cumberland Historical Society; Thomas Bennett at the Prince Memorial Library in Cumberland Maine; Tinker Crouch at the Deer Isle-Stonington Historical Society; Marion "Toosie" Scharoun and Claudia Bell of the Farmington Historical Society; Jennifer Griffiths at the Fenimore Art Museum; Jennifer Lewis and Brandan Roberts of the Hamlin Library; Laura Johnson at Historic New England; Jane Lury of Labors of Love; Barbara Sellitto of the Lubec Historical Society; Peter Mallow at the Maine State Archives; Kirk Mohney, John Mosher,

ACKNOWLEDGMENTS

and Leith Smith of the Maine Historic Preservation Commission; Kate McBrien, Emily Schlemmer, Jacqueline Field, Jamie Rice, Sophia Yalouris, Tilly Laskey, Holly Hurd-Forsyth, and Abby Zoldowski of the Maine Historical Society; Jill Piecut of the Maine Maritime Museum; Erin Early-Ward and Rachel Snell of the Mount Desert Island Historical Society; Lauren Whitley, Jennifer Swope, Pam Parmal, and Rebecca Carpenter at the Museum of Fine Arts, Boston; Maribeth Quinlan at Mystic Seaport; Kay Peterson at the National Museum of American History; Nathan Sowry and Tanya Thrasher at the National Museum of the American Indian; Arlene Cole at the Newcastle Historical Society; Laura Lane and Pam Weeks at the New England Quilt Museum; Nan Lee and Lydia Brown at the North Haven Historical Society; Peggy Wishart and Pat Fitzgerald at the Old York Museum; Jane Stinchfield at the Phillips Historical Society; Kimberly Smith at the Presque Isle Historical Society; Vicki Magnum at Quilts, Inc.; Bryan Fennimore at the Redington Museum; Ann Morris at the Rockland Historical Society; the staff of the Ruggles House; Kara Vose Raiselis, Carolyn Parsons Roy, and Leslie Rounds at the Saco Museum; Tom Denenberg, Barbara Rathburn, Katie Wood Kirchhoff, and Allison Herrig at the Shelburne Museum; Karen Asherman and Amy Aldredge at the Yarmouth Historical Society; Abby Dunham and Patricia Hutchins at the Wilson Museum; and Linda Eaton, Jeanne Solensky, Catharine Dann, Susan Newton, and Rebecca Duffy at the Winterthur Museum, Garden, and Library.

At my own Maine State Museum, Brewster Buttfield, Linda Carrell, Bernard Fishman, Angela Goebel-Bain, Natalie Liberace, Sheila McDonald, Teresa Myers, Toosie Scharoun, Dona Smith, Gabrielle Stanhope, Ben Stickney, Amy Thompson, Joanna Torow, Ryan Walker, Kate Webber, and Paula Work all contributed to the success of the book and the exhibit. Doubtless I have missed someone on this list. I will bake you a pie to make amends.

Thanks, too to Jim Julia, Nancy Noonan, Mike Fredericks, Katya Tilton, and members of the photography crew at James D. Julia, Inc., and to Mike Taylor and Sonia MacNeil Taylor, who took most of the images in this book, for their photographic and editing chops. Tim Gould was a great bloodhound and yenta, finding and matchmaking quilts, not to mention being great fun to travel with. Thanks to Kraig Anderson for a photograph of the original Portland Breakwater Light. A special thanks to Tim Gould, to Dale Flagg of the *Maine Antiques Digest*, and to Ed Hild and Patrick Bell of Olde Hope Antiques for their sleuthing abilities.

Michael Steere, thank you for your help and support in bringing the book to life. Jennifer Bunting, Sheila McDonald, and Jean Oplinger, thank you all for your help and advice with the manuscript. Thanks, too, to Lynne Bassett, Judy Roche, and Sue Rivers, who looked it over and offered excellent advice. A special debt of thanks to Lucie Teegarden, for her wise, professional, and patient approach to editing the manuscript, and to the late Karen Ackermann and the editors at Rowman & Littlefield, for their patience.

My mother, Joan LaBar, was an avid and prolific quilter. She loved to make quilts and was astonished at what one could learn from historic quilts. She would have so enjoyed this project. Mary Alaniz, Dale and Jeri Bergdahl, JoEllen and Ron Force, Michael and Angela

ACKNOWLEDGMENTS

Goebel-Bain, Pete and Kay Hannah, Patty Heather-Lea, Dale and Alice Hyerstay, Jack and Pat Lindsay, Sheila McDonald and Debora Price, Jennifer and Matt Milligan, and David and Peggy Murray gave to the *Maine Quilts* project in Mom's memory. Thank you for your gifts of friendship to my family and me, for the rays of light you provided at a dark time, and for your support of *Maine Quilts*.

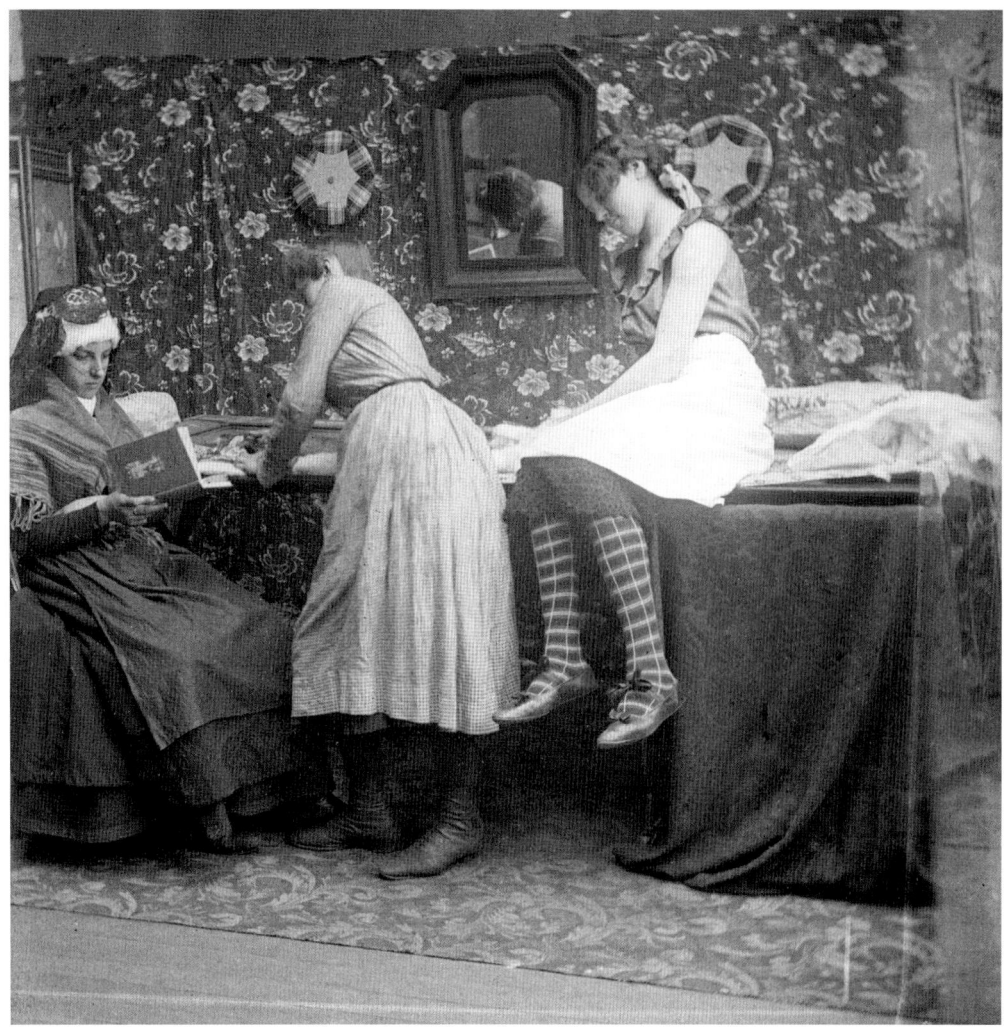

Peep Show Quilting Bee
E. Joseph Leighton photographer or producer
Newcastle or Alna, Maine, ca. 1900
Maine State Museum, 91.26.2664

Little is known about this series of twelve peep show images that purports to depict a quilting bee. This is number five in the series.

LAUREEN A. LABAR is the Chief Curator of History and Decorative Arts at the Maine State Museum. After a career as an archaeologist focused on textile and pottery technology in prehistoric northeastern North America, she received her master's degree in Early American Culture at Winterthur and the University of Delaware, specializing in Wabanaki trade silver. LaBar then returned to Maine and a curatorship at the Maine State Museum. She has written two previous books. The first, Uncommon Threads: Wabanaki Textiles, Clothing and Costume, co-authored with colleague Bruce Bourque, won the R. L. Shep Ethnic Textiles Book Prize from the Textile Society of America in 2010. She lives in Dresden, Maine.